JAMAICAN GREATS

Lives of Famous & Notorious Jamaicans

JAMAICA INSULA
a DREAD Editions series

- Also available:

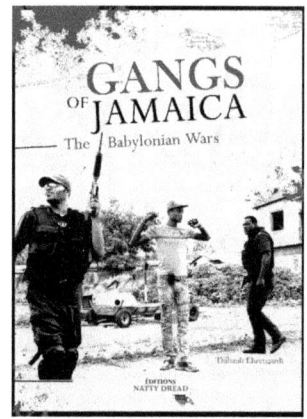

- *The Gangs of Jamaica: The Babylonian Wars*,
by **Thibault Ehrengardt**
(Ja. Insula 05).

An independent inquiry into the underworld of gangs! The author was granted the rare authorization to follow the mobile reserve patrols in the most volatile areas; he also met various *Dons* (gang leaders), in order to give an impartial insight into the post-Dudus Jamaica.

«Thibault Ehrengardt pens a provocative work that transcends the violence and mayhem that bleed through its every page. (...) It is insightful, investigative and written with sheer brilliance.»

G. Ashby, *The Gleaner* (Ja).

www.gangs-of-jamaica.com

Jamaican Greats: Lives of Famous & Notorious Jamaicans, by T. Ehrengardt
Copyright(c) 2014 T. Ehrengardt
Artwork & picture front cover (c) DREAD Editions 2014
Natty Dread Editions / Jamaica Insula 06 / ISBN: 978-2-9533982-7-4

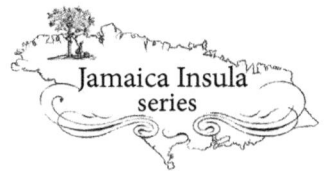

Jamaica Insula series

JAMAICAN GREATS
Lives of Famous & Notorious Jamaicans

By Thibault Ehrengardt

Sous l' œil de Dieu.

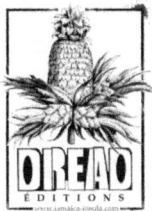

www.jamaica-insula.com

Author's note

I've always been fascinated by historical dictionaries. Because they contain thousands of incredible lives, of course; but mostly because the use of alphabetical order creates unexpected chronologies of lives and events, juxtaposing periods of time centuries apart, giving way to villains over saints, bringing together kings and beggars, murderers and humanists. A *mighty maze* I find irresistible. And that's exactly how I've discovered the history of Jamaica. Music alone brought me to this island, where I soon came across dozens of lives: a serial killer, a prophet who unwillingly gave birth to a living God, a producer who wrote the Third Testament with his music, some cold-blooded politicians who brought their country on the verge of chaos, the ruthless buccaneers of The Point, whose laughs still echo in Port Royal... Great or notorious, all these portraits draw the burning one of the boiling island of Jamaica.

This is how I enjoy life, in a puzzling disorder, with fleeting and haunting emotions rushing me like visions. This is Jamaica to me, and this is what this book tries to render. I borrowed from historical dictionaries the use of alphabetical order, deliberately trying to catch my readers off-guard; make him jump unprepared into the stream of history, let him follow unknown currents, hoping for the best while risking the worst. Beware! Jamaica is no fairy tale country; it's a beautiful and dangerous beast. Sometimes gorgeous, sometimes ugly and disgusting—naked life. But one good thing about reading—when it hits, you feel the pain.

Thibault Ehrengardt

Contents

- **GARVEY,** Marcus, *In His Own Country* ---------------------------- 01

- **HENRY,** Claudius, *The Repairer of the Breach* ---------------------- 19

- **HUTCHINSON,** Lewis, *First Serial Killer* --------------------------- 45

- **JACKSON,** Vivian (Yabby You), *Born Strange, Born Free* ----------- 51

- **MARLEY,** Bob, *The Skipper* --- 77

- **MARTIN,** Vincent, *The Two-Gun Killer* --------------------------- 109

- **MORGAN,** Henry, *Sir Ain't No Saint* ----------------------------- 123

- **SEAGA,** Edward, *Blind Man With A Pistol* ------------------------ 157

- **TACKY,** *Not Enough with You, Mr Long!* -------------------------- 213

- **WILSON,** Trevor, *Johnny-Too-Bad* -------------------------------- 229

- *About the author* --- 238

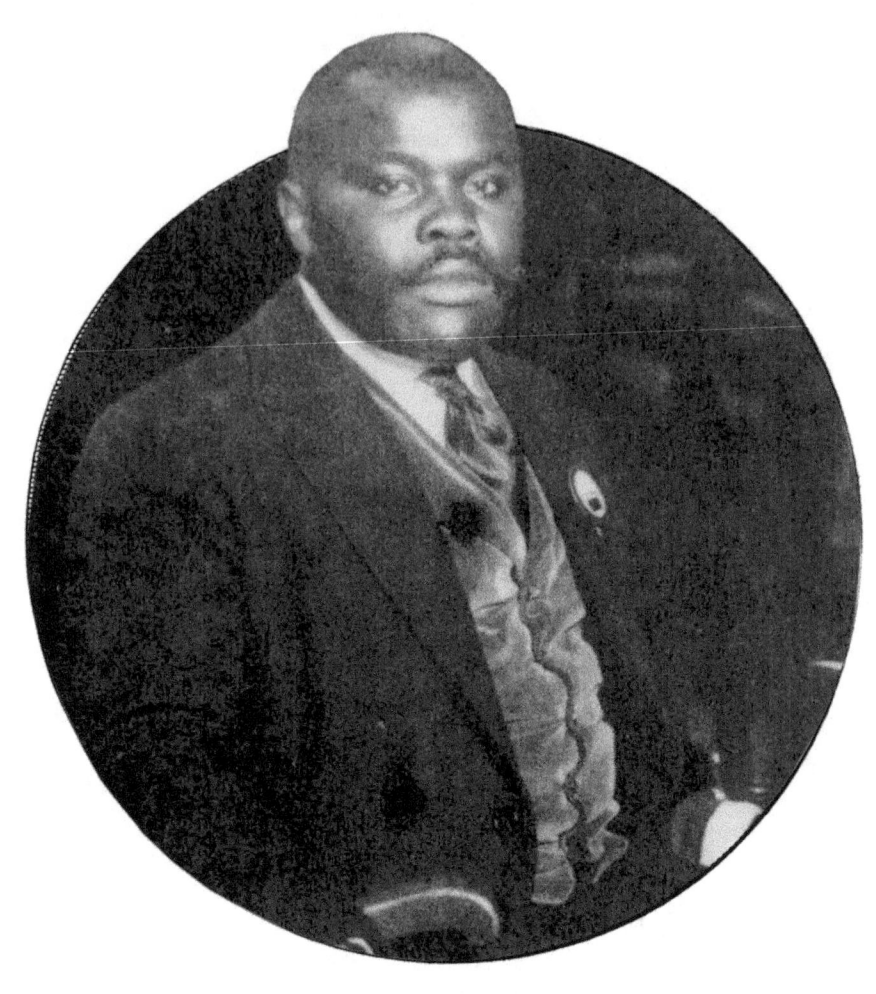

Marcus Garvey, spearhead of self-determination
and father of the *Back-to-Africa* movement.
(DREAD Archives)

Garvey, Marcus Mosiah
(1887-1940)

In His Own Land

In 1974, the nagging and anxious burden of Burning Spear's hit song *Marcus Garvey* resounded all through Jamaica: *Marcus Garvey words come to pass / No food to eat, no money to stand it / Who knows the right and do it not, shall be spank with many strife / Weeping and wailing and a gnashing of teeth, you've got yourself to blame.* These apocalyptic lyrics brought back to life the somewhat forgotten message of Marcus Mosiah Garvey. Since 1964, Garvey had been a national hero—the first of all, thanks to Edward Seaga (see portrait). But enthroning him, the heirs of his enemies had frozen his message in history. In 1974, it fiercely resurfaced through the unique voice of Burning Spear. This song is a story from the North Coast; from the parish of Saint Ann, to be more precise. The local producer Jack Ruby used to export *ganja* (marijuana) in tourist airplanes, and to reinvest his profits in music. He was a renowned producer and sound system owner. His raw sound and the thrilling voice of Burning Spear fitted perfectly. He met Burning Spear on a beach, one day, at a time when, disappointed by his first professional experience in Kingston, the singer had come back home to wait for better days.

Just like Marcus Garvey, Burning Spear (real name Winston Rodney), was born and raised in the parish of Saint Ann—a geographical filiation that soon became philosophical.

Papa Garvey

Marcus Garvey was born August 17, 1887, from Sarah Richards and Malchus Moziah Garvey. His father was a mason by trade, and the son of a slave. A determined and ambitious man, he read like others breathed, avidly piling precious books in his house; but he was also an irascible man, violent with his wife, without any compassion for his son whom he once trapped into a cellar for hours, insensible to the child's terror—a tough education, even according to the standards of the time. At the end of his life, Garvey Senior had to face repeated humiliations. Too short-tempered, he got caught in a series of lawsuits, lost all of them, and ended up as a ruined and bitter man. Exiled in his inner self, he spent his last days prisoner of his dark feelings.

Marcus Garvey grew up in a society based on racial separatism. In the West Indies, slavery had left deep invisible scars, and Jamaica was no exception. In the early 20th century, there were in the island 800,000 black people, some 15,000 mulattos and only 5,000 white people, who controlled almost all the wealth. All these considerations were far from the joyful kid of Saint Ann, but the dream vanished one day. He was fourteen when he learnt that the daughter of his neighbour, the respectable Reverend Lightbourne, would never play with him again—because of his complexion. Marcus Garvey's skin wasn't just black, but so black it bordered on blue. He also had intense and powerful African features, far from the aquiline noses every one was anxiously looking up to. The shock was even more violent as he had been friends with the Reverend's daughter since childhood—the awakening was brutal, and it was just a start. Marcus acquired his political consciousness when settling in Kingston in 1904. There he dwelled in the popular district of Smith Village, the future Denham Town—it looked like a tropical *cour des miracles* populated with mad preachers, purse robbers, thieves and visionaries. For the young Marcus, Smith Village was like a rejuvenating bath. He rapidly made friends with a lot a people, taking and avid interest in foreign news. Anytime he came across his friend Isaac Rose, he would take a newspaper out of his pocket to read him an article that had attracted his attention. The world was vibrating, and Marcus was listening keenly. In 1907, Jamaica trembled. The terrible seism cost the lives of 600 people, and partly destroyed Kingston. Fires started everywhere; corpses lay half-decomposed in the open and much of the city was in ruins. In the midst of chaos, the Governor of Jamaica couldn't prevent two American ships that were cruising nearby to accost. The G.I's disembarked to organize help—without anyone asking them anything—, shooting on sight at the looters. For several weeks, Marcus and his relatives survived in this dreadful situation.

This drama reinforced the fragility of a country permanently on the edge of the abyss because of social instability. At the time, the bosses used thugs to physically fight the unionists in the streets, and Kingston resembled a burning furnace—people assembled on the sidewalk to talk for hours about politics, religion, and to discuss international news... Garvey learnt this new way of life, and later confessed his being fascinated. He soon got involved, and even shut the mouth of Tom Prang, a tough guy who worked for the bosses, thanks to his rhetoric revolving around the struggle of races—his first exploit.

But in November 1908, Garvey's back was against the wall. The employees of the printing office where he worked as a white collar went on strike. He had to take side, and it cost him his job. Tired of the endless speeches on Victoria Peer, he launched the first Jamaican nationalistic party, The National Club, and demanded the dismissal of Governor Sir Oliver as well as a ban on Indian immigration. Marcus Garvey was both determined and humble. The story goes that he was first mocked for his country accent—he endured the remarks, followed some lessons of diction and eloquence with Robert J. Love, a learnt man known for his radical political positions who became his mentor. Every evening, Garvey looked up new words in the dictionary, and forced himself to use them in various sentences. In fact, the Word lay at the heart of his fight. He launched many publications such as *Garvey's Watchman* or *The Nation/El Nacion*; the latter was published soon after his arriving in Costa Rica as the supervisor in a banana plantation of the mighty United Fruit Company (UFC). His articles denounced the economical octopus—meaning the UFC—, and supported the workers. His first newspapers didn't last; they were just rough works. Nevertheless, this long period of time spent in the region of the Panama Canal—the nerve centre of the Americas—, gave him an international vision of the struggle. He came back to Kingston in 1911, before heading to England the following year.

A Prophet

Internationally, Marcus Garvey was the spearhead of the *Back-to-Africa* movement, a strong black man who owned a maritime company, and whose Negro Improvement Association (UNIA) had more than ten millions members in the US. Jamaican people are aware of this Garvey. But they also know of the other one, the spiritual one—almost divine. For once, a prophet is honoured in his own land—by Rastas.

In 1927, worried by the importance taken by the UNIA, J. Edgard Hoover (head of the CIA) seized the first opportunity—an alleged mail fraud—to bring it down. Marcus Garvey was arrested, and then deported to Jamaica. Just before he left, he allegedly uttered his famous prophecy: "*Look to Africa, when a black King is crowned, deliverance shall be near.*" In fact, this statement was published on November 8, 1930, in Garvey's *Blackman* newspaper. The article he personally signed was a tribute to the newly crowned Ethiopian Negus Haile Selassie 1st, aka Ras Tafari: "*The authors of the Psalms have announced that the Princes would come out of Egypt and that Ethiopia shall stretch forth her hands towards God. We doubt not that the time has come.*

Ethiopia is indeed stretching her hands. This mighty Kingdom in the East has remained secret for centuries but, little by little, it stands up to play a key role in the World; it is our duty, as black men, to grab and raise the hand of the Emperor Ras Tafari." At the time, the prophecy stood on a moving ground. But, as underlined by the *University Report* about Rasta published by two searchers in 1960, *the truth has two levels in social matters. You have real facts and the statements about real facts. Statements considered as true are often sociologically more important than the true ones.* In his song *Marcus Garvey*, Burning Spear thus crowned Garvey *the first prophet*. Indeed, three days after Garvey's article, *The Gleaner* dedicated its front page to the newly crowned Negus of Ethiopia, Emperor Ras Tafari—a worldwide event. The feverish Garveyites made the link; they looked up in their Bibles, and read the Revelations: *And I saw an angel coming down out of heaven, having the key to the Abyss and holding in his hand a great chain. He seized the dragon, that ancient serpent, who is the devil, or Satan, and bound him for a thousand years. He threw him into the Abyss, and locked and sealed it over him, to keep him from deceiving the nations anymore until the thousand years were ended. After that, he must be set free for a short time.* Thus was born the living God, Rastafari—the Ethiopian Negus.

Garvey never saw the Negus as the returned Christ. At the end of his life, exiled in England, he even came under harsh criticism from the revolutionary avant-garde for blaming the Emperor too much. He thought the Negus shouldn't have fled his country when the Italian troops of Mussolini invaded it. But in 1941, the victorious Negus came back to Addis Ababa, fulfilling another Garveyite prophecy foretold in the Bible: *And the beast was taken, and with him the false prophet that wrought miracles before him, with which he deceived them that had received the mark of the beast, and them that worshipped his image. These both were cast alive into a lake of fire burning with brimstone.* The Jamaican career of Garvey was quite humble, compared to the American one. Nevertheless, that's where he became a prophet, giving birth to a living god. Preachers like Leonard Howell—the *first Rasta*—worked his prophecy into their own systems. Garvey became inexorably linked to Rasta, though he never directly dealt with the movement. His philosophy revolved around culture and race, not that much around spirituality; the UNIA believed in the black Christ but remained far from any sectarian doctrine. But the aura of Garvey developed among Rastas through parallel and apocryphal prophecies.

Apocryphal Prophecies

Though he died a solitary and isolated man, Garvey wasn't forgotten. Praised in Africa or in America, he had already become a forefront figure of the international black liberation struggle. In the US, the Nation of Islam, Malcolm X, Martin Luther King Jr. and the Black Panther Party were directly inspired by his ideas—from his political platform to his tactics. Jamaica also honoured her own hero. In 1964, Minister Edward Seaga had his remains repatriated, and crowned him the first National Hero. He was buried in George VI Memorial Park—today the National Heroes Park. In 1983, the same Edward Seaga asked the US authorities an official pardon for Garvey's mailing fraud of 1923, and was at once tackled by the Garveyites. To them, Garvey had done nothing wrong—he had just been the victim of a plot—, and if someone should ask for pardon, then it wasn't him. And when Jamaica celebrated Garvey's centennial in 1987, the establishment unanimously praised him as a unique black hero.

Nevertheless, Garvey came back on the map in the 1970s, thanks to Rastas and, more precisely, to the Rasta artists—and especially Burning Spear. A lot of people in Jamaica had learnt about Garvey in school, but never realized he could have a direct impact on their lives. But as Jamaica was going through the terrible decade of the 1970s, some people remembered the words of Garvey, and saw it clearly: these were the last days evoked by the prophet. The world as they knew it wouldn't survive the 1970s because Judgement Day was near! To prove their point, they frantically read the news, looking for signs. The most significant one they came across was the crowning of the Negus—seen as the return of Christ. In the meanwhile, Jamaica was going through its worse historical period, because of political frictions. The election of Michael Manley in 1972—with a socialist program inspired by Garvey's theories—hurled the island into the Cold War. Political corruption and violence turned the tropical paradise into a nightmare. Each community chose its political colour—in fact, it was imposed on them—and started to fight against the rival ones. Invisible frontiers were drawn overnight, blood started to run down King Street and heads were rolling down Sandy Gully. This apocalyptic scenery was reminiscent of Garvey's prophecy.

Following the hit song of Burning Spear, many artists entered the studio to talk about Garvey. They quoted his prophecies at length; not the official ones to be found in history books, but those perpetuated through oral tradition—Jamaicans have always been suspicious towards official history; they usually believe nothing but what the street says. Colin Grant attributes seven apocryphal prophecies to Garvey in his book *Negro With A Hat* (2010). One is about the 1970s, indeed. An obscure reggae band appropriately named The Survivors adapted it in a song at the time. It went like: *I don't know if you remember / I remember very well, what Marcus Garvey said: live out the seventies, you'll live forever.* It was a refrence to the Revelations, when a sign on the door of the righteous shall differentiate them from the wicked to be chastised.

No one knew the precise date of this dreadful day, but some predicted it would take place when the two 7s meet—the first day of 19-77 (some point out the 7th of July—the 7th month of the year—of 1977). A Garveyite reggae band named Culture entered the musical legend in 1976 with the hit song *Two 7 Clash: My little prophet Marcus Garvey prophesize say Santiago de la Vega* (the first name of Spanish Town, and the first capital of Jamaica) *and Kingston would meet.* This reunion was supposed to be another miracle foretold by Garvey. He was incarcerated in Spanish Town for three months in 1928. Before entering the prison, he allegedly declared: "*No one else shall enter through this door until my words come to pass.*" Culture quoted this prophecy in their song. And up until today, the malicious Rastas point at the former door of the Spanish Town prison that was walled up long ago.

Burning Spear evoked another apocryphal prophecy: "*Bag O Wire, the first betrayer who gave away Marcus Garvey!*" Bag O Wire is a Jamaican mythological character, a beggar, a pariah. Garvey, as the story goes, was betrayed by a friend of his, Bag O' Wire, whom he then sentenced to an eternal life of hardship with his female accomplice Madda (for Mother) Muschett. Both traitors ended up their lives in misery; but there's no evidence of such a story in Garvey's life.

In the 1970s, the bloody prophecies of Garvey seemed to come to pass. Hadn't he foretold that the community of Swallowfield, in Kingston, would become a battlefield? And indeed, the political warfare had turned the capital into a deadly battlefield! "*This is Marcus Garvey time,*" reminded us The Gladiators on their song *Jah Jah Go Before Us*. "*Everything he said, is true / Man on top of the roof fighting their brothers.*" Garvey had also foretold that *blood would run down King Street one day*—the blood spilled by the hundreds of youths caught in the war. "*Blood in the country, blood in the country, blood in the woods... Marcus Garvey words,*" added Big Youth. "*And there will be a false leader he said! And he shall be stoned with stones!*" The last line probably displeased Prime Minister Michael "Joshua" Manley, who had almost taken the stand of a prophet during the 1971 general election. But Big Youth and the other Rasta artists weren't afraid, their music was a divine warning—and if God was with them, who shall be against them? Furthermore, Marcus Garvey had also told them that *black people's backs would be against the wall, and that the righteous would stand while the wicked would fall.* The time had come to rise to the occasion.

UNIA Triumph

Garvey launched the UNIA in Kingston in 1914, but it became a major force in New York, where Garvey went two years later. Several black associations he had come in touch with while in Panama—including the Universal Loyal Negro—joined it right away. The era was chaotic and rebellious. More than 370,000 black men were sent to Europe to fight in World War I; when they came back, they were despised and rejected despite what they had done for their country. As a consequence, they developed a strong sense of racial community. Among themselves, they felt safe. And Garvey wanted them to love themselves, physically and intellectually. He advocated the theory of *race first*, called upon the artists, the historians and the preachers to see the world through their black eyes. The black race had to get strong, to take example on other races in order to become sovereign and free. *"If you can't do what other races have done to survive, then you'll die,"* he said. The black race had to breed her own geniuses and monsters, to feel the bitterness of her own defeats, and the sweetness of her own victories. All complexions, from the lighter to the darker, were indiscriminately accepted and treated in the UNIA—but neither Whites nor women were tolerated. The idea of equality between different complexions was already unthinkable in Jamaica, and Garvey was obsessed by this problem; a direct consequence of his education.

Garvey's strength came from his determination never to be victimized. He was as proud as his father, and he never promised his black kinsmen happiness without blood sweat and tears—he never pretended to be a messiah neither. His aim was to unite black people, as shown by the motto of the UNIA: *One Aim, One God, One Destiny*—and he put his words into action. In the 1920s, the UNIA was organizing many activities in Harlem, New York, and employed more than a thousand people! The most influent black people of the time knew and respected Garvey. Elijah Muhammad, the founder of the Nation of Islam, was a member of the UNIA; Malcolm X's father used to organize UNIA meetings where he would carry his son—it eventually cost him his life, as he was murdered by white nationalists in front of his son's eyes; Jomo Kenyatta from Kenya defined himself as a Garveyite; Tony Martin underlined that Ho Chi Min, the spearhead of the Vietnamese resistance against the US, used to attend the meetings of the UNIA when living in Harlem. From Sierra Leone to Guatemala, Garvey's influence spread, and he soon found himself at the head of the most powerful African-American organization of all times.

But his enemies were also many, and quite determined. His publications were banned, his emissaries arrested; laws were voted against the UNIA. Garvey also succeeded in upsetting the FBI *and* the Russian Communist Party, who both disliked his concept of *race first*. Garvey also made some political mistakes, including meeting the Imperial Wizard of the Ku Klux Klan.

The Black Star Line

To own a maritime company in the 1920s was a privilege; only rich and influent people could afford it. Everything transited by sea, goods, men and ideas. For a self-taught black man to reach that level, it was almost unbelievable—and yet. The Black Star Line became the biggest achievement of Marcus Garvey, a thumb nose at the white elite, and a powerful signal sent to the *black race*. To gather the necessary funds, Garvey opened a subscription for the members of the UNIA in October 1919. One year later, he had collected 600,000 dollars—he bought four boats. The name of his company is an irreverent allusion to the White Star Line—it notably chartered the Titanic in 1912—, which symbolic name had probably irritated, or inspired, Garvey. The Black Star Line vessels started to cruise the West Indies, celebrated in every harbour. Unfortunately, despite a very encouraging start, the line of the black star was soon indebted for 47 million dollars.

Repatriation to Africa was going along separatism, an idea bitterly criticized by the black American writer W.E.B Dubois—the nemesis of Garvey—, who saw it as a utopia, intellectual fraud and a call to racial confrontations. Was the idea behind the Black

Star Line to embark black volunteers for Africa? The official anthem of the Black Star Line seemed to confirm it: "*Brothers, Sisters, countrymen / You'd better get on board. / Six steam ships want to sail away / Loaded with a heavy load / It's gwina take us home (...) Flying home on the Black Star Line.*" Garvey got in touch with the Government of Liberia, which agreed to welcome every migrant from the African diaspora. Garvey wanted to build a black empire there. Yet his ships were doing nothing but classical freight in the West Indies. At least in the beginning... Anyway, the symbol was so magic, so powerful, so fantastical, that he became a source of hope as far as Jamaica. In the 1970s, several Jamaican artists sang about Black Star Line ships entering Kingston Harbour to pick them up *en route* to Africa—what a vision! Yet, these boats had stopped sailing dozens of years ago. What happened? Should we blame it on internal embezzlements, a disastrous management, or on external malevolent forces? There was a very bad idea, to begin with, which discredited Garvey and his movement, and weakened the unity of the UNIA: the meeting of Garvey with the Klan.

On June 25, 1922, Marcus Garvey went to Atlanta, Georgia, to meet the Imperial Wizard of the Ku Klux Klan. This became the most controversial exploit of the black leader. Right after the meeting, Garvey sent a telegram to Liberty Hall, the headquarters of the UNIA in Harlem. While he thought he would be celebrated, he was actually booed and condemned. The other black organizations were puzzled. What was the aim of such a meeting? The Ku Klux Klan (KKK) was then experiencing a regain of popularity in America thanks to the mute movie *The Birth of A Nation*: some activists wearing white hoods revenged an innocent Southern girl who had chosen death rather than dishonour in the hands of an ugly black villain—the latter was duly lynched at the end of the movie. Between the ending of the Civil War (1865) and 1922, the KKK had allegedly been responsible for the lynching of 3,000 black people. Many black organisations, including the powerful National Association for the Advancement of Coloured People (NAACP), were trying to have the KKK officially banned in America. Meeting the Imperial Wizard, Garvey gave it an untimely legitimacy. During a speech given in New York in July 1922, Garvey justified himself: *"I met the Imperial Wizard of the Ku Klux Klan to know the position of the Klan over races. Believe it or not, I made several statements to which he answered that the Klan had never intended to interfere with black people—or to suppress them. The Klan was created in order to protect the interests of the white race in America."* Garvey was accused of complacency—worst, of coming to terms with the enemy when the UNIA officially announced that *Garvey intended to reorganize the Black Star Line shortly, and that* (the Imperial Wizard) *Clarke might buy some parts in the new company.* Garvey was wrong, but he insisted. He kept on saying that the KKK was a racial institution that stood for the *real and honest America*—ugly as it might be, it was still better than the hypocritical one.

To team up with the Ku Klux Klan was highly controversial, but at the end of the day, it was the strict application of Garvey's realpolitik. If white people were tired to see black people in their country, then they should help them to migrate. But Garvey had gone too far. He wasn't teaming up with black people's enemies, but with their executioners! The news spread rapidly among his followers, and excited disgust and mistrust. Weakened in his organisation, Garvey enabled his detractors to come on the forefront, and had no choice but to repudiate the entire Executive Committee of the UNIA during the third convention of the organisation. He thus silenced his opponents, indeed; but at which cost? The UNIA was left shaken and divided. Soon after, the Black Star Line went bankrupt. The ship was sinking. To crown it all, Garvey was accused of mailing fraud in 1922, as he allegedly sold some shares of the *Orion*, a ship he didn't yet own at the time. On the photograph coming along with the proposal, the name of the ship had been roughly crossed out and substituted. A swindle? Probably not. Apparently, the transaction was on the process. Garvey pleaded: "*My ideal goes far beyond money, it aims at the liberation of my people.*" He also said: "*None shall believe that I am so ill-intentioned that I could rob my black brother.*" He was arrested, and temporarily released. He tried to restore confidence among his followers, blaming his problems on the rival organisation of W.E.B Dubois, the NAACP. Did his enemy operate in connection with the European and American secret services to destabilize the Black Star Line? Anyway, Dubois welcomed Garvey's arrest with relief: "*Ruin and despair shall follow his downfall, until another false prophet rise again.*" Garvey was sentenced to five years in prison. He did three years in a penitentiary of Atlanta, and was then deported to Jamaica in 1927. End of the American epic journey—the sunset of the UNIA.

Rasta has faced many reverses of fortune; the most violent one being the death of Haile Selassie in 1975. Bob Marley had then to reinvent the movement in emergency (see portrait). The failure of the Black Star Line was another theological contradiction to cope. But the coming of the Negus to Jamaica in 1966 provided Rastas with a coherent spiritual explanation. While privately meeting some Rasta elders, the Emperor allegedly spread a new word: *liberation before repatriation.* Jamaica had become a new frontline, and repatriation had been conceptualized—for some, it even turned into an inner journey.

Poor Marcus

The UNIA didn't sink at once. But Garvey's triumphant come back to Jamaica was in fact a failure. And as he moved the crowd to tears with his speech, the powerful of Jamaica were already planning his downfall. To them, the arrival of Garvey was nothing but *a source of problems,* to quote *The Gleaner.* Garvey probably didn't intend to remain in tiny Jamaica. Nevertheless, he inaugurated a new Liberty Hall in Kingston, and applied his eternal recipe: printing newspapers and setting up cultural events. The UNIA was first and foremost a cultural revolution. In the very first days, the UNIA openly ambitioned to *improve eloquence and the literary taste of the youths.* The association launched a musical group that played three days a week for free at Victoria Gardens; it also regularly raised funds through concerts. Later in the States, the headquarters of the UNIA—the famous Liberty Hall—, were the meeting point of dozens of chorales, literary clubs or theatre companies. Garvey wrote several songs himself, including *Keep Cool*, and many poems; his wife later published them in two volumes: *Selection from the Poetic Meditation and The Tragedy of the White Injustice*. The title shows that art and politics were indivisible for Garvey. As a matter of fact, he disliked the book *Home To Harlem* by the famous Jamaican writer Claude McKay; he described McKay as one of these *black men who prostitute their intelligence under the yoke of white people, to show the worse sides of our people*. He also wrote: "*We must encourage our black writers who have some character, who are faithful to their race and feel proud to be black.*" To him, art should be deeply rooted into the struggle, accountable for its productions, subdued to censorship not to be prejudicial to the struggle—even out of sincerity—, and dedicated to the community. Which is exactly how Rastas consider art. Dancers, actors, painters or writers, the UNIA supported all black artists—in Harlem, it even invested in aeronautic under the influence of Colonel Julian, the first official American black pilot who would come to the meetings by jumping from a plane with his prototype parachute—he once went through the window of the police station. Such was the seed Garvey planted anywhere he intended to settle.

In 1926, Marcus Garvey travelled. In London, some white women of black members of the UNIA welcomed him, shouting: "*Africa to the Africans!*" First step towards a modernisation of the movement, Garvey gave his agreement for the creation of a subsidiary branch of the UNIA, where white people were accepted. In Paris, he was also well received. But in Montreal, he was prevented from speaking; he wasn't welcome in the West Indies neither. Eventually, tracked down and cornered, he came back to Jamaica in November 1928, and he entered the political arena. The UNIA headquarters were open at Eldeweiss Park, on Cross Road—the National Convention gathered dozens of thousands of people, who blocked the streets. Elected Counsellor, Garvey ran for the election of the Legislative Council under the banner of his own People's Political Party (PPP)—another pioneering move. Anytime he gave a speech, the crowd was overwhelmed, but his attacks on the judicial system owed him three months in prison at the Spanish Town penitentiary. Released, he challenged George Seymour-Seymour in the constituency of St Andrew. Seymour-Seymour was the owner of the Banana Producers Association, a direct competitor to the *octopus*, the United Fruit Cie. To convince the electors, he talked to their bellies. Just before the election, he offered a free meal to everyone: beef with rice and peas. Garvey was defeated. Ever since, the Rastas have bitterly reminded this treason: *Them never love, never love poor Marcus!* sang the Mighty Diamonds. *And them betray him; his own brothers sold him for rice and peas!* Bob Marley sang it too: *I'll never forget no way, they sold Marcus Garvey for rice.*

Garvey had to step back: "*My own people, unfortunately, have been fed on rum, sugar, water and sandwiches for their votes.*" Did it totally justify the overwhelming victory of Seymour-Seymour—1,677 votes to 195? *The Gleaner* had clearly cast aspersions on Garvey, and the Governor had sent the troops in various polling stations to intimidate his followers. But was the program of the PPP—*the first realistic and concrete program against imperialism*, according to the historian Ruper Lewis—, founded as usual on the reject of immigrants and the concept of *race first*, close enough to the expectations of Jamaica, isolated as it was from the international intellectual currents Garvey was accustomed to? Was Jamaica too small for Garvey? Anyway, it was becoming harder for the UNIA to raise funds in America—the organisation slowly drifted away; Garvey went bankrupt and had to sell Edelweiss Park in March 1934. He eventually left for one of the rare countries willing to welcome him, England. *"I've come to join friends,"* he said on arrival. *"I couldn't trust Jamaica any more. I come as a broken man, financially and spiritually, in my heart as well as in my wallet... And I will never go back to Jamaica, never, never."* He was right. Isolated, trapped in a vain and counter-productive criticism of Haile Selassie, criticized by the young generation of activists, Marcus Garvey suffered a first strike in 1940—this man, so powerful, was left mute and half-paralyzed. The rumour had it that he was dead and several tributes were made, that praised a man jeered a few hours earlier. This early funeral oration was like an ultimate humiliation for a man who had once held the black world of the West in the palm of his hand—it was the sad symbol of his last and lonely days. On June 10, 1940, a second strike had the better of him. Marcus Garvey died silently, far from the tribulations of a world he had partly shaped.

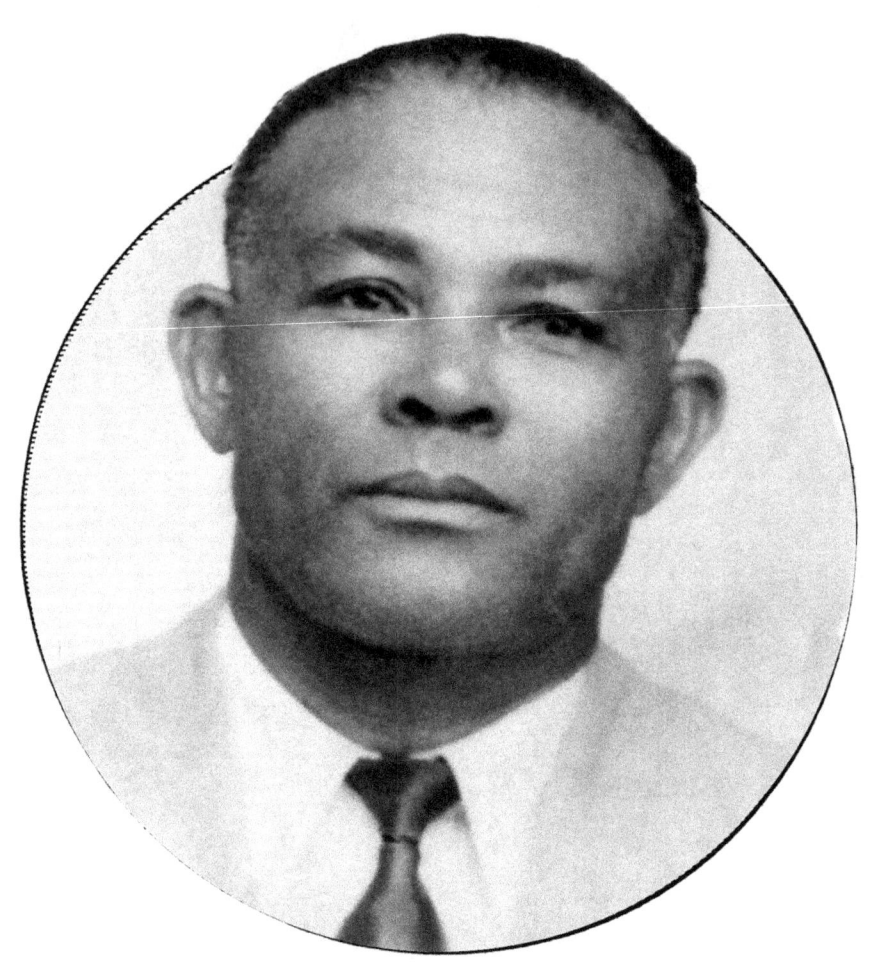

Reverend C. Henry.
(DREAD Archives)

Henry, Claudius
(1904-1986)
The Repairer of the Breach

In the early 20th century, Jamaica bred numerous apocalyptic souls, who perceived the world as a riddle to be deciphered through the Bible and deep personal meditation. These self-appointed prophets frantically read the Holy Scriptures and international newspapers and elaborate complex and feverish systems. Thirsty for godliness, Jamaica was a safe haven for visionaries. At the dawn of the century, Alexander Bedward promised he would fly away to Africa from the Tamarind Trees in front of his church in August Town. The news spread as far as Panama, from where many came to witness the miracle. But Humpty Dumpty jumped from the trees and *Humpty Dumpty had a great fall...* Bedward was sent to Bellevue Asylum; he came out several years later, feet first. The Bedwardites have always refuted this story; they denounce a governmental propaganda. God was on everyone's mind and in everyone's heart. Haile Selassie was crowned Emperor of Ethiopia in 1930, and at once identified by the most attentive observers as the returned Christ. The Bible was right. So was Marcus Garvey (see portrait) who then rallied more than 10 million people around his *Back-to-Africa* movement in America. Just before being deported to Jamaica in 1930, he exhorted black people to *turn to the East and to hold the hand of the Emperor Ras Tafari*—Haile Selassie's title. His words were interpreted and analysed as a true prophecy foretelling the defeat of the beast of Babylon, the eradication of evil and the reward of the righteous. The Negus was a Christian, and the heir of a dynasty tracing its origins from King Solomon and the Queen of Sheba; as such, he chose the Biblical title of *King of Kings, Lord of Lords, the conquering lion of the Tribe of Judah*, as tattooed on the thigh of the rider of the Apocalypse. In Jamaica, some made the link; among them was Leonard Howell. Howell was an itinerant preacher who had travelled around the world before coming back to Jamaica to eventually become the *first Rasta*; he was the first, indeed, to preach Selassie's divine character—but he afterwards changed his mind, and from the bottom of his separatist community of Pinnacle found it more comfortable to preach his own divine character.

In Kingston, street preachers stood on boxes to preach; they warned their *brethren* about Judgement Day. Among them was Nathaniel Hibbert, a freemason banana planter, and Archibald Dunkley from the mighty Atlantic Fruit Company—both had travelled the world, listening, analysing, feeding their own reflexion, and building a system from scratches, following spiritual currents and divine inspirations. These men turned shacks into temples, then into locals of the Ethiopian World Federation. Disagreements, feuds—they spied, supported or criticized each other—, and alliances were their everyday lives. They weren't so many, at first. Nevertheless, the police grew interested in their activities—Howell's, especially. In 1933, in Saint Thomas were he had been preaching for a while, he sold some 5,000 portraits of Haile Selassie as passports to Ethiopia. The government never tried to see if this *rhetorical judo hold* made any sense spirituality speaking. Legally, it was a fraud—and Howell was sent to prison for two years. Meanwhile, the Ethiopian fever spread all over Kingston and the invasion of Ethiopia by Mussolini seemed to confirm the prophecy: *And I sew the beast, and the Kings of the Earth and their armies, assembling together to declare war to the one who rides the horse*. *Time Magazine* wrote an article about the Niyabingi tribes based in Congo and Ethiopia, describing these fierce African warriors as determined to overthrow the worldwide white supremacy. Some even alleged that Haile Selassie was their secret leader. The speeches of Kingston preachers grew more radical—including Howell's—, and the police intensified their actions. Dunkley was sent for one month to jail after a speech given on Bond Street. Hibbert was arrested three times in 1935. As a result, the movement went out of breath. Most of the organisations went to sleep, Howell retired to his isolated community of Pinnacle in 1940, and in 1950, only a dozen of Rastafarian organisations were to be found in Kingston—they regrouped between 50 and 120 members each. The rest of the society ignored them; they weren't despised but regarded as dirty, especially those who wore *dreadlocks*—or dread knotty locks of hair—as the symbol of their Nazarene vow—the Nazarenes were Biblical fighters who refused any comb or scissor to touch their head. But in the early 1950s, the government— identified as a modern *Babylon*—raided Howell's Pinnacle, and scattered his disciples. It was like blowing on a bed of hot ashes. Some reached West Kingston, and set it on fire.

Kingston 12

Pinnacle had something of the Maroons camps. The Maroons were the runaway slaves from the 18th century, who almost drove the colony to its decline by systematically defeating the regular troops of His Majesty with their guerrilla tactics. They had sought refuge in the asperities of the Blue Mountains, and their lifestyle was centred on war. Violence was a vital component of their society, to such an extent that after having forced the English to grant them their freedom, they started to chase runaway slaves for the benefit of their former enemies. The same kind of hard-core dedication was to found at Pinnacle—a sort of autohypnosis. Close to their living God, the disciples smoked marijuana all day long while listening to their own imprecations. They survived by selling marijuana and sometimes raiding the nearby communities. Ganja, or marijuana, imported to Jamaica at the turn of the century for the sake of Indian workers, had become a pillar of the Rasta faith—or should we write the Howellian faith in this particular case? It was cultivated at Pinnacle, but not only. The island had become one of the biggest producers in the world. The authorities grew concerned about the parallel economy generated by this trade, and by 1957 even the Maroons from Accompong were deprived of the privilege to grow marijuana in their camps. In 1954 the police raided Pinnacle; some disciples ran away to Vere, but most of them ended up in West Kingston in the unhealthy ghetto of Back O' Wall. There they started to preach to a new and fascinated audience, the *rudies*—or juvenile delinquents. The police were harassing them. Some groups walked on North Street, asking for freedom—they were arrested. Some were beaten, and others shaved by force. The government realized how huge the movement had become, and decided to cope with it. A few months later, the honourable Ethiopian World Federation Inc. sent a messenger to Kingston, Maymie Richardson, to create antennas for the imperial church. She formed not less than ten locals, each one wearing a simple number in a revolutionary style. Right away, the Ethiopian Emperor who had just recovered his throne, decided to thank the members of the diaspora who had sustained his war efforts against the Italian troops of Mussolini by granting them some land in Ethiopia. The myth of repatriation had turned into reality! At last, Africa that had been awaiting her creators was stretching forth her hands unto them.

Some people were overwhelmed with emotion. One Mr Brandford, a Trench Town resident, claimed that he had seen His Majesty Haile Selassie in a vision; the Emperor, he said, had told him to take the first plane to Africa—having no passport, he was turned back at the airport. Drunk with hope, several groups of people also uselessly gathered at quays 1 and 2 of the Kingston wharf, looking for the ship they had seen in a vision, and that was to carry them to Liberia.

This was a spiritual movement, but also an artistic one—at night, chants reverberated through West Kingston over hypnotic drum rhythms. It was all about a burning Babylon, agonizing oppressors and the triumph of the oppressed. In the middle of this spiritual furnace, the bolder spirits exalted. Hundreds of disciples attended hundreds of little churches, avidly looking for signs. Some chased the truth between the lines of the Bible; others decided to imitate Christ by re-enacting His life under the tropical heaven. One thing was for sure: these were the last days. Times were not serious but crucial.

At the end of the 1950s, the two young parties of the island, the People's National Party (PNP) and the Jamaican Labour Party (JLP), started a merciless war. Independence was near (1962) and the stakes were important. After its humiliating defeat in the federal election of 1958, the PNP intended to win the general election of 1959. The party's henchmen were sent to Back O' Wall to spread a rumour: if elected, the PNP would organise repatriation for the *locksmen*. But Rastas have always distrust politics. They saw beyond the polls, they were part of a spiritual uprising. And when in March 1958, the self-anointed Prince Edwards C. Edwards decided to set up a Rasta convention in Kingston Pen, the temperature of West Kingston rose a little bit more. That's when Claudius Henry came back to Jamaica.

And you shall be called the repairer of the breach

The late Prince Edwards, better known as Prince Emmanuel, was the founder of a Rasta congregation called the Bobo Ashantis. The story of Emmanuel is quite obscure, his coming to the *throne* was curious, some talk about an unorthodox succession. His convention crystallised an era; it was grandiloquent, pompous, and terribly offbeat. But to make a step sideways to see the world from an original angle has always been the favourite *spiritual judo hold* of Rasta—and may God be merciful unto those who went a step too far. The Convention was advertised all through the island,

and somewhat misrepresented—or at least amplified; when the news reached the North Coast, it was described as departure day for Africa. Consequently, many Rastas sold their belongings and converged to Kingston, the first stage towards the Promised Land. These pilgrims eventually joined a consequent crowd of 3,000 souls, composed of preachers, disciples, and friendly observers. Piles of tires were set afire behind the Tivoli movie theatre while drums and Rasta chants raised in the suffocating atmosphere. Preachers succeeded each other on a handmade stage to deliver fiery speeches through a portable speaker to a stoned and devoted audience. At 4 a.m., a delegation led by Emmanuel walked on Victoria Park to *capture* the city. The police intervened and quickly dispersed everyone. This march was a minor event, but it betrayed the radicalisation of the movement. The moderates were losing ground as violence seduced more and more disciples. Furthermore, a lot of robbers had let their hair and beard grow to infiltrate the movement—the lucrative *ganja* trade was their target. Rasta became a nest of vipers where anarchists, thieves and genuine disciples mingled.

Claudius Henry sprang from the middle of this not so ill assorted mob. Born in Jamaica, he was then living in New York where he had experienced his first vision in 1921 at age seventeen: "*A voice talked to me, the same who once talked to Jeremiah, and she said: before I find you in the belly, I know you; before you were born, I sanctified you, and I made a prophet out of you.*" Guided by the angel's voice, Henry joined the Anglican Church, and was ordained priest in Cleveland, Ohio, in 1953. According to him, he was then literally living on his knees, his hands joined in prayers, fortifying his faith through fasting. His psychiatric records were opened in 1935 after he was confined for unauthorized preaching. "*The first night the messenger came to me to tell me: they want to send you to the lunatic asylum but you won't stay there more than three days.*" Once Henry freed, the angel manifested again, exhorting him to read Isaiah, chapter 58, verse 12: *you shall rebuild the ancient foundations and you shall be called the repairer of the breach*. From this apocryphal vision, he earned the nickname of *the repairer of the breach*. We don't know when or how he became a relative to Prince Emmanuel but, apparently, the latter personally invited him to speak at the National Convention. Henry was already in Kingston, where he had arrived on December 9, 1957. Indeed, God had urged him to inform the poor people of the absolute necessity to head back to Africa. Among those who paid attention to his speeches was Edna Fisher. Moved by his words, she humbly approached him, and told him about her house at 78 Rosalie Avenue in the community of Waterhouse, Kingston. She invited him to open a church in her backyard and even provided a part of the necessary funds. Her help was welcome as Henry was broke. Indeed, he had spent all his money on clothes for the needy; the Reverend practiced what he preached—amen.

* * *

Henry's church wore the baroque name of *The Seventh Emmanuel Brethren*. It was first linked to the *Ethiopian World Federation* (EWF) but Henry was a prophet of his own, and tensions led him to part with the EWF. Cecil G. Gordon, then in charge of the EWF in Jamaica, published an official letter of rupture in *The Star*—he had probably foreseen that Henry was up to no good. The preacher rechristened his church *African Reform Church of God in Christ*. At the door now stood two disciples holding iron rods—very convenient to break the bones of the curious. The church was located in the backyard, passed a V8 Ford car and a van; it was a humble building with a notice pinned on the door. It read: *no smoking during meatings* (sic). At this point, one usually met Miss Edna, the first disciple of all, who retorted to the inquisitive visitor that the Reverend was resting. "Come back later," confirmed the devoted Mr Jarrett, an elderly disciple wearing a beard and a pair of seamless trousers. The Repairer of the Breach was a busy prophet. A stout man with a light complexion, Henry was also a mysterious man. "*Long time now I wrote His Imperial Majesty an' I don't get no answer,*" quoted *The Gleaner*. "*I spent fifteen an' three pence an' register the letter to him. When I don't get no answer I go an' see the Postmaster General and the Postmaster General say him trace the letter to England and that if I want to trace it any further I have to pay fourpance. I paid the fourpance but I don't get no further so I spent five hundred pounds and go to Ethiopia go-see His Imperial Majesty miself.*" When he returned, hundreds of beard men had gathered in front of the 78 Rosalie Avenue. They were singing liturgies and playing drums despite the rain, waiting to embark to Africa. Most of them had pinned their blue tickets on their shirts. Some 15,000 had been handed all over the island—supposedly for free, but in fact sold for 1 shilling each. But they were priceless to their lucky owners as they represented the promise of repatriation.

We bring back the Messiah of Israel

Man is obstinate in his mistakes. Howell had already deceived many people by selling some portraits of Selassie as passports to Africa. But nothing could quench the thirst for Africa, and repatriation was a collective obsession. So when the blue tickets of Henry started to circulate through the island, cohorts of Rastas hit the road to reach Kingston; some walked, others jumped on a bus or in a taxi. They held their precious ticket in the bottom of their pocket. Some had hurriedly sold their belongings or their small plot of land at a very low price. Their neighbours laughed at them, but they stood firm, asserting that they were about to kiss the soil of the motherland. "*Idiots!*" giggled their neighbours. "*With your blasphemous beliefs, your so-called prophet and your dirty hair! You will soon come back to beg bread!*" But *blessed is the one who reads the words of this prophecy (...) because the time is near.*

In front of the 78 Rosalie Avenue hundreds of people were now waiting. Some wore dreadlocks, others a simple beard; conscious of the solemnity of the instant some had put on their nicest uniform. Rasta flags were floating all over: red *for the blood that they shed*, yellow *for the gold that they stole*, and green *for the lands of Africa*. They were told that the Reverend was in Africa, and that he would be back by the morrow. They just had to wait. So they started to load their chalices with ganja and to play drums to give thanks to the Lord—O glorious day! The rain started to fall—then stopped, *as ordered by the Reverend*, went the rumour. The mud that testified of this miracle was celebrated. And suddenly, here he was! The Repairer of the Breach! Straight from Ethiopia. He even led a few prayers. But time was fleeing, October 5 was closing in, and the Prophet started to wait for the mailman with growing anxiety. In order to organise repatriation, he had approached the government of several nations such as Ghana, England, Cuba, the USSR or Liberia, asking for assistance; but so far, he had received no answer. The State Secretary of Jamaica alone wrote back, reminding that no African country seemed willing to welcome him or his disciples. *A highly unsatisfying answer*, moaned the prophet. On October 5, the consequent crowd in front of the church grew impatient, and the prophet claimed he was sick. From the bottom of his bed he wrote to the newspapers and to the Secretary of the United Nations. As people outside got ready to embark, the Reverend evoked a misunderstanding. He had never planned to go back to Africa *today*, but to hold a conference on repatriation—the Jesophat Conference. He blamed it on the journalists: "*Them print a whole pile o' lie in the paper and make all these people come here and some o' them can't even go-back home now.*" Yet, the beard men were asked to clean before the journey—some were even allegedly asked to shave their heads and beards. Food was sold to them, and their generous donations were accepted—the money came from the sale of their belongings. The sun eventually rose on Waterhouse on October 6, and Africa remained as far as ever. Outside, people stood in the rain, in a stoning silence; from time to time, someone would cry out for *the man who gives away passports*—in vain. As awaken in the middle of a dream, the beard men seemed to be more abased than angry. The police who stood nearby didn't have to intervene. The authorities had smelt something fishy from the start; they were waiting for Henry when he landed in Kingston, to make sure he was really coming from Ethiopia—he was. But what did he exactly do there? Who did he meet, if he ever met any one?

The most reasonable left the place—others, those who had sold all their belongings and who had nowhere to go, remained. They demanded an explanation, and were told they had misunderstood the whole thing, and that it was time to move now. Anyway, food was running short. The stunned Rastas eventually walked away—another setback on the long and painful road to the Promised Land. Following this sad day, Rev. Henry was fined a hundred pounds. But he remained as determined as ever: "*Them hang Paul Bogle, them betray and sell out Marcus Garvey, them crucify Jesus Christ*. But none o' that gwine happen to me! We have power in America and when the time ready, when the Gentile dip him off in blood we getting two ship and plane and machine gun, for if we can't go-back to Africa by peace we going back by force.*"

Dear Dr Castro

Following the aborted repatriation, the Reverend became more radical. He blamed it on the *Babylonian governments* that hadn't supported him in spite of his acting in the holy name of Haile Selassie. They would pay for such an offence, one day—just like Pharaoh who opposed Moses. More and more people attended his church. But on Rosalie Avenue, the mood had changed. Noticing that his people were somewhat undisciplined—especially the Rastas—, the Reverend bought some dark uniforms for his disciples and forced them to wear them; because of the berets, the Rastas had to shave their dreadlocks. The church started to resemble a military camp. Was it linked to *the powerful connections in America* mentioned by Henry in his press release?

---

* Bob Marley later used these lines in his song *Guiltyness*.

He hadn't lied; he was in touch with an African-American small group of activists based in New York, the First Africa Corp (FAC). This small secret organisation was located at 332 Beekman Avenue in the Bronx, and composed of black police officers who ambitioned to liberate Africa trough armed struggle. They committed armed robberies to finance their project. One of them, the young Noel Agard—the driver during the robberies—was born in Jamaica, and had come to live in New York as a kid. He had kept in touch with some relatives in Jamaica. Furthermore, Reynold Henry, the Reverend's son, was a member of the FAC. No one exactly knows how or when he joined the group, but he had grown up in New York, where he acted as an agent for the African Reform Church.

At the time in Jamaica, Henry's church also came under the influence of one Calvert Claude Beckford, aka Thunder. Was this mysterious disciple linked to the FAC? Or was he an undercover FBI agent? When did he precisely join the Church? Sybil E. Hibbert, a retired journalist, recently published an article in *The Observer*, relating her encounter with the Reverend at Rosalie Avenue at the time. She knocked on the door and was told to come in: *"I pushed my head in and straightened up to find myself staring into the barrels of seven rifles. The men behind the guns were bearded and wore dreadlocks. Heavy puffs of smoke were exhaled into my confused face. The smell of ganja was unmistakeable."* She depicted Calvert "Thunder" Beckford as the most aggressive disciple: *"After about four hours of grilling it was "Thunder" who announced: "The woman is a spy. We have to get rid of her."* But the Reverend opposed his decision, eventually taking the journalist around the church to show her the carvings in wood of the Black Jesus and the Black Virgin Mary. One thing is for sure, *Beckford started to control the church,* as later testified Wilfred Brown in court—Wilfred was a peanuts seller in Kingston, one of the first disciples of Henry whom he had met in Spanish Town in 1958; he had helped building up the church.

Calvert "Thunder" Beckford replaced liturgies by physical exercises; physical abilities, he stated, would be required to go back to Africa. He even set up training sessions at Rosalie Avenue. One day, Miss Edna worried over dozens of machetes and batons scattered all over the church—she was told that they were stocked on Beckford's order. One Monday, the peanuts seller Wilfrid Brown saw Calvert Beckford as he was carrying some boxes and jute bags inside the Church. Wilfrid saw him opening one of the boxes, taking a pistol out of it, and sticking it into Henry's drawer. In the yard, several disciples were making double-edged machetes in a Biblical fashion. *"Those without weapon won't go to Rocky Point!"* warned Beckford. Rocky Point, in Saint Thomas, had been chosen to become the grandiloquent scenery of an incredible production. Henry and his disciples gathered in front of a photographer from Kingston hired for the event. Wearing their nicest clothes, they brandished swords and machetes in front of the camera. These pictures were later used against Henry to prove his violent intentions—unfortunately, the author was unable to locate any of them. Two months later, the Reverend went to the States, leaving his precious Church with Beckford. *"When Henry left, Beckford started to preach violence and to eat dirty things like pork, rabbits and all that,"* explained Higgins, an early disciple. All these testimonies uttered during Henry's trial might have intended to put the blame on Calvert Beckford—who wasn't here to defend himself anymore. Blame it on the dead.

Henry swore he had discovered the arsenal when he returned from America. There were knives, sharpened machetes, batons of dynamite, a revolver, and a rifle. Henry said he was upset, as many scared disciples had deserted the Church that now resembled a training camp. In the neighbourhood, people whispered that the Reverend had threatened to play football with the head of Prime Minister Norman Manley, and that he accused the PNP government of being *stained with blood.* The intelligence apparently came to the Jamaican government from the British secret services through the US. On April 6, 1960, Deputy Superintendent McIntosh was sent to raid the 78 Rosalie Avenue; officially, he was looking for *ganja*. At 5:30 a.m., the police cordoned the area, and McIntosh knocked on the door. "*Who dat? Who dat?*" answered a voice inside. "*Police! Open the door!*" said the Deputy Superintendent. Henry opened up, read the warrants, and then whispered: "*All right, Sir. Do what you have to do.*"

The police who were looking for *ganja* found the weapons: seven batons of dynamite, first, inside a chest; eleven more, behind a curtain. Then weapons like rain, including 2,500 electronic detonators, a rifle, an Ivor Johnson pistol calibre 32 and dozens of ammunitions, shells filled with dry cement, a spear. Meanwhile, McIntosh crossed the yard to enter the small church where twenty disciples were sleeping on the benches, armed from head to toes. One Rupert Ellis war carrying a double-edged machete while one Vidal Valentine had three knives and a handmade gun. Among those sleeping wolves, some banderols read: *God's Righteous Army, Lion of Judah,* or *Freedom.* This was already quite an exceptional raid but there was more to come. A policeman discovered several letters inside a suitcase, typed with the Underwood typewriting machine found in the next room. They contained a list of squadrons with the names of their respective soldiers, the Black Savage, the Black Snipers, the Demob Squad—it sure looked like the chart of a paramilitary organization. Then came the unbelievable! A copy of the letter sent on August 18, 1959, to Fidel Castro, in Cuba. Clarice Atkinson, who worked at the post office in Whitfield Town, later identified Claudius Henry as the sender of the original. The contents left McIntosh breathless.

"Dear Dr Castro,
We wish to draw your attention to the conditions which confront us today as poor underprivileged people which were brought here

from Africa by the British slave traders over 400 years ago. We now desire to return home in peace, to live under our own vine and fig tree, otherwise a government like yours that gives justice to the poor. All our efforts to have a peaceful repatriation have proven a total failure. Hence we must fight a war for what is ours by right. Therefore we want to assure you, Sir, and your government that Jamaica and the rest of British West Indies will be turned over to you after this war which we are preparing to start for Africa's freedom is completed, and we her scattered children are restored. We are getting ready for an invasion on the Jamaican Government, therefore we need your help. We have the necessary men for the job. The Black people of Jamaica are with you and your government one hundred percent and desire to see that Jamaica gets into your hands before we leave for Africa."

Fidel Castro had not yet become the favourite *red threat* of America, but his *coup d'état* of February 1958 had drawn international attention—and Jamaica was close by. Of course, Henry's arsenal was derisory but what if Castro had backed him? This letter was an act of felony signed by twelve traitors, including Calvert Beckford, Miss Edna Fisher, and Jarrett. But Henry's signature didn't appear. Some disciples later confessed they had signed without reading; others reminded the court that they couldn't even read or write. Henry was arrested, so were Miss Edna and a handful of disciples—but Calvert "Thunder" Beckford wasn't among them. The investigations led the police to two disciples named Noel Bryan and Lincoln Braham, who lived in the community of Cockburn Pen. When they reached, thirty bearded men welcomed them by shouting: *"Ras Tafari is God!"* Dozens of handmade bombs were found in the backyard. The newspapers covered the story extensively. At one point, *The Star* was even accused of making unnecessary publicity of these insignificant Rastafarians by multiplying articles and inquiries. On April 30, columnist Clinton Parchment denounced *the rascal Rastafarians*.

> "The majority are lazy, dirty, violent and lawless scoundrels mouthing religious phrases to cover up their aversion to work and their ill abilities (...). It looks in fact strongly as though the Government too is afraid of the Rastafarians! (...) They constitute a highly dangerous nucleus capable of exploding in any crisis (...). Lawless, disorderly, ignorant, irresponsible and pugnacious, the Rastafarians are an anti-social group doubly dangerous in a country where blood runs hot and law and order are anyway little more than skin-deep (...) The banning of their sect and the repression of their habits is something that no Jamaican government with claims to public service ought to hold back from."

About her visiting the Church at the time, the retired journalist from *The Observer* Sybil E. Hibbert wrote: "*The premises were full of chanting Rastafarians clad in black uniforms. There was singing and dancing and smoking and the beating of drums.*" But Henry never claimed to be a Rasta. He preached the divinity of Haile Selassie, indeed—asked about the portrait of Haile Selassie hanging on his wall, he answered that he was his God; but asked about Marcus Garvey's *Back-to-Africa* movement, he retorted that he was much more into *Moses' movement*. A former disciple still alive today, and who lives next door to what was once Henry's church—it has been totally razed—, disdainfully shrugged when asked about Rasta: "*No, man. This wasn't a Rasta thing, we were no Rastas.*" Yet, the relationship between Henry and Rasta appears to have been complicated. Some Rastas followed Henry, who stated during his trial—according to *The Gleaner*—that many of them were *undesirable* as they refused to reform. But Henry had borrowed many concepts from Rasta, and the press sometimes referred to him as a *beard man preacher*. All this bad publicity eventually attracted the attention of some foreign journalists. On May 2, 1960, the Jamaican government banned the issue of *Time Magazine*. Page 17, an article about Henry entitled *Jamaica The Lion of Judah's Men*, was illustrated with a picture of the Reverend surrounded by his disciples*. The caption read: *Fire, Lightning. White people must fall, blood must run.* The ban wasn't politically motivated, though; but linked to the on-going trial of Henry and fifteen of his men for treason; it was actually a matter of impartiality.

Henry was tried under the Treason Felony Act, the first case ever recorded in Jamaica at the time—the law had come into effect in 1869. Outside the courthouse, dozens of Rastafarians demonstrated by singing, shouting and showing banderols reading: *Give us back our leader or get prepared to jail 20,000 of us.* Inside, Claudius Henry, Kenneth Morgan, Nelson Dawkins, Vernon Washington, Sylvester Jarrett, Lascelles Stone, Edna Fisher, Wilfred Brown, John Bryan, Lincoln Graham, Gifford Higgins, Hazel Collins, Reuben Jackson, Fitz Albert Brooks, Cecil Moore and Rupert Davis faced the Judge. They were accused of having around December 5, 1959, *incited to rebellion against the government of this island*. Outside, some Rastas stoned the police vehicles, before being chased by tear gas. But while the entire nation focused on the 53 year-old Reverend, things got out of hand at 78 Rosalie Avenue. Indeed, Henry's son arrived from New York to take control of the church.

---

* The author was unable to find a copy of this magazine, and the one advertised on *The Time* website featuring the date of May 2, doesn't feature any article about Henry. These following details are reproduced from an article of *The Gleaner*.

I thought Henry was joking

While his father was tried for felony, Reynold Henry—sometimes referred to as *Ronald*—came down to Jamaica with seven fighters from the FAC; they were former G.I.'s. They went to the Red Hills outside Kingston to build a paramilitary training camp. Several disciples of Henry surreptitiously joined them, but things went wrong up there. Did Beckford and Reynold become rivals? Or was Beckford, already responsible for the radicalisation of the African Reform Church, an undercover agent working from the government, as Reynold later claimed? Anyway, on June 15, at approximately 7 a.m., a disciple named Al Thomas came out of his tent, and witnessed a curious scene. Reynold Henry was standing in front of five soldiers, including Beckford, whom he accused of felony. Leaning towards the cook Albert Gabbidon, he asked him to go for the automatic pistol. To the rebels he said: "*You five are here tried for felony, and I will expel you from the camp.*" Beckford inquired: "*What are you going to do? Deliver us to the government?*" Henry shook his head: "*No, I can't do that.*" He then ordered the five men to lay on the ground, and asked Gabbidon who had just returned with the gun: "*You sure you told me the truth?*" Then Thomas heard the surreal order: "*Kill them!*" But he didn't take it seriously, this made no sense, why should he ki...?—gunshots exploded. One—two—three. Then Gabbidon turned to Henry, said a few words, and put an end to the killing. The two survivors stood up, they were spared. But Beckford was among the three victims. Alvin Irving was shocked. "*I had come from the States to train Rastafarians,*" he later told the Court. "*I paid for my plane ticket and wasn't expecting any salary (...) I thought Henry was joking (...) As I was digging the graves, I asked* (Eldred) *Morgan why they had shot these guys, and he said he had heard that Beckford was a Private Investigator.*" Henry's son and his American friends weren't joking. Did they ambition, as written in *The Time*, to turn Jamaica into a *Rastafarian republic*? That sounds quite unlikely. The FAC didn't seem to be of Rasta obedience, they were just gathering weapons to prepare an armed insurrection.

Informed of their presence, the police spotted them in July; 250 men were sent after them. Unfortunately, it included some British soldiers from the Royal Hampshire Regiment that resided in the island. According to the Jamaican law, these foreign soldiers had the right to carry unloaded weapons only. Ambushed by the members of the FAC, they thus surrendered at once. They were ordered to kneel down, and shot at blank point. Two of them died on the spot, while three others were seriously injured. The members of the FAC then jumped into a van and drove away. The government added a hundred men to the hunt, sent a plane over the hills, and exhorted the peasants to inform them on the fugitives—but they were too scared to comply. Jamaica is a small island and the Red Hills are even smaller. The members of the FAC were soon caught and brought to Court—little is said about the circumstances of their arrest. Gabbidon, who had committed the murders, and Reynold Henry, who was the mastermind behind the insurrection, were both sentenced to death. The son of the Reverend was hanged shortly afterwards at the Saint Catherine District Prison—an inglorious ending. Meanwhile, his father was condemned for treason, and sentenced to six years of hard labour. The Henry family was going through a rough time. But the Reverend hadn't preached his last sermon yet.

They make the concrete blocks

When Walter Rodney came back to Jamaica in 1968, he wasn't a simple Guyanese student of the University of the West Indies anymore. A brilliant orator, he had became the spearhead of the black liberation struggle in the Caribbean. Appointed Professor at the same university at the end of his studies, he first fascinated his students, then the whole society. His lengthy speeches about Black Power drew attention in a country where books like the autobiography of Malcolm X or Eldridge Cleaver's *Soul On Ice* were banned. Crowds gathered on the campus to hear his violent and revolutionary rhetoric that contrasted with his sweet and gentle manners. The Rastas from West Kingston regularly invited him to their conferences, and he became a bridge between the two worlds. On August 17, 1968, he spoke in George VI Park in front of a crowd of activists. Among them stood Rev. Henry, and several members of the New Creation Tabernacle Church. Ever since he had come out of prison in 1966, Henry had transformed his doctrine from *Back-to-Africa* to *Building-Africa-in-Jamaica*. His disciples hadn't forgotten him. When he left Kingston to settle in the parish of Clarendon, they all went with him.

A few days after his speech in George VI Park, Walter Rodney went to Clarendon to visit Henry's church. The New Jerusalem of Henry was still young, but already quite impressive. Beyond the Church and its one hundred active members, there were a concrete blocks plant, a bakery and several houses. Henry was then sixty, and not such an orator as his host; but this very day, Rodney didn't speak, he listened, observed keenly and then reported:

> "At Kemp's Hill, in the middle of a most depressed area which is the Prime Minister's constituency, Rev Henry has gathered a number of black brothers and sisters, and they have turned themselves into an independent black economic community. In less than a year they built themselves an attractive church and several dwelling houses—all of concrete for they make the concrete blocks. They have proper plumbing and electricity, and in case the local supplies are inadequate they have their own water tanks and electrical generator. They operate a fish shop from the outset and later they set up a bakery. In spite of massive persecution by the government, the police and the army, the Henry community has extended to several other parts of the island and at Cross they are doing the same thing all over again—except that this time they are achieving it

all in a matter of weeks instead of months. The importance of the above example of economic re-awakening is that it proves the great capacity of our people once they are resolved to strike out for themselves."

The *massive persecution* evoked above wasn't a mere revolutionary expression. The Jamaican authorities kept an eye on Henry's activities, as well as on people close to him—including Walter Rodney. In 1968, the teacher attended a conference in Canada but couldn't come back—his Visa had been revoked. "*The government accused me of plotting with Reverend Henry,*" he wrote, "*which means they consider Henry as a criminal. These accusations come from a small group of people terrified by the demonstration of black solidarity.*" This arbitrary decision linked to the Reverend—whose past was then evoked at length—, started some riots in Kingston that cost the lives of several persons. Rodney was never readmitted to the University, and trod his revolutionary path until he was murdered over politics in Guyana in 1980.

The 1972 elections
Michael Manley was only 44 when he first ran for election in 1972. Though he had officially inherited the PNP from his retired father in 1969, he was lacking experience, and his campaign was a mere warm-up for the 1976 election. But Manley had charisma; a refined and elegant young man, he soon captivated the country. The dinosaurs from the JLP hung on to their colonial privileges, trying to get the angry street under control while Manley was blowing on the embers. Everything in Jamaica was crying out for a change. In 1968, a new music was born, *Reggae*. Through deep and spiritual rhythms, it translated the Africanist aspirations of a society suffocating under racial prejudice. Black pride exploded all other the world, and Rasta was its Jamaican echo. Of course, the Henry Scandal and the Corral Gardens Incident—some Rastas murdered a gasoline intendant, an incident that launched

a brutal and blind national repression—had given Rasta a bad name. But the official *University Report* of 1960 about the Ras Tafari movement, as well as the official missions to Ethiopia resulting from this report, and the visit of Haile Selassie to Jamaica in 1966 (Henry was then imprisoned), had changed the image of Rasta. These *blackheart men* said to take little children away, had become the symbols of black integrity in a corrupt Babylonian system. Michael Manley felt, and reinforced, the power of Rasta. He put on his lion's skin and started to roar with the brethren. But he needed an adviser, so he got in touch with Rev. Henry. How did the candidate and the former convict connect? It remains quite obscure, though M. G. Smith, one of the three authors of the *University Report*, was an active councillor of the young Manley—a report recently questioned by the Jamaican professor Robert A. Hill who describes it as *an intelligence document prepared by the anthropologist MG Smith, acting covertly on behalf of N*(orman) *W*(ashington) *Manley*. Could Smith be the missing link?

Anyway, Henry was a very good choice—he knew about the cultural codes of a movement that was born before his eyes. Not to mention the few thousand disciples he sent to support Manley during his meetings. Henry did even more; he made Manley legitimate among Rastas. First, he gave him a meaningful nickname, *Joshua*—it was adopted at once, and quoted in many reggae songs and various articles. The Biblical Joshua—Moses' brother—was responsible for entering the Promised Land with his people after his brother's passing—a powerful symbol. Every successful legend needs to be rooted into history so Henry dug up the story of a young Michael leading an angry mob in front of the buildings of the JBC in 1962, where he shouted: "*These are the walls of Jericho!*" Manley had a new name, but he still needed a new language. Henry taught him the *I-words*. Rastas built them by replacing the first syllable of positive words by the personal pronoun *I*, symbol of unity and purity—creation became *I*-ration, for example. When talking about himself, Manley said *I-man*, and all his speeches started with a loud *Hail that man!*—a Rasta reference used in a few *Joshua songs* recorded at the time. Denouncing the colonial system, promising to share the wealth and to establish racial equality, Joshua convinced the intellectuals and the middle-class with his rhetoric, and the *sufferers*—or underprivileged—with his promises. He was yet missing an accessory—that's when Claudius Henry came up with the idea of the rod of correction. Henry had a rod himself, and was photographed with it in New York in 1956 by the famous photographer James Van Der Zee. But Manley's rod couldn't be an ordinary one, not even an extraordinary one—it had to be exceptional. As a matter of fact, Manley had allegedly received his own from Haile Selassie in person, during an official visit to Ethiopia in 1970. Henry's idea wasn't good, it was magic.

Now, Michael "Joshua" Manley had become unbeatable. During the 1971 campaign, he hit the stage during the free concerts his wife had set up with Clancy Eccles, holding his rod in front of a delighted crowd. Without a word, he raised it above his head, creating a wave of bliss. Backstage, his JLP opponent Edward Seaga was infuriated—*he* was reputed as a powerful *obeahman* (a voodoo master), not Manley! How could a stupid rod defeat him on his own ground? The rod became a central element of the campaign, and an obsession to Seaga who went as far as counterfeiting it. He held a fake rod in front of a camera, skinning his teeth—and then published the picture in the newspaper. The caption read: *I've got it now!* But this trick mostly underlined his powerlessness and anger. Trying to undermine the power of the rod, he reinforced its legitimacy.

Rev Henry then unwillingly came on the forefront of the campaign. The JLP printed a pamphlet, since known as the *bogus pamphlet*, that underlined the suspicious links between Manley and Henry, described as a former convict condemned in his time for treason. *How come the father of a traitor had become the adviser of the PNP candidate?* asked the JLP. Especially as Henry's son was tried and hanged under a PNP government led by Joshua's father! Three pictures illustrated the pamphlet, representing a mocked Trinity: Haile Selassie, Joshua and Henry. Edward Seaga accused Henry of manipulating the PNP. *The JLP lies!* retorted the incriminated party.

At the end of the day, and despite the efforts of Seaga, Michael "Joshua" Manley wan the 1972 general election by a landside. Jamaica entered the decade on a dream—and left it eight years later in the middle of a nightmare.

I was hiding in Egypt

What went wrong after Manley's victory? How come Henry didn't benefit from it? On the contrary his bakery and his church were burnt down—a divine intervention, giggled his detractors. Once again, the Reverend had to retire from the forefront. Nevertheless, the days of the 78 Rosalie Avenue were past and gone. In 1974, a Jamaican journalist named Alex D. Hawks visited Henry's property in Sandy Bay, Clarendon. He gave an impressive description of the settlement. The land originally belonged to Sadie, the Reverend's wife, who had inherited it. Apparently, the couple settled there as soon as Claudius came out of prison, and they started to grow tobacco. Too demanding and harmful to man, it was soon replaced by vegetables, and an army of chickens.

By 1974, Sandy Bay had become a community with several rum shops, well-kept alleys, warehouses and various shops. Henry gave a job to many people around, and the economical success of Sandy Bay soon crossed the borders of his kingdom. As usual, spirituality was at the heart if his project; he called his church The Ethiopian Peacemakers School of Ancient Traditional Bible Story. Everyone between Old Harbour and May Pen praised the former traitor. His turf was developing rapidly; the same year, he bought more land, and gave a portion to the government in order to obtain the power connection and a main sewer as counterparts. To irrigate the pens where the goats roamed, the Henrys invested 25,000 dollars. Sandy Bay, just like the Ark, sailed a raging sea. The dry climate of Clarendon was pernicious to the cattle, so the Henrys had to build water tanks. Restrictions on imported goods were also an obstacle, but nothing could discourage Henry, who erected a new building on the nearby main road to sell his own products. He also opened the Peacemakers Bakery in Green Bottom. Aged 71, the Repairer of the Breach never got weary despite political harassment. Indeed, his former allies from the PNP apparently disliked his projects—whether foes or friends, politicians hate to witness the rise of a leader whom they perceive as a natural opponent. About politicians, Henry was outspoken: "*They know I'm not on their side since they have betrayed the people. So they try to get rid of me.*" Bankers under influence became reluctant to lend him money, administrative harassment intensified, and the authorities threatened to seize his properties. "*They might do anything the devil tells them to do, I'll keep on doing the works of God despite their provocations.*" The political acquaintances of the Reverend had turned to bitterness. The progressive ideas of the PNP inspired by Garvey's theories didn't attract Henry anymore. In 1976, violence was at its peak—both parties had armed their supporters who fought daily in the streets. The comedy had turned to tragedy. Manley declared the State of Emergency, and even had some opponents arrested whom he accused of terrorist activities. Some feared a *coup à la* Castro—a close friend of Manley. Eventually the oil crisis, the IMF demands and an unofficial civil war brought Jamaica on the verge of chaos. On Christmas day of 1977, the Reverend talked to his disciples, saying that for many years, he was hiding in Egypt but that the time had come for him to take a stand. He focused his speech on Michael Manley, without calling his name, but comparing him to Saul: "*When he started to rule Israel, the spirit of God was with him and he respected the law. But when God forsake him, people came to ask him: why do you want to destroy us, Saul?*" Getting closer to Cuba and the USSR, Michael Manley irritated the Reverend who saw the pagan Communists as his worst enemies—the days of the FAC were far away. Furthermore, the PNP supported Mengitsu, who had overthrown and murdered Haile Selassie in 1975. "*Wh does our leader keep on talking about Communism? Is it because he refused to follow the instructions of God?"* The Reverend prophesised the end of Manley, promising him a slow and painful agony; the evil was to slowly consume him from inside, till his ultimate death. These words became very dull twenty years later, when Manley died from cancer.

Claudius Henry entered eternity on September 26, 1986—aged 83. Ironically, the communist Workers' Party of Jamaica officially saluted him, as he had *followed the footsteps of Marcus Garvey in a religious way, enduring the same calomnies and sufferations from those who tried to belittle his actions.* The community he left behind—which still exists—is the testimony of his vision, the result of a life that led him from Jamaica to the Ethiopian Court, to jail. His son was hanged for treason, his name slandered—yet he almost offered the seat of Prime Minister to the son of the man who had his son executed. Eventually, Rev Henry built up his own Jerusalem in the remote parish of Clarendon, faithful to his living God murdered in 1975, and whom he worshipped until his very last breath.

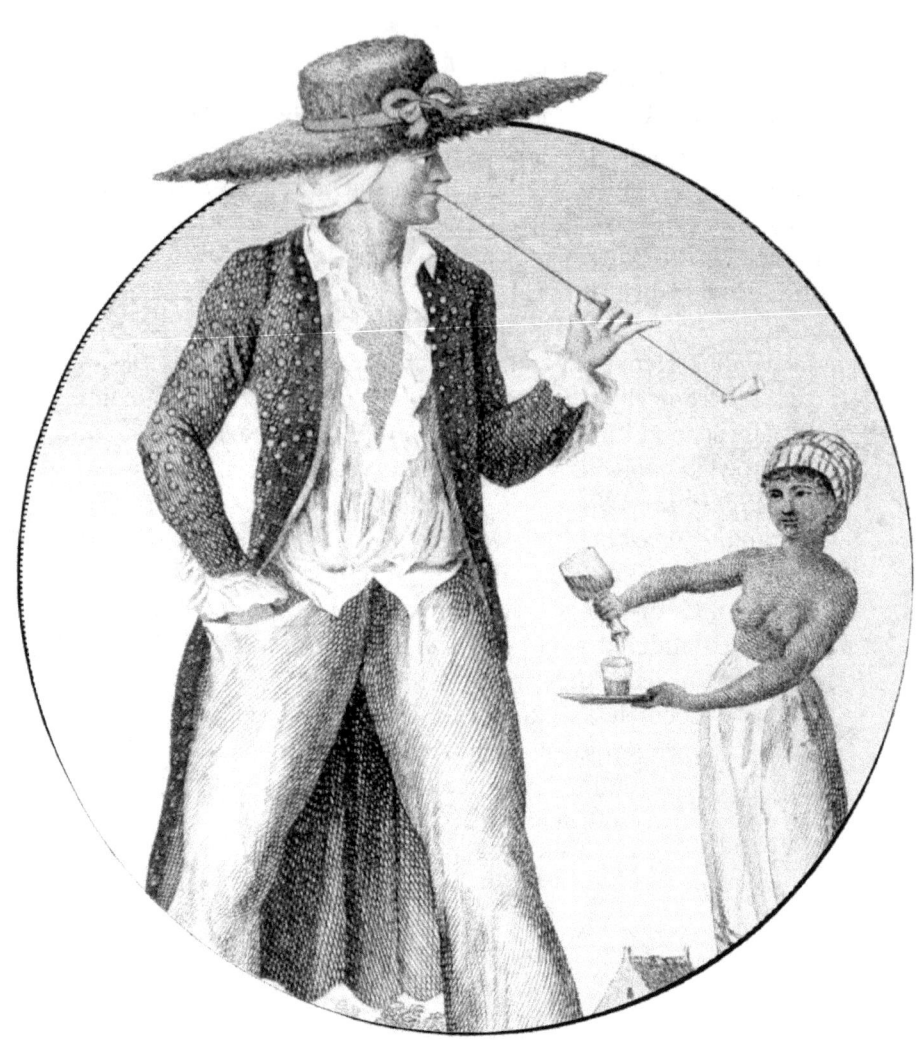

There's no known portrait of Lewis Hutchinson but this planter of the New World (Surinam) drawn in the late 18th century by George Stedman is very close to what Lewis Hutchinson might have looked like.
(DREAD Archives)

Hutchinson, Lewis
(1733-1773)
First Serial Killer

Lewis Hutchinson lived in the 18th century in Val Pedro, in the parish of St Ann, where his name awoke fear in the hearts of his contemporaries. Many bloody tales circulated about this Scottish surgeon who had come to Jamaica in 1760, and who had bought a mansion pompously called Edinburgh Castle— actually a simple two-room mansion with two turrets overhanging the only path leading from Kingston to the North Coast. Hutchinson lived there with some twenty slaves freshly disembarked from Africa; contrary to those born and raised in Jamaica, they were still entangled in their dark and pagan African beliefs. Hutchinson, also *feared* as the mad master, terrorized the whole parish. His name regularly popped up in discussions about unexplained disappearances and dead bodies stuck into hollow tree trunks and left for John Crows— vultures—to devour. Hutchinson was a quarrelsome man who extended his cattle herd with any errant animal crossing his path. But no one dared confronting him. Thus he peacefully ruled his small and evil empire, surrounded by decomposing corpses piled in a nearby natural pit. When the kids of Saint Ann weren't quiet, they were threatened with the *ol' Hutchinson* who beheaded his victims in the middle of the night and dipped the blade of his knife into their blood to lick it clean with a maniac laugh. And indeed, although a lot remains to be discovered about Hutchinson, there's no doubt he was the first serial killer of Jamaica.

Dr Lewis and Mr Hutchinson

A young man—let's call him Edward—on his way to the North Coast, weakened by a bout of fever and hardly holding on to his horse, reached Val Pedro one fine day. On the side of the path appeared Edinburgh Castle. Edward asked for Hutchinson's help, who kindly welcomed the poor wretch. He nursed him, and gave him proper medical treatment, being a former surgeon. The young Edward quickly recovered thanks to the care of his host. Back on his feet, he warmly thanked his benefactor, offered him assistance at any time, jumped on his horse, and then hit the road. But Hutchinson, who had gone up the stairs of one of the turrets of Edinburgh Castle with his rifle, was already waiting for the young Edward to cross his line of sight. When he did, the mad master shot him in the heart. Hutchinson was a very good shooter, the young Edward probably didn't live long enough to even hear the gunshot—he was dead before his body hit the ground. The gunshot was still echoing through the valley when Hutchinson's slaves ran out Edinburgh Castle to drag Edward's body in; they dropped it at the feet of their mad and triumphant master.

Later at night, the slaves laid Edward's body on a plank and walked to a nearby pit—it was so deep, some said it was bottomless. They put one end of the plank on the edge of the pit then lift the other end until the corpse slid into darkness. After a few seconds of a silent fall, Edward's body hurt a rock, bounced back, eventually crashing at the bottom. Down there, it now lied on the rock, blind to the dozens of dislocated corpses around that would share its terrible fate for the rest of days.

In 1828, Reverend George W. Bridges published a very valuable piece of work entitled *Annals of Jamaica*. This author has a sad story; one day, his four daughters embarked on a small boat to enjoy a bucolic sail on a lake, but their boat was unexpectedly overturned, and the four of them drowned. Bridges went on living but never really recovered from the blow—he left Jamaica, and spent the rest of life drifting all over Europe, waiting for death. He was the son of a rich tradesman, and he had come to Jamaica in 1815—he was the Rector of Saint Ann from 1823 to 1837. A learnt man, he was the first to write about Lewis Hutchinson. His catchy style was full of sensational expressions, and he described Hutchison as animated by *a fierce hatred for mankind,* rejoicing at his victims' agony, *beheading their still throbbing bodies* to satisfy his dark soul with the sight of *a flow of blood.* The portrait he gave of the mad master is particularly interesting as he obtained many details from a slave who lived on the nearby Bonneville plantation; and slaves were the keepers of the oral history of Jamaica. Bridges' gothic description of the crimes committed by Hutchinson gave birth to many dark legends, but another account was to soften his own, Annie E. Cork's. She was the grand-grand-daughter of Mary Hutton, whose father, Doctor Hutton, almost died at Hutchinson's hands. As a retired soldier from the Navy, Dr Hutton spent his time between England and Jamaica, where he possessed two plantations nearby Edinburgh Castle, Bonneville Pen and Lebanon Pen. He quarrelled one day with Hutchinson over the demarcation of their properties, and made a deadly enemy of him. Animated by the thirst of revenge, the mad master struck a first time in the heart of the night. The Doctor was then riding back from a meeting of the parish militia where he served as a Colonel; one if his slaves walked behind him, carrying his weapons and his material. The slave had been distanced by his master when Hutchinson suddenly came out of the blue, riding straight at him. The mad master caught the Doctor's sword from the trembling hands of the slave, brandished his loot, and then galloped away: "*My kindest regards to the Doctor! Let him know I am the happy possessor of his sword!*"

Apparently, Hutchinson didn't try to get his sword back. Did he fear his neighbour's reaction? Anyway, Lewis Hutchinson grew bold. A few months later, aware that Hutton was on his way to Kingston with his daughter, he ambushed them at Grier Park with a handful of slaves. Rushing out of the wood on his horse, he violently hit Hutton on the head with his own sword, throwing him down. Then he rode away, leaving his unconscious victim for dead. But Hutton's servants took him to Kingston where, after a few days of recovery, he lodged a complaint against his aggressor. Unfortunately, leaving the island shortly afterwards he couldn't follow the case; the mad master of Edinburgh Castle remained unpunished—at least for the time being. Hutton was trepanned in England and the silver plate placed in his head became the cruel reminder of the insult he had received. He was back to Jamaica within a year's time, where he tried to enrol some men to go for Hutchinson. But the case was delicate: everyone was scared of Hutchinson; not only was he a mad man, but he was also a damn good shooter. Only a white soldier named Callander dared taking the head of a posse of volunteers. But Hutchinson shot him on sight as soon as he got close to Edinburgh Castle! The bullet went straight to Callander's heart, killing him on the spot. Standing at his loophole with the smell of powder in his nostrils, Hutchinson laughed at the disbanding posse. The slaves loudly rejoiced over their master's deed, but Hutchinson had gone too far: he had murdered a white man in front of other white men. During this dark period, only a white man could testify against another white man—the incredible stories later told by the mad master's slaves in Court couldn't be legally registered, and despite overwhelming testimonies, Hutchinson was tried for the murder of Callender only.

Informed of this new crime, the authorities sent a consequent troop of men from Spanish Town. The mad master had no choice but to run away. He headed south, to Old Harbour, where he jumped on a bark and sailed away. Nevertheless, he was quickly intercepted by a ship sent by Admiral Rodney himself—before meeting a glorious death at Trafalgar, the English hero was stationed at Port Royal for a while. Hutchinson was arrested and tried in Spanish Town. Two skilful lawyers defended the scornful Scottish master. But Jamaica soon realized who he truly was.

The testimonies of his slaves were inadmissible evidences but they still gave an idea of the motus operandi of their master. As soon as he spotted a traveller, he would run for his rifle and wait at a loophole to shoot him down with a single gunshot. His slaves would then slander the victim and throw the body in a nearby pit that has never been clearly identified. There are too many pits in this part of the island and the one currently known as The Hutchinson Hole—which is 700-meter deep—, is probably not the right one. Hutchinson, who stripped his victims, was fond of watches. Searching Edinburgh Castle, the authorities found no less than forty-three of them in a chest! One had once belonged to Timothy Cronin, a teacher Hutchinson apparently strangled in front of one Mrs Suzanna Cole, one Elizabeth Thomas, and one Dorcas Maddix—the latter was married to Roger Maddix, a planter who lived close to Edinburgh Castle, and who partook in several murders orchestrated by Hutchinson. Roger Maddix was sentenced to death. So was James Walker, another planter also convinced of complicity. These names have surfaced through Bridges' writings but the judicial archives in Spanish Town have apparently lost the minutes of the trial, and many details are yet to be told about this incredible association of killers.

Hutchinson pleaded non-guilty, and was hanged on March 16, 1773—aged 40. Bridges wrote that he left a sum of money to erect a monument to his memory with the following inscription:

Their sentence, pride and malice, I defy,
Despise their power, and, like a Roman die.

The authorities opposed his
last will. No epitaph
for the villains.

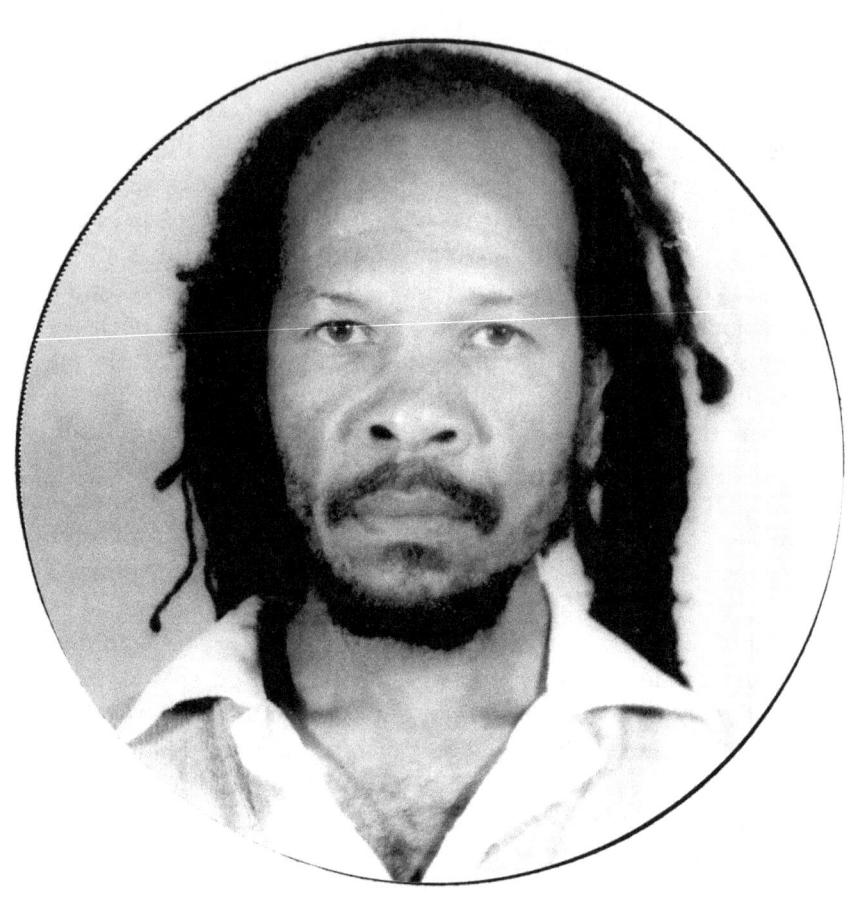

Yabby You.
(DREAD archives)

JACKSON, Vivian
aka Yabby You
(1946-2010)
Born Strange, Born Free

I was born strange but free, whispered Vivian Jackson. On August 14, 1946, Vivian was extracted from eternity, and thrown into the ghetto of Waterhouse, Kingston. Born Lion in a house spiritually divided between the ancestral Jankanoo cult of his father and the obtuse Christianity of his mother. Vivian was a disobedient child—so his mother used to say; and when he turned seven, she sent him to Sunday School, where he started to meditate on Christ. A few years later, he decided to live a spiritual life in imitation of this strange and fascinating man, and left home. He was positive about the fact that his parents had never beaten him—he just wanted to be free. He said his heart was full of weird and powerful thoughts—so much for his young age, he sometimes thought it was about to explode. In the alleys of Waterhouse, the child also heard voices. At night, sleeping outdoors rolled up in a blanket, he carefully listened to them, and observed the firmament above—His handiwork. Under a stormy sky reminiscent of Biblical times, Vivian explored the *I*—the essence of life. At daytime, he roamed the streets, looking for something to eat. But he refused to touch anything he hadn't cooked himself, or that had grown up underneath the earth—not to mention meat. As a consequence, he suffered from deficiencies, and his body soon wore the stigmas of street life—to buy his lunch, he also used to fight for the *badmen* of his community. Waterhouse was a sort of village, bordering on slum—a gangsters' paradise. In the middle ran the famous Sandy Gully, one of the most important evacuation canals of the city that drove the rain to the sea; people used it as an open dump. Rubbishes where left decomposing under the sun for days, and the smell could become unbearable; until the rain fell and dragged all the pestilence down to the sea—the wages of sin.

In the 1960s, Waterhouse was like a boiling pot, where the worst and the best were cooking. Any illuminated guy opened a little church of his own, and attracted disciples by building systems that were mixtures of genius, ignorance and divine certainties. In the late 1950s, Reverend Claudius Henry (see portrait) promised repatriation to all volunteers. People came by the hundreds to his place on Rosalie Avenue, selling their belongings and leaving their incredulous relatives behind; but Henry eventually claimed the whole story was a misunderstanding—he was jailed for swindle. Among his disappointed followers was Solomon Wolf, the grandfather of singer Beenie Man, who had his own little church on Unity Lane. He had invited the young Vivian to come along with him to Henry's—and then to Africa. But the kid was an iconoclast as far as the Rasta faith was concerned. He considered it blasphemous to claim that a living man, the Emperor Haile Selassie, was God. He stayed away.

Yout I-an

Vivian then met Mr Walker, a Rasta who taught him how to recycle iron to earn a living—or rather to survive. He bought old objects from people, and melted them to make cups or plates; then he sold them—mostly to tourists. Vivian keenly observed the tricks of a trade that was to feed him for more than ten years. He motivated a dozen of Rastas from the nearby slum of Back O' Wall to team up with him. They were strange guys who lived like priests—far from women. They ate *I*-tal—for *Vege*-tal—, refused to eat salt or to drink milk; they even refused to wear clothes made from animal skins—leather. Consequently, they went barefoot. At night, they hung their hammocks where night caught them; at daytime, they went from slum to slum, living a life of contemplating meditation. They saw themselves as rebellious to the system, some kind of urban hermits. But Vivian saw them as a bunch of lazy guys. What was the use of refusing the yoke of Babylon, if it meant living like beggars? He was the youngest of the group, but it was he who motivated them to melt iron. They started in a yard in Waterhouse they called *the moulding shop*. To build their furnace, they dug a hole in the ground, plastered the sides with bricks sealed together with clay; on top was a grate upon which the crucible was heating up—the overheated air coming from the blower was harmful to health, as it burnt the lungs. Once melted, the iron was poured into a mould where it eventually took its final shape. Vivian was already perceived as a strange kid with peculiar ideas. He spoke the *I-language* fluently—which consisted in replacing the first syllable of every word as a tribute to the great *I*, a sort of grammatical purification. For example, Youth *Vivi*-an was baptized Youth *I*-an. The Rastas at the moulding shop also purified themselves using the holy I-prefix, including I-an Dudley, a deeply spiritual man who inspired the kid a lot. Sometimes, they could afford to buy raw iron, but most of the time, they obtained it from generous people who pitied them: these poor wretches lived in a slum with no running water, or electricity; they were quite ignorant, slightly crazy and wore dreadful locks of hair—perceived as a stigma of squalor. They always found some old frying pan to collect. One or two car repairers were also glad to get rid of used parts.

Vivian crossed the whole island with his iron pots, looking for buyers—mostly among tourists. As soon as he had collected enough money, he left for solitary tours, walking alone for days—sometimes for weeks, or months—in the Jamaican wilderness, singing liturgies. When he ran out of everything, he came back to the moulding shop and to its burning clouds of hot air.

Solomon Wolf

Vivian attended various churches in Waterhouse, homes of the most eccentric people. Solomon Wolf, for example, lived his life in the imitation of Solomon. Just like his Biblical model, he had several wives—seven, to be precise. The Ethiopian World Federation operated by the Ethiopian Negus' wife soon granted him the right to open a church in Kingston, Local 37. There, Solomon reigned over some admiring courtesans—but Vivian was none of them. Seven women? Blasphemy! Solomon didn't like contradiction, but he respected this strange kid. Did he fear his power? To defy the authority of a youth who could hear voices was quite risky in a spiritual environment full of signs. Furthermore, Vivian—who was now a teen-ager—preached a life of spiritual righteousness, not of physical tenderness. Down in the ghetto, he had learnt it hard-core. He was a notorious youth—his knife could hit a target with the handle or with the point, depending on his mood. He was also affiliated to a small local gang of youths who knew no fear. Thus was he able to defy the Sons of Negus when he met them in the late 1960s. That's when music entered his life, thanks to Brother Joe, a Rasta from Rosalie Avenue.

Joe was a shoemaker by trade, who had come to Kingston years ago. He soon converted to Rasta and started to attend Solomon Wolf's Local 37. In the meantime, playing percussions with various people, he had developed an artistic network in Waterhouse. Music was the main vehicle of the Rasta faith. The first activists gathered on the top of Wareika Hill, outside Kingston, to play and sing together all night long while smoking the *chalice* (water pipe of marijuana). The producers realized they had some potential, and took them to the studio. First, because their doctrine fascinated them; but also because they hoped to capitalize on this new movement that was taking on in West Kingston. A few artists distinguished themselves at the time, and the percussionist Ras Michael was one of them. He soon met Bother Joe, and then invited him to partake in an exciting cultural project: the recording of the Ethiopian anthem over a Rasta rhythm. The band hired the most sought after studio of the capital, Studio One. But when the legendary owner Clement "Coxsone" Dodd realized that the group had overrun studio time and had no money to pay, he came up with a bargain: he wouldn't charge them for extra-time should they freely record two songs for him. They agreed and recorded *Blacker Shade of Black* and *Drumsong*, two of the most enduring rhythms of all times. Brother Joe worked for a while at Studio One, where he met Lloyd Brevett, another Waterhouse resident and a prominent musician; indeed, he was a member of the former Skatalites. Lloyd and Ras Michael were also friends and when they decided to launch a new band, The Sons of Negus, they enrolled Brother Joe. The rehearsals started at Local 37.

During those sessions, dozens of curious gathered at the window, including Vivian who knew nothing about music apart from what his mother had taught him: *do, ray, me, fa, sol, la, si, do*. But he realized he had a musical ear. One day, as Lloyd's students failed to sing a note, Vivian sang it out loud from outside. Lloyd came out to find out who was disturbing his lesson. Vivian stepped forward, defiantly staring at him. Lloyd didn't get mad, but took the kid inside. The group then included Ras Michael, Roy, Jack, Martin and Brother Joe: the legendary Sons of Negus. "*The Songs of Negus? A bunch of criminals*," laughed Vivian. According to him, the Sons of Negus weren't a musical band only, but a larger set of people from Waterhouse, some of whom involved in criminal activities. "*When one got caught, another testified for him at Court so they could peacefully murder people*," said Vivian. "*You can tell them*," he added, "*but make sure you used my exact words.*" But they still had a spiritual motivation. Living an alleged guilty life of crime, they sang universal songs of redemption.

The 7 o'clock Show

1970. The musical journey of the Sons of Negus started. Thanks to the interest of the intellectuals for the *Back-to-Africa* movement—or was it political?—, Ras Michael and Lloyd Brevett had the opportunity to enjoy their own radio show at Jamaica Broadcasting Company (JBC). It was a short program, but quite an opportunity to spread their ideas. Some producers from the JBC came along with them to the ghetto one day. Upon hearing the rehearsal of the band, they decided to broadcast them on television. So one fine day, Youth I-an left Pirate and Cleo—his two new friends with whom he was melting iron—at the moulding shop, and headed to the JBC studio. The Sons of Negus wore African clothes for the occasion—but not Vivian, who didn't worship Selassie; he wore a purple vest as a sign of disapproval. As the *7 O'clock show* started, the Sons of Negus sang *Run Come Rally*, a traditional Rasta liturgy. But the sound engineer cut Ras Michael short. "*Your lead ain't good, man,*" he said. "*This guy singing harmonies, over there—with the purple vest. Give him the microphone, man. Let him lead the song.*" Thrown in front of the camera, Youth I-an sang six songs, including *Love of Jah*. At the end of the session, the same engineer took him aside: "*Want a piece of advice, my youth? Forget 'bout these guys, they're up to no good. Go and record these tunes for yourself, man. They have a potential.*"

Vivian claimed that Ras Michael got forty dollars for each singer from the JBC, that he handed Vivian four, before asking back for two—to buy weed. Vivian was soon back to Waterhouse, to the moulding shop and his penitent life; there he slept on the floor, upon a mattress, alongside Cleo and Pirate. His two new friends were Rastas, but had little in common with the priests from Back O' Wall. On the contrary, Pirate—better known among Rastas as I-rate—was a real Don Juan; his pretty face worked miracles with women. He also sold the best marijuana in town. The trio wasn't rich, but this humble way of life was partly resulting from a choice. As the Bible reads, *the birds have their nests, the foxes their holes but the son of Man has nowhere to rest his head.* And indeed, Youth I-an was no son of Negus—he was the son of Man.

Go to I-on

When Brother Joe and Ras Michael went their separate ways, Joe launched his own band, Brother Joe & the Rightful Brothers, with the help of two young musicians from the nearby community of Waltham Park, Albert Griffiths and Clinton "Bassie" Fearon—the Gladiators, one of the most celebrated reggae bands of the 1970s. Albert and Clinton had just met—and the latter wasn't yet the exceptional bass player he would become. When he first heard him, Joe got upset. "*Learn how fi' play and come back later, man!*" he shouted. Offended, Clinton practiced for hours before he had the guts to face Joe again. This time, he passed the test, and the group started to rehearse every evening. Various musicians came by during those sessions, including Roydel Johnson—who later became famous with The Congos. To attend, Vivian Jackson had to cross the entire community of Waterhouse, crawling in the streets at night to avoid the rival gangs—he would have been killed on sight. The Rightful Brothers were eventually booked for a date in the countryside. The Gladiators got a handful of weed for the backing—but they had to throw it away in a gully when the police stopped them for a routine search. The best was yet to come! As a matter of fact, Joe booked some studio time at Harry J to record their first tune.

On the evening of the great day, everyone met on Rosalie Avenue, including Youth I-an, Roydel Johnson and Cedric Myton—the other legendary member of the Congos. Once the truck loaded with the instruments, Joe turned to Youth I-an: "*Gwaan* (go) *get the last chair inside!*" When he came back, Vivian froze. The truck had gone without him! Vivian stood motionless for a while, as if lost—outraged. Then someone called his name out loud—a taxi driver who had just dropped a client down the road. He knew Vivian; the kid was famous in Waterhouse, as a very good cricket player, first; but also as a bookmaker. This last occupation came as a necessity. Growing in the street, the kid was affected with pneumonia, stomach ulcer, diarrhoea, malnutrition and arthritis—and he was in his twenties! In the early sixties, he was hospitalised in emergency, and underwent surgery; he narrowly escaped death that day. As he was still a juvenile, his parents were informed; he saw his mother for the first time in five years but it seems like the reunion wasn't that moving. When Vivian left the hospital, he went back to Waterhouse. But he was weak, and could hardly walk. The doctors were positive, should he keep on working at the moulding shop, he would never recover. That's why he started to advise gamblers at the racetrack, earning a few bucks from the wisely advised winners. Being quite good at it, he made a name for himself in the middle of horses, where the taxi driver had met him. When Vivian told him about his misadventure, he drove him straight to Harry J studio.

Vivian discreetly entered the place, and hid behind a door to spy on all *these little idiots who worshiped Selassie*, and who were trying to record his songs. Joe was here, guiding Roydel Johnson who couldn't voice *Carnal Mind*. The session was a nightmare, and Joe was upset. There was only fifteen minutes left, and they still had nothing. They tried every song in their songbook, from *Carnal Mind*, to *Love of Jah*, to the mighty *72 Different Nations*. The latter was the most powerful of Vivian's compositions; it had come to him on a stormy day. Exhausted by a long discussion about God, Vivian's friends had fallen asleep around him in the yard when the storm spoke to Vivian from the heavens; following the rolling sound of fury, the kid started to hum a melody that would later change his entire life. But at this precise moment, Vivian was far from recognition. At one point, Joe stepped out of the recording room to have a word with the sound engineer Sylvan Morris; that's when he bumped into Vivian. He was surprised, but soon pulled himself together. Without a word of explanation, or an excuse, he asked Vivian a favour: "*You know the tune, man. Sing it for me!*" Vivian complied and thus recorded his very first song, *Hail The Children*. The lyrics were taken from Psalm 2, and uttered in an original style, the *sing-jay* style—at the cross roads between singing and deejaying.

This story wasn't confirmed by Joe or The Congos—curiously, they hardly remembered anything about this period when questioned, and happened to be quite evasive. Several questions remain. First, how come Vivian recorded a tune totally different from the ones featured in his songbook? Second, how come Joe didn't sing the song himself? He *did* record one song that evening—*Go To zion*, which came out as the A-side to *Hail The Children*. So, what happened? Did he run short of breath, or was *Go To Zion* recorded later on? Why did Vivian accept to sing for the group that had just tried to double-cross him? Of course, he wanted to sing badly. Then, he probably didn't have much choice. Waterhouse was a small world where you had to learn how to live with people, whether friends or foes. No one could stand alone in this environment. Born free, yes—but Youth I-an was just a poor kid who melted iron. Opportunities were few. Plus, Joe was ten years older than Vivian, and probably had a certain influence on the kid. Last but not least, was the doctrine of Christ: *turn the other cheek*.

At the end of the day, the record was pressed. *Go To Zion,* on the A-side, was an interpretation of the *Carnal Mind* liturgy led by Joe, and clearly backed by Vivian Jackson. *Hail The Children* appeared on the flip side. Both titles were credited, music and lyrics, to *Bro. Joe*. And who ended up riding his bicycle through Kingston to sell the record? Youth I-an, of course. He made sure to return every penny to Joe—and never got anything from him. How many times do you have to turn the other cheek? Joe described Vivian as a little youth who *sang so badly nobody wanted to rehearse with him*, and considered it was very kind of him to give him a chance. He appreciated the humility of this kid, yes—but they eventually quarrelled over Selassie.

The Prophets

Vivian now spent his days on Higglers Rest, downtown Kingston, to sell Joe's records. In the evening, he jumped on his bicycle and rode back to Waterhouse. One day, a woman lost her wallet in front of him while coming out a taxi—he picked it up and called her; she was then standing in front of her gate, looking for her keys. When she turned back and saw a ghetto youth in rags coming at her, she got scared. But he simply handed her the wallet, with all the money inside. She thanked him, and then hurried inside her home. "*You're an idiot!*" shouted Joe and his wife upon hearing his story. "*You spoilt your luck!*" Vivian didn't say a word. He was shocked—he expected some congratulations! "*God had sent this money for you!*" said Joe. That was too much for Youth I-an, who secretly took the resolution never to see these people again—they were just a bunch of hypocrites who lived in corruption. He would save money and record *72 Different Nations* on his own. There was no time to lose. Joe had the tape of the Harry J session with Cedric Myton singing his tune; not properly, but he sang it anyway.

The following morning, Vivian talked to Cleo and Irate. What about giving up the moulding shop to start selling records? The Rastas from West Kingston represented a consequent market; furthermore, he had to earn a living and they refused to let him melt iron again. Indeed, Vivian's life was at stake and should something happen, they would be blamed—no doubt. A couple of days later, as Irate and Cleo were still considering the offer, Leroy "Horsemouth" Wallace came to the moulding shop to buy some marijuana from Irate. Horsemouth was a professional drummer from Waterhouse—the residential part of it. A former student of the Catholic Alpha Boys' School—attended by so many great Jamaican musicians over the years—, Horsemouth was then playing with the Generation Gap, the band of the singer Freddie McGregor.

Vivian told him about his project and sang *72 Different Nations* a capella for him. He couldn't have found a more complacent ear; Horsemouth defined himself as a *ghetto musician*. He attended as many parties as possible, always on the look-out for something new, some unusual sound. Horsemouth was not a mere musician, he was living for music. What he heard at the moulding shop left him breathless. He ran to check Aston "Familyman" Barrett, Bob Marley's bass player, and took him to Vivian. The musicians then set up an impromptu rehearsal. Horsemouth surreptitiously borrowed the set of instruments from the Generation Gap, and carried them to the Sandy Gully. The musicians climbed an electronic post to illegally access the electricity, and started to play. The guitarist Earl "Chinna" Smith was part of the group, and he couldn't believe his eyes; as the song went on, dozens of people started to dance on the gully banks, singing and shouting. Mesmerized at the whole scene, Chinna looked around and thought... *Woaaa!*

Vivian & the Buckers

Irate and Cleo had made up their minds, it was time to record the song! They walked to Harry J studio with Vivian to meet Horsemouth, Familyman and Chinna Smith. But a problem arose at once, money. The three singers had nothing but silver coins. This might have been enough to buy a two tracks tape, and to hire the studio for half an hour—but then? What about the musicians? The money left couldn't even pay for their bus fare. "*And where are the others?*" asked Horsemouth. "*The others?*", replied Vivian. "*The other musicians, man! Three is not enough to make a song.*

- Really?"

Horsemouh sighed, this was going nowhere fast; they'd better leave. Familyman cooled him down. Since they were already here, and since the song was so strong—why not? They hired the B studio that was cheaper than the A, but the place was still too sophisticated and psychedelic for Youth I-an. It left him at a loss, and unable to let out a single note. It took Horsemouth's kindness to comfort him. Inspiration came back, and Vivian started to sing. Inspired by his melody and his *vibes*, the musicians built a rhythm track—a *riddim*. A slow and powerful drum pattern, a sumptuous bass line and an incredible introduction written by Chinna; it sounded like a thunder roll—a God-fearing music. They created more than a song, this day—a genre, that the world would one day celebrate as *roots reggae*. Familyman then recorded the keyboard on the second track of the tape. The result was so incredible—especially for 1972—that the sound engineer Karl Pitterson rushed inside at the end of the recording: *"I wanted to quit this job anyway,"* he said. *"And this song is the last one I shall record here!"* It was beyond his understanding: how could these nobodies coming from nowhere get such a sound? During the same session, the group also recorded the rhythm track for *The Man Who Does the Work*—which features the same almost unbearable strength. The Rastas and the musicians shared the fruits of the session: a drum and bass cut for each musician, as well as for Irate and Cleo, and a full version for Vivian who, as a counterpart, left the full version of *The Man Who Does the Work* to Irate and Cleo.

To record a song at the time, you had to lay the rhythm track first—it implied to pay some musicians and to hire an expensive studio in Kingston. Then you had to record the voice—but this part was cheaper if you chose to record at King Tubby's studio, in Waterhouse. Born Brad Osbourne, Tubby—or Tubbs—is another legendary figure of reggae music. In his tiny studio of Dromilly Avenue, he simply invented Dub music. An electrician by trade, he had developed an unconditional love for dances. With his sound system, he entertained his friends during small privates parties before becoming the most popular sound system of Jamaica. To have a wider access to music, he opened up a little studio in his backyard. You couldn't record a whole rhythm track in there; it was too small, and not equipped for that—though Lee Perry, a legendary and eccentric producer did it once. But Tubby had set up a voicing booth in his former bathroom, and with derisory means, he obtained staggering results. He was first and foremost an artist, who loved twisting sounds, isolating a note from a rhythm, distorting it for awhile; then he would throw it into a new musical dimension where it faded away on a remote echo; then the song came to a full stop—and started again for the listener's greatest joy. His creative thirst for new sensation gave birth to Dub music.

When Vivian first went to Tubby's studio, he knew no one there, and he had no money. But Tubby always lent an ear to what strangers brought. He ran the tape, listened *from the top till the very last drop*—and was left speechless. He stared at Youth I-an for a few seconds: "*I tell you, I ain't giving you back this tape, my youth. It's too powerful. I'm going to keep it until you're ready to record.*" Tubby knew he had just heard something exceptional. He mixed the rhythm track and pressed a unique copy on acetate—it was called a *dub plate* then, or a *pre-release*—to play it at his dances. The instrumental became so popular that it was baptized, *The Buckers*. Tubby even gave a *Buckers Dance*, once—on the name of the instrumental.

Meanwhile at the moulding shop, the trio was rehearsing. Sometimes, Horsemouth would pass by to play melodica with them. Weeks went by, but money was still short. So that Vivian had no choice but to melt iron again. He knew that Cleo and Irate would prevent him from doing it, so he went to another slum called Back Toe—without telling them. The inevitable happened: after a while, Youth I-an collapsed. Carried to the hospital, he was transfused in emergency—and he survived. Now, he had the money! He hired Tubby's for two hours, in the middle of the night; the said evening, the place was rammed with some of the greatest people in the music business like I Roy or the producer Bunny Lee. Impressed, Irate and Cleo couldn't sing their part properly. Everybody gave his piece of advice, trying to be helpful. But nothing came out if this session. The trio came back a few days later, and failed again. Irate and Cleo got fed up, and started to wonder. Were they meant for music? Melting iron was their thing, not singing. "*You know what, Youth I-An? We keep a rhythm track that you'll record for us and you can share the other one with Horsemouth. We're out of it, man.*" They had a deal.

The Ralph Brothers

On the other side of the gully, on a *captured*—or squatted—piece of land, lived two guys who had just arrived from the parish of Mandeville; two brothers who could play music, the Ralph Brothers. One of them had already recorded under the name of Bobby Melody. In 1966, he had even won the parish selection for the National Festival, a major singing contest. His brother Alrick Forbes was a very good guitarist. But they couldn't believe Youth I-an when he told them that *The Buckers* was his song. *You? A Tubby's favourite? Come on, man...* He took them to Dromilly Avenue where they listened to the tape. They rehearsed for three hours, entered the voicing booth and recorded *72 Different Nations* in one cut—at last! Coming out of the studio, Alrick whispered to Vivian: "*We gonna buy ourselves a Benz with this song, man!*" This remark foretold much strife.

* * *

Errol Smith from Commercial Studio stopped the tape, looked at the two guys in front of him, and smiled: "*You'll never leave this place with this tape, guys! I love this song, and I want to put it out!*" Alrick Forbes laughed and hit Vivian with his elbow—they had a distributor. The song came out on the *Now* label. Standing in front of the Specialist pressing plant a few days later, Youth I-an discovered his very first record, and realized the title had been misprinted on the label; it read *Conquering Lion* instead of *72 Different Nations*. The original title was a Biblical reference and a tribute to the on-going year of 1972. Well—no big deal. With his box of singles, Vivian pedalled around town. He sold his records to the record shops, to the people in the street. He didn't even think about giving promotional copies to the radio stations. Yet, Irate told him one day that he had just heard it on the radio. "*They played it three times straight, man!*" The Yabby You phenomenon had started. People linked the song to *The Buckers* and asked Tubby about the singer: "*You know, the song that goes 'you, yabby yabby you'.*" But the shy Youth I-an had asked Tubby not to reveal his identity—the surest way for Tubby to keep the song exclusive for his sound system. "*It's a foreign group, man,*" he replied. When

Vivian entered the record shops, the sellers rejoiced: "*At last, man! Everybody is asking for the tune that goes 'yabby you'. Ah who sing it?*

- *Me nah know,*" whispered Vivian. "*Me just ah sell it fi Tubby—I don't know, I'm just selling it for Tubby.*" In fact, he was selling it for Errol Smith, according to their deal. But Alrick Forbes grew nervous. He came to the moulding shop one day, and claimed someone had cast a spell on Bobby Melody; he urgently needed money to see an *obeahman*—a local voodoo sorcerer. Wrong pick! Vivian refused to deal with superstition—blasphemy! He sent Alrick away. "*I'm gonna call the police!*" threatened the guitarist. Bobby Melody then allegedly came out of the blue, a stone in each hand, insulting Vivian. The discussion was tensed, and when the Ralph brothers left, Vivian went to build a *spliff* (joint) in his yard. He picked up his Bible, worried. He knew of this kind of guys, and he took them seriously—mostly when they felt they had been taken in. He was still thinking when he heard Alrick's voice at his gate. Talking to someone in the street, the guitarist was turning his back to Vivian, leaning against his gate.

Suddenly, something hit the gate! Alrick started, turned back, and saw Vivian's knife still trembling a few inches from his head. He started to shake from head to toes: "*But... Youth I-an, did you try to kill me? But we... we're friends!*" He left for good this time, but a few hours later, someone informed Vivian that Alrick and Bobby had gone for their friends in Grant's Pen to besiege the office of Errol Smith. Vivian jumped on his bike, and headed to Commercial Studio—there, push quickly came to shove. Alrick lifted a heavy stone, threatening Vivian who took his knife, trying to slash is enemy's throat. Livid, Errol Smith intervened, and offered to settle it down: all the money collected so far would go to the Ralph brothers who, as a counterpart, would give up all claims on the song. Everyone agreed.

In the street, Vivian was trembling with rage; he had tears in his eyes. The Ralph brothers rejoiced, but they had just given up their rights on one of the most important songs in the history of reggae music.

*   *   *

As promised, Vivian recorded *The Man Who Does The Work* for Irate and Cleo during the *Conquering Lion* session. But Irate's passion for women turned soar when one of his deserted girlfriends threw some acid in his face. His pretty look spoilt, he felt downtrodden and didn't care about the song anymore. Vivian got it back for his first album. Meanwhile, *Conquering Lion* put an end to he hegemony of another historical hit song, the Africanist *Satta Amassa Gana* by the Abyssinians. Vivian reinvested all his profits in music. For the recording session of *Love of Jah*, he asked Familyman to build a rhythm track and, of course, went to Tubby's to voice it. He started to spend a lot of time in the studios, but still knew little about business. To print a record, to build an artwork—it was all beyond his capacities. He knew of the importance of using others' talent, though. And when he met Herbie Carter, who was then working for the renowned producer Joe Gibbs, he asked for his help. Herbie put out *Love of Jah* on his *UMR* label. The contemporary label credits one Leighton Young as the producer—Vivian reproduced the mention when he later repressed the record on his own *Prophets* label. The same Leighton Young popped up again on a strange record that came out in 1975 on the English *Roots* label—this is the same *Conquering Lion* but entitled *72 Nations Bow*! But Vivian was positive, he knew nothing about this Young—whom he yet credited on his own label—, or about this particular song. He cried out piracy, but have all the mysteries of his story been revealed? He had some connections in England. At the same period, he apparently pressed 200 copies on a blank label of a song entitled *Beggy Beggy Licky Licky*, and sent them to England. "*Just to try a thing*," he said. But was this song really linked to Yabby You? The copies that have resurfaced thanks to the Internet are on the Jamaican *Melrose* label and credit the song to *S. Thomas* and *H. Thomas*. And although the vocal style sounds a little bit like the Prophets', the voice of Yabby You can't be heard on the song.

* * *

Falilyman and Yabby You became close friends. Every Saturday they ate together at the musician's place, and then went to the bush to smoke weed and rehearse. Thus was born the fantastic *Love Thy Neighbour*, in 1973. Carlton Barrett, Familyman's brother and Bob Marley's drummer, played bass on this song and Bunny Wailer played percussions. Familyman left the bass to his young disciple Robbie Shakespeare, who probably signed here the first bass line of his brilliant career. The song came out on the *Defenders* label with the mention *produced by A. barrett*—but the musician didn't own it, just the drum and bass version he later put out under the title *Distant Drums*.

You, yabby yabby you

Before being *delivered from his enemies*, Yabby You had to compromise with them. He worked several times with Alrick Forbes, but succeeded in replacing Bobby Melody by a dubious guy, Da Da Smith, whom he described as a *politician*—meaning a *gunman*, fighting the political wars in Waterhouse. Da Da Smith could sing, so Vivian invited him to the recording session of another classic, *Jah Love*, aka *Warn The Nation*. Behind the microphone, Yabby You started: *Dreadlocks sent down ina Babylon to warn the nation, tell them about Jah love...* Tubby stopped the tape—Da Da was off key. After several aborted attempts, Yabby You left the lead to Da Da, and sang the harmonies with Alrick. The latter became jealous: "*Why him? Me want to lead a song too!*" Vivian said he financed another session to offer Alrick an original rhythm track. The singer recorded a terrific version of the song, and put it out on his own *Forbes* label under the name of The Prophet Alric Forbes. Curiously, the original records are dated from 1978.

The burden of *Conquering Lion* goes like this: *You, yabby yabby you*—it means *be yourself*, and don't let anyone *turns you a fool*. The rest of the song is a divine warning whispered over the apocalyptic *Buckers riddim*, that hurls the listener into the mighty kingdom of Vivian Jackson; this song tells of his determination in life, of his fight for integrity. As a producer, he learnt rapidly, and declined his hit song: Tommy McCook, Dicky Burton, Wayne Wade, Big Youth or Trinity, all gave their interpretation of the *riddim*. So did Tubby, of course, who signed two different mixes, and two masterpieces of dub: *Yabby Youth Fight Against Capitalism* and *King Tubby's Rock*. It had become impossible for Vivian to hide his identity. Furthermore, the song was a success. "*What?*" wondered everyone, staring at him. "*Ah-you Yabby You?! You are Yabby You?!*" Hence his artistic name.

With a few bucks in his pocket and music on his mind, Vivian went to check Albert Griffiths and Clinton "Bassie" Fearon from the Gladiators, and took them to the legendary Black Ark studio of the bizarre Lee Perry—Bassie was to remain there for six months, recording a handful of splendid bass lines for the producer. The group recorded several rhythm tracks, including those of *Jah Vengeance* and *Run Come Rally*. Lee Perry listened to them, and went mad. No one but himself was supposed to get such a sound in his studio! The Gladiators became Vivian's official backing band, and even sang three songs for him—as they were under exclusive licence with *Virgin Records*, they put out these songs as The Prophets.

Yabby You was moving on, but things took time and when Dennis Harris came from England to buy a full album from him, the singer only had eight songs available. Dennis Harris was an immigrant from Clarendon who had launched his own DIP label in England; he gave Vivian an advance and, in 1975, the *Conquering Lion* album saw the light. The surprising sleeve jacket was signed Cogil Leghorn, the accountant at Tuff Gong—Bob Marley's studio. Cogil also co-wrote *Them Belly Full* with Bob, and *Talking Blues* with Carlton Barrett. The Barrett connection, once again.

Devilish Marley

Conquering Lion has become a reference as it helped defining a genre, *roots reggae*. This is raw and fierce music from Jamaica, a violent and initiatory one; this sound will crush your bones and leave you trembling. The Biblical lyrics denounce the antichrist and covetousness—they explore the dark side of Man, and send the listener back to the days of Moses, under the watch of a jealous and dreadful God! This is the voice of ancient blood, a trip through the Valley of Josaphat.

Dennis Harris put out the LP in England, under the name of *Ram A Dam*, an alleged tribute to his Muslim faith. The pre-release featured a picture of the Prophets; and the official one a black jacket—they have both become very rare. Harris renamed some songs, obtained some exclusive mixes and added the song *Beyond The Hills* by Cleopatra Williams. But who was this obscure singer? And how did she end up on Yabby You's first album? She was just a female singer, who hung out at various studios, waiting for an opportunity. When she met Yabby You, she begged him a chance. He complied, and pressed two hundred copies of her adapted song on the discreet *Hot City* label—adding her song to the track listing was probably a way to complete the album. Anyway, Yabby You built his musical empire betting on young talents. Cleopatra Williams never established her name in the business but some of Yabby's creatures did, including Michael Prophet. The story of the latter is quite relevant to Yabby You's musical vision.

In a warring Biblical sky, the archangel Michael defeats the dragon and throws him down on Earth. Humiliated and broken, the outraged dragon establishes his dark empire on Earth and starts to harass mankind with the help of *the beast from the sea*. This is a tale of the Revelations. And Yabby You wasn't reading the Bible, he was *living* it. To him, the Revelations were a reality, and reggae music was the modern Gospel—the missing Biblical link. He studied his environment and soon identified the false prophet the Bible speaks of, Bob Marley. What was wrong with the star?

He had signed a contract with the devil to get money, big cars—some B(ob) M(arley) and the W(ailer)s—, and pussies—Bob was a pathological Don Juan. Signs, always signs; analysed, deciphered, and meditated. Yabby You decided to arm an exterminator angel, whom he met in front of the Channel One studio in the late 1970s. He was a poor ghetto youth in his twenties who, despite working sometimes as a mechanic, wore torn shoes without soles. Though shy, he approached Yabby You and sang a capella for him. He had a voice no doubt, and his name was Michael—a sign. God had sent Yabby You the anointed one to overthrow Bob Marley. Vivian took the young Michael under his wing, rechristened him Michael Prophet—a reference to his mission—, and offered him a cover version of The Heptones' *Fight It to the Top* that became a hit song in 1979. With his disciple, Yabby You wasn't demanding but terrible. Every day he drove to his place, climbing his stairs on his motorbike—because of his diseases, Yabby You had serious difficulties to walk—, and took him to rehearsals. His project about Marley was no secret to the impressed young singer who didn't dare to contradict his mentor. How could *he* challenge Bob Marley? He didn't even reach his ankle. But his producer believed in him, so Michael Prophet went with it. Yabby You's sound and Michael's voice fitted perfectly. The association gave birth to the masterpieces *Vocal & Dub* and *Serious Reasoning,* also known as *Know The "Right"*—featuring strange inverted comas. On top of dark and fierce rhythm tracks laid by the Gladiators, the sweet voice of Michael Prophet runs like a refreshing river. He sings about the destruction of Babylon, corrupt friendship, and the forthcoming reign of the rootsman. In a Jamaica described as a Valley of Josaphat, Michael fears no evil, and slews all sins. His album came out on *Island Records*, Chris Blackwell's international record company, where Marley himself was signed. But something went wrong. Michael had a disagreement with *King Sounds,* the English distributor of the album. Step by step, it affected his relationship with Yabby You—the archangel had had hit songs, and he naturally flew away from his mentor. Remained the producer's vision, a musical testimony. Despite a hit song, *Gunman*, and several good albums, Michael Prophet never beat what he did for Yabby You. In 1981, the *devilish* Marley died, but Michael Prophet had little to see with it.

Tubby the King

Several young engineers worked for King Tubby at Dromilly Avenue, but the King had his privileges, and no one could mix Yabby You's songs but he. He personally signed the dub counterpart to *Conquering Lion, Prophesy of Dub*—500 copies only were pressed in 1975. To speak about Yabby You, one has to speak about King Tubby. This musical genius gave the best of his art to Yabby You—and to Augustus Pablo, two of the most strange and spiritual reggae producers. As a matter of fact Yabby You was now sort of living at Tubby's, where he voiced various young talents while working on his second solo album, *Deliver Me From My Enemies*. He had become an institution, a close relative to Tubby. As such, he was approached by the young Lloyd "Jammy" James one day. Back from Canada, Jammy wanted to become a part of Tubby's team, but the former singer Pat Kelly was standing on his way. Kelly had been working for Tubby since 1975, but had become somewhat overwhelmed by the work, and Jammy could feel it—he asked Yabby You to talk to Tubby on his behalf. Yabby You didn't like the request—Jammy, he said, was a *serious threat* to Pat Kelly. He thought about it and decided to help Kelly—after all he was a talented singer who had enjoyed a handful of hit songs back in the days. He earned 40 dollars a week at Tubby's, not a fortune. Why not coming back to music? Yabby You set up a session at Channel One. When the song *How Long* came out, the producer bought an ad in *The Star*—a first for the producer who, as a result to his independent status, hardly appeared in the newspapers. When the stamper of the song broke off a few weeks later, Yabby You gave 900 Jamaican dollars to Pat Kelly who left Tubby's—giving way to Jammy.

Deliver Me From My Enemies

When *Deliver Me From My Enemies* came out in 1977, Yabby You was an established producer. He always controlled his catalogue, and only signed a few licences in his life. A lot of his productions are to be found on the English label *Groove Music*, which he apparently co-founded; when it became *Grove Muzik*, it allegedly licenced some albums to *Island Records* without Yabby You's consent. Yabby You then focused on independency, printed his face on his label and put out dozens of singles—with almost no weak song. Nonetheless, recognition from a wider audience wouldn't come before 1997, with the release of the beautiful compilation *Jesus Dread 1972-1977* by the English label *Blood & Fire*. The breath-taking artwork and the quality of the dozens of songs were like a roots revelation for thousands of listeners around the world. At last, Yabby You's music was made available, and treated with the care it deserved.

Yabby You wasn't the type of man to bear someone a grudge for too long. He teamed up with Brother Joe again, produced and distributed his song *Freedom of Life*; he also worked with the Brevett family, producing *Stop Your Gang War*. In the mid-2000s, most of the people he had met in his early life had disappeared. Da Da Smith died in 2003. Irate and Cleo were no more. Solomon Wolf was already quite old when he eventually fulfilled his dream in 1975: he left for Ethiopia, and no one has ever heard about him again. Bobby Melody enjoyed some hit songs in the 1970s with his cover versions of *Jah Bring I Joy in the Morning* and *Let It Be*. He even recorded for Lee Perry, as the Divine Brothers. He spent his last years in England, where he died from throat cancer in 2010. Lloyd Brevett died in October 2013. Albert Griffiths is sick, but still alive and Clinton "Bassie" Fearon keeps on touring and recording. Brother Joe is still alive in Kingston, where he records sporadically, building drums to earn a living.

Youth I-an ended up living in the street at a very young age. Despite his health problems—he was apparently the subject of an American medical thesis—, he built a powerful reggae catalogue.

Jamaica hardly seems aware of his work; probably because he was independent, and maybe because of his straightforward personality that owned him a few enemies—especially when it came to Rasta and Haile Selassie. Horsemouth still remembers the animated discussions he had with him and other artists. But Youth I-an feared no one except God. He saw himself as an humble servant—a very weak one, in fact. So weak he couldn't understand how an entity powerful enough to create the Earth and the Universe could expect anything from him. The best for God was to expect nothing from Yabby You—He could work things out by Himself, *don't*? Rasta artists are no fundamentalists, and they love theological discussions with a passion—contradictions are always welcome. Yabby You was appreciated for his strange statements, and was a righteous man. But most of all, he was true to himself—and nothing else can earn you the respect of Jamaicans. It doesn't matter how different you are, as long as you don't pretend. Deejay Trinity started to work with Yabby You in the 1970s, as an imitator of Big Youth with whom the producer had fallen apart: "*Yabby You was told by the doctors that he would never walk again because he was sick. But through his faith in God, he walked again without stands. You can't say anything against that, man.*" Yabby You was one of them, from near or far. His music wasn't meant to entertain people—it was, and still is, the vessel of God's voice, a musical missal. A major record company once offered Yabby a US million dollar for his catalogue—he refused. You could buy his music, yes; but it wasn't for sale.

I first met Yabby You after a few-hour drive, in the Parish of Clarendon. I can still see him standing in the middle of the hallway of his house, leaning on his stand and greeting me with a strange smile: "*You—a white man! You came from so far to see me, so I know you really want to know the truth. But are you sure you're ready for this? Knowing makes you miserable, and you'll end up a lonely man.*" The prophecies of Yabby You never scared me; on the contrary. There is too much care, too much love in his music—and mischievousness enough in his eyes. Yabby You wasn't the blind sheep you would peacefully bring to the slaughter—he refused to suffer anyone's yoke, and was offended to see that the dumb stone had come forever while flesh was bound to disappear. But he eventually had to pay the terrible tribute due to his Creator; a creator Yabby You praised all his life in music. On January 12, 2010, he kissed his wife good-night, went to sleep—and never woke up.

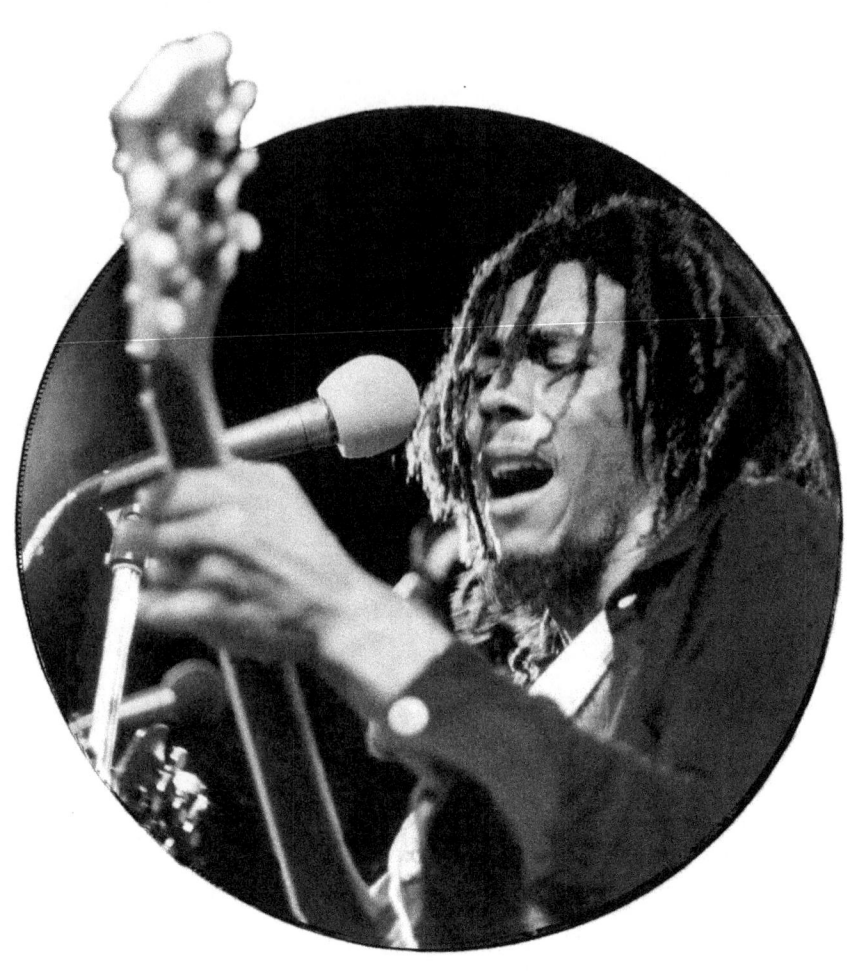

Bob Marley.
(Dread archives)

Marley, Robert Nesta
aka Bob Marley

(1945-1981)
The Skipper

In the 1970s, in fair Jamaica, *two households both alike in dignity, from ancient grudge broke to new mutiny where civil blood made civil hands unclean*—though far from the Verona of Shakespeare, the Jamaican Labour Party (JLP) and the People's National Party (PNP) did fight a Capulet-Montague war that bordered on civil war. Things got out of hands under the two successive turns of the PNP Prime Minister Michael Manley, from 1972 to 1980. The opposition led by Edward Seaga (see portrait) destabilised Manley's government by tagging it as communist, and plunged the country into chaos. The communities of Kingston came under political influence and received arms and orders from their respective master; that's when the *sufferers*—the poor among the poor—, started to kill each other for the sake of ruthless politicians. This war was forced on them; even the half-hearted had to take side. A few resisted, though—but it took determination, as they lived in the lion's den. They relied on deep spiritual beliefs, and Rasta became their haven. The *Ras Tafari brethren*—or Rastas—had never expected any reward but from their living God Haile Selassie, whose crowning in 1930 foretold the near end of time. Thus, the bloody events that were rapidly leading Jamaica to a breaking point appeared logical to them—

just like written in the Bible, the dragon had gained control over Man, but it would only last for a while, and it was crucial to hold on to one's faith. Rastas saw Jamaica as the Valley of Josaphat, and rejected politics; they blamed both parties, perceived as the offspring of the *bakras*—or slave masters—, the tools of a corrupt Babylonian system bound to fall. As it refused to deal with politics, Rasta was of course highly political. The successive governments had always kept an eye on these rebellious bearded men who preached social disobedience. But Rasta was permanently mutating, like a malleable spiritual paste taking on various shapes—it was hard to understand, and even harder to apprehend. And when it infiltrated the Jamaican society, it became even more complex, slowly remodelling the minds of the youths. Kids loved the idea of a black God, and wanted to be proud of their black selves. They also loved *ganja* (marijuana); and Rastas smoked it as a holy sacrament—*without any apology*. The plant soon took possession of the local music, and polished it. The brutal *ska* rhythm played by rum drinkers slowly gave way to the subtle and delicate *rock steady* in 1966, a jewel of precarious balance between the drums and the bass. This vital principle did not disappear with the rise of *reggae* in 1968; it just became subtler. Ganja is definitely linked to this music sometimes described as a *peace and love music* by neophytes. But violence in reggae music is absolute and dreadful; it hides behind a fake nonchalance, just like *ganja* eases up the pressure without erasing it. Beneath the sensuality of gorgeous bass lines lies a burning fire. Rasta and reggae never had a lot in common with the hippie movement. The two collided in the 1970s, indeed—a happy coincidence. The word *peace* in a reggae song rarely refers to the international situation; but to the *tribal wars* fought daily in the streets of Kingston. The name itself, *tribal* wars, is a terrible mistake. It sounds like they've been imported from Africa, when they were initiated by the politicians. They are *political* wars, if not *politicians'* wars. Bob Marley had enough talent to turn his local stories into universal parables, but if you pay attention to his lyrics, you'll realize he has almost never sung about anything but his ghetto of Trench Town. Jamaica is an island; and islanders hardly talk about anything but themselves.

From 9 Miles to Kingston 12

Robert Nesta Marley was born on February 6, 1945, from a guilty relationship between Cedella Booker and Captain Marley, a white officer who was consequently disgraced by his family. Of *daddy Marley*, we are shown a photograph—always the same one, currently hanging on a wall of the official Bob Marley Museum in Kingston. It shows the handsome white man riding his horse, wearing an elegant hat. Of his father, Bob had probably kept mixed memories. When the boy turned seven, his father sent him to Heywood Street, in Kingston, to take care of an old sick lady. Bob—everybody called him Nesta at the time—remained there for one year, all by himself in the heart of the concrete jungle. His father remarried—without even bothering to divorce—, and never came back for his son. One day, someone from the boy's village came across him in Kingston and reported to his mother who sent for him—back to Nine Miles, his childhood village in the parish of St Ann. Apparently, his relationship with his mother wasn't that satisfying either. She was unable to take care of him, and kept on leaving him with other people, until she couldn't recognize him anymore. Once her son had become a worldwide star, she reinvented herself as an African queen, wearing dreadlocks and *boubous* sewn with golden strings. Nowadays, she attends some reggae festivals around the world to dedicate her autobiography—usually surrounded with a deferential and ageing court without magnitude or humility.

As a child, Nesta roamed the country paths of Nine Miles, a small village with neither electricity nor running water—a hard life with few pleasures and a lot of housework. Furthermore, the kid starved for affection. He had too light a complexion, the stigma of the forbidden love of his parents. Nowadays, we talk about half-blood people; but at the time, Nesta was just a mulatto, a masters' kid, envied and hated.

One day, a sophisticated kid from town came to Nine Miles. His name was Neville Livingston but everybody called him Bunny. His father owned a thriving shop in Kingston, and had been dating Cedella for a while. The two kids got along at once. Bob revealed Bunny the secrets of country life—how to ride a donkey, or to catch goats—and Bunny told him about Kingston, and bought candies with his pocket money. One day, they made a guitar with a tin and a few strings, and started to sing together. Bob was fascinated. Before heading back to town, Bunny left the instrument with his new friend. Bob spent hours and hours practising—the roots of a legend.

* * *

Bob's life underwent a crucial change when he came to live to Kingston with his mother in 1957—two years after his father's death. They stayed for a short while on Regent Street, and then ended up in the community of Trench Town, Kingston 12—at 19 2nd Street. It wasn't yet the awful place it would become—life was precarious but the environment was relatively peaceful, and the houses were well built. Bob was to witness the slow agony of his community as it sank into chaos and despair—and he would never forget it.

West Kingston was already a furnace haunted by bad boys, illuminated bearded men, and kids contaminated by music. Trench Town was the cradle of an unbelievable amount of artists—it seemed natural at the time, but to quote their names nowadays makes you feel dizzy. Among the patriarchs was Joe Higgs, who had earned the respect of the community thanks to his talent and a local hit song recorded for Edward Seaga—he also had been arrested following a social demonstration. Joe Higgs welcomed everyone on his doorstep, on 3rd Street. Artists still refer to the veranda of his small house as a *musical college;* his many students later rocked the world. Kids in Trench Town dreamt of becoming the Four Tops or the Supremes, and focused on vocal harmonies, probably the most difficult part of popular music. First, you need to have an ear and a voice. Then you must work, work, and work again. But these kids usually had a lot of spare time; jobless, they spent their lives in the famous *government yards* of the community, where they discovered *ganja* (marijuana), music and girls.

Bob invited his friend Bunny to Trench Town, and reminded him of their musical experiments in Nine Miles. Bunny smiled, he had forgotten the handmade guitar. Bob hadn't, who took him to Joe Higgs'. They soon launched a group, trying to be distinct from others by featuring five members. Among them was already this tall and gangling kid from Trench Town, Winston McIntosh— aka Peter Tosh. They called themselves The Wailers, probably from an American white rock group. Later on, they became the Wailin' Wailers. Asked about the original formation, Bob would simply answer: *"Whosoever wails over Justice is a Wailer."* Full stop. For more details, he sent you to Joe Higgs.

Back to Trench Town and its scorching atmosphere. Bob eventually met Rita Anderson, the woman of his life—a ghetto girl who sang with the Soulettes. The two lovers needed a place to enjoy a little privacy, and the *rude boy* Vincent "Tartar" Ford let them spend some time in a small room on 1st Street. At nighttime, in the same yard, Georgie—a kid from the neighbourhood— made the fire light shine all through the night, as related in the song *No Woman No Cry*. But Trench Town was also a devils' nest, as rendered in the same song: *I remember when we use to sit in a Government yard in Trench Town / Observing the hypocrites, as they would mingle with the good people we meet along the way.* These lines express the anxiety of an ambitious kid facing an uncertain future—as well as Bob's usual wild melancholy. In the 1960s, Trench Town was a social dead-end—and it has crushed many souls over the years. Bob used music as a vessel to get out of this bottomless pit. But he first had to endure the claims of tyrannical producers who didn't even pay their artists—sometimes because the local market wasn't lucrative enough, sometimes because they thought that betting on ten songs that didn't work gave them the right to recoup on a hit song.

Bob recorded a song for the first time thanks to a kid whom he heard playing the piano at Leslie Kong's studio. Bob congratulated the kid who shook his hand: *"My name is Jimmy Cliff."* Then he introduced Bob to the owner of the place, the famous Leslie Kong. The producer had turned down the skinny teen-ager a few weeks earlier; but that day, he recorded his song *Judge Not*, a Biblical parable with a catchy melody. Nothing really came out of this first experience—except a good song—and Bob went back to Trench Town, lending a keen ear. When he heard a catchy saying, he bought it from the surprised author to use it in a future song, as underlined by the journalist Hélène Lee in her book *Voir Trench Town et mourir*. In 1962 he was seventeen; his mother went to work in the US, and left him with Bunny's father, who had also become the father of Pearl, Bob's half-sister. But the teenager quarrelled with his stepfather, and ended up living on his own in Trench Town, where only a few compassionate friends helped him out. This place was to haunt him for the rest of his life; here is where his art was rooted, where his inspiration came from—and he never forgot, even when he went to live uptown at Chris Blackwell's villa after he had signed with *Island Records*. Trench Town had become his musical obsession, as heard in *No Woman No Cry*. The connoisseurs also consider *Trench Town Rock* as one of his best songs—it was recorded in the early 1970s with the original trio, Bob, Peter and Bunny. The rhythm track is raw, almost dirty and as punchy as an uppercut—*one good thing about music*, sings Marley, *when it hits, you feel no pain!* West Kingston haunts this song; the heat of the place is palpable, and you can feel the creative fever as well as the bloody mood of the place. There's a rock and roll dimension to this composition, a cry of both despair and rebellion. *Don't turn your back, give the slum a try,* implores the trio. *Grooving, in Kingston 12 / Grooving, in Kingston*

12. But there's a distinctive threat behind the plea, and the song ends up on a disturbing line: *Don't call no cop, we can take care of our trash.* Trench Town was also a school of crime, the breeding ground of heartless murderers let loose by their political masters. Bob grew among them—and was inclined to badness himself. He was nicknamed *Tuff* (tough) *Gong* because he hit hard—probably also as a reference to Leonard "Tuff Gong" Howell, the first Rasta. Though short and skinny, he knew how to earn the respect from the wolves around him; and he could petrify people with a single look. He always remained close to the ghetto, and to the *gunmen* from West Kingston—from his friend Tartar to the notorious Claudie Massop. The latter was the Don—or godfather—of the most powerful gang of Jamaica based in Tivoli Gardens (see Edward Seaga portrait). In the 1970s, this man was feared by the entire nation. Not only did Bob spend hours smoking *ganja* and playing football with him, but he even took him on tour to the US, and bought him a BMW. From this period of his life, Bob had kept an attitude and a daggering look. He also loved to exercise his power. Invited to the 56 Hope Road, the singer King Kong was challenged by the superstar who threw a pair of boxing gloves at him. Just before the fight started, one of Bob's bodyguards whispered to his ear that if he dared touching Skip'—for *Skipper*, the nickname of Bob Marley, as the one who steers the boat—, he would regret it. Apparently, they regularly tied unruly guys to a tree in the back of the yard to teach them discipline with a baton. Don Taylor, the former manager of the star—who was fired after he had charged the state of Zimbabwe for a show Marley had said he would perform for free—reported in his biography that he was once beaten by Bob Marley as his friend Alan "Skill" Cole held him at gunpoint. In Bob's world, you had some good guys and some bad guys—but mostly bad guys. Some petty criminals like Skill Cole; a childhood friend, a professional footballer and a swindler, always running into problems—he sometimes led a complacent Marley behind him. Trench Town inside, like a curse, or a disease—a dirty little angel with his broken wings and his divine look. Bob dedicated several songs to his ghetto, even on his ultimate and posthumous album: *Trench Town, come from Trench Town*. In this particular song, entitled *Trench Town*, the name of the community is repeated over and over, like an incantation.

It is a popular saying in music that *the West is the best*. The artists who came from West Kingston are many, indeed. Ken Boothe, Joe Higgs, The Wailers, The Heptones, The Maytals, The Wailing Souls, Stranger Cole, Alton Ellis, etc. All brag about their protected designation of origin, aware of the worldwide reputation of these wretched streets where everyday life has always been so hard. The title *Mama Say*, by Leroy "Heptones" Sibbles, vibrates with suffering. The singer relates a difficult childhood, telling of his single mother battered down by poverty. This song is the chronicle of a physical and spiritual wreck. Thirty years later, sitting in his brand new Jaguar coupé, Leroy looked away for a while. After a short silence, he shook his head with a weary smile: "*Trench Town, man...*" In this ghetto, a drama was played behind closed doors—a parable of Jamaica, who was slowly, but surely sinking into darkness. Everything Bob Marley knew about politics, he had learnt it in Trench Town. *Never let a politician grant you a favour, or he will always want to control you forever.* Unfortunately, when you lived in the lion's den, you didn't necessarily have the choice. Just as anyone, Bob had to take side—and to pay the consequences.

The Toughest

The political consciousness of Bob aroused at the turn of the 1960s, with the rise of the *rudies*. More than a mode, this phenomenon was orchestrated by the impatient and disheartened youths of West Kingtson. The nearby slum of Back O' Wall was populated with illuminated preachers, robbers and thieves. In the foggy heart of this settlement were bred political manipulations, the most notorious criminals but also Rastas. The sound and the fury poured from Back O' Wall into the neighbouring communities. The rebellious kids hung unto some of the apocalyptic sermons of the elders—it flattered their wounded pride, bandaged their open psychological scars, and promised them a brighter future—hope granted to a whole generation. The independence of 1962 only accelerated the rotation of this supernova. Lots of *country boys* who had no time to lose came to Trench Town, where they used their *ratchets* knives to make their way out of misery. The fire was fuelled from various sources: the anger of a frustrated youth, political corruption and, to a lesser extent, music. A sound war was also opposing the various producers of Kingston. The *Generals* like Duke Reid or the newcomer Clement "Sir Coxsone" Dodd recruited sound soldiers among their most zealous admirers. They sent them to the competitors' dances to spy, but also to crash them. A few bottles thrown over a fence were usually enough to create a wave of panic among the patrons. Sometimes, it was necessary to start a fight. This chaotic but creative atmosphere was rendered in an endemic sound created by a handful of musicians in the late 1950s, The Skatalites. Their name was a tribute to this sound, as the pounding rhythmic guitar went *ska, ska, ska*. Their music was brutal, unrefined, but powerful and energetic. It soon overshadowed the local Calypso, Mento—a music mostly played by hotel bands for the tourists. Born in the polluted streets of Kingston and not in the hotels of the North Coast, *ska* became the voice of the street, and more precisely of the *rudies*.

The Wailers had already become one of the *rudies*' voices when they entered Studio 1, recently opened by the visionary Sir Coxsone at 13 Brentford Road, a few miles from Trench Town. Coxsone —his nickname derived from a famous cricket player— was a tough guy who often used his 38-calibre to put an end to a discussion. He looked like the ideal son-in-law but was a *rude boy* in his own way, a self-assured man who called everyone *Jackson*, and who treated his artists without any consideration—Joe Higgs even lost an eye after Coxsone hit him in the face with his gun butt for telling other artists about royalties. You probably couldn't do business with the *rudies* from Trench Town if you couldn't keep them at bay. Glad to read their names on a record, the young artists were sometimes paid with mere *patties*—some small local sandwiches—, or with a pair of short pants that the producer imported from America. Most of a time, a slap on the back and a *Good job, Jackson!* was their only reward. The local musical industry was still emerging, and the market wasn't that huge; opportunities remained few and all these kids saw Studio 1 as an Eldorado. The Wailers recorded their first hit song there in 1963, *Simmer Down*—Bob was eighteen. They exhorted the *rudies* to simmer down over an hypnotic *Ska* rhythm. The lyrics contained another Bob Marley's trademark, popular sayings—including the famous *sweet nanny goat have a running belly*, a scatological interpretation of the academic *the grass is greener on the other side of the fence*. The Wailers thus made a name for themselves, and started to record on a daily basis for Coxsone. They rehearsed in the yard, under a tall tree, meeting established or upcoming artists. The mood was musical, they played guitar, sang harmonies for other artists, learnt how to arrange a song—a musical college, to quote most of the artists who *studied* there. But a local hit song wasn't leading you far—you might seduce a girl or two, and get a free drink now and then, but the Wailing Wailers had greater views. Unfortunately, none of the numerous songs they recorded afterwards hit the top of the charts. They nevertheless established themselves as an authentic group. Was Coxsone particularly attentive to Bob? He let him sleep in a room at the back of the studio and developed a special relationship with the singer, who was obviously missing a paternalistic figure. The place was uncomfortable, though—at night, some *dupies* (spirits) harassed Bob who asked Rita to stay with him one night. Together they confronted the devilish spirits and came out victorious of this initiatory fight. From now on, Bob would fear no evil—he had become a *duppy conqueror*.

Though paternalistic and caring, Coxsone's yoke was still a yoke. With the Wailers, he hardly talked about money. The youths were stagnating, and time was fleeing. Bob's mother asked him to join her in the Delaware, USA, in 1966. There he worked eight-hour shifts in the cold, slowly perishing—and missing the coming of Haile Selassie to Jamaica; he had to satisfy himself with what Rita reported him. Still hanging to their glorious hopes, The Wailers realized they had to become the masters of their destinies. When Bob came back to Jamaica, the three friends launched their own label.

Wail'N Soul'M

The artwork of their *Wail'N Soul'M* label bore all their aspirations: three hands holding each other on a black, gold and green background formed a solidary triangle with their names written above, *Bunnie, Peter, Bob*; the trade mark mention written in tall letters betrayed their pride and determination. The Wailers had grown fed up with being called *Jackson*, and had put the Rasta teachings of self-determination into action. They even opened a little record shop downtown, buying ads in *The Gleaner* and in *Swing* magazine. Unfortunately, the music business was a jungle, notwithstanding the unpredictable hazards of life; Bunny got caught with a *spliff* (joint) of *ganja* (marijuana) and was sent to prison for one year—the song *Battering Down Sentence* relates his painful experience. The Wailers knew it by then, salvation could only come from above.

At the time, the Wailers teamed up with the black American singer Johnny Nash and his villainous producer Danny Simms. They met through Mortimer Planno, the Rasta mentor of the Wailers. Nash, who had heard about Rasta, attended the Ethiopian Christmas organized in Trench Town by Planno. Impressed, he got in touch with Planno who introduced him to a group of young and talented musicians from his community, The Wailers. The opportunity seemed almost unbelievable; Nash told the Wailers of success, fame and wealth. Dannys Simms taught them how to adapt their music to the aimed US market. In the attic of a villa of Russel Heights, the Wailers recorded dozens of more or less anecdotal songs that keep on coming out of nowhere nowadays, labelled as *forgotten jewels*. Everything Marley is gold, and even his third-rate compositions are sought-after.

Johnny Nash got along very well with his new Trench Town friends, he laughed and joked with them, but, at the end of the day, he still called them *Jackson*. The only thing he was really interested in was their songs. He interpreted several of them on his solo albums, but the association soon came to an end. "*We thought he had come to help us,*" later told Marley to *Swing*, "*but he had come to help himself.*" We'll hold no grudge against the Wailers for these gutless songs and these syrupy melodies—they are the results of their frustration, and their fear of a dark future. Salvation could only come from above, and it was worth trying.

1969 was a crucial year for the Wailers, as they started to work with the independent producer Lee "Scratch" Perry; a weird guy, bordering on autism, but a musical genius. Scratch remains one of the most respected figures of the Jamaican music—a pioneer who started in the 1960s as an engineer for Coxsone, and who went on to produce a personal and haunting music.

In 1973, he opened his mythic Black Ark studio, where he attracted the best artists of the island—he totally reinvented them for the occasion, going as far as changing the names of the most established formations. In their career, nothing can be compared to what they did for him. His Black Ark studio resembled a bunker with no window; it was equipped with a rudimentary material, but he made the best out of it, and created a unique sound; both fiery and sharpened like a razor. Perry was first and foremost a rhythm master—that's what makes most of his productions irresistible. But he was also a disturbed man, who suffocated with ideas and who could go through pernicious black holes. During the last years of his reign, the skipper of the Ark had lost his head—he spoke to flowers and cooked stones from his yard; to chase away undesirable visitors, he wrote *I am a battyman* (homosexual) on his wall—that was meant to Rastas who've always abhorred homosexuality. Nothing was simple with Perry, and his tormented soul made dozens of detours to reach the point. In the end, even his wife had become scared of him. But in 1979 a mysterious blaze sent the Ark to the bottom of darkness. Ever since, Perry's been living in Switzerland, the shadow of the producer he used to be. He has now become a provocative character who plays fool but hardly ever catches the wise—and who hasn't recorded a good album in the past 30 years. Reggae is an endemic music—it has rarely been happily transplanted into another country. Far from Jamaica, it becomes tedious and weak, and it perishes.

But in the late 1960s, when he first met the Wailers, Perry was animated by the same fiery desire for recognition. Together they defied the three big producers of the time, warning them in a song: *If you are the big tree, we are the small axe ready to cut you down.* Perry launched his label, using a skilful band for his recording sessions. As a matter of fact, this band—The Hippy Boys—was what he had kept from all these years working as a *Jackson* in the biggest studios of Kingston: the essential. The Barrett brothers, Aston and Carlton, led the group. They started out playing with tin cans and cardboard boxes, and ended up rocking the world under the name of The Wailers. Who could have guessed it? Bob, who, as soon as he heard Slim Smith's hit song *Watch This Sound*, asked the producer Bunny Lee to introduce him to the musicians. Meeting the Barrett brothers was a crucial turn in Bob's career. When he finally parted with Perry, Bob took them with him. In-between, The Wailers had undergone a crucial change. Before their association with Perry, they were a nice local group; after, they had the potential of the greatest international bands.

The recording sessions took place in what has become a sanctuary, Randy's studio, located on Parade, downtown Kingston. There, in the middle of the urban fury, among *higglers* (peddlers), noise and pollution, on the first floor of an old building, the Wailers, the Hippy Boys and Lee Perry recorded some everlasting pieces of music. The period was exciting and creative—Kingston was vibrating to new sounds, original and bold; a generation of independent producers endeavoured to establish themselves through excellence. The idea wasn't to stick to mainstream music to sell records, but to create a sound never heard before—to leave one's mark on music. Reggae was officially born in 1968, but it was still far from what we can hear today: rhythm tracks were still dry and stiff, and sometimes very weird. Creativity led to many experiences and Scratch's productions like *Mr Brown* or *Duppy Conqueror,* for instance, are quite daring; but others like *Natural Mystic* or *Kaya* featured a dark and abyssal atmosphere that Bob Marley would never forget. This tensed music was telling of the morbid lanes of Trench Town upon dark ancestral rhythms from Wareika Hill. Reggae has always been an emphatic music depicting urban tragedies—it's the mythology of a people deprived of history, and who had to build its own story through visions and memories. Of course, it has evolved over the years, and adapted to commercial purposes. In fact, reggae music has many faces, but if you take this fundamental dimension out of it, then it's not reggae anymore. And this isn't a conscious phenomenon—this mystic is just natural.

Forever Loving Jah

The political message of the Wailers is linked to the Rasta faith they embraced in the early 1970s. They were tutored in this conversion by Rasta elders from Trench Town, especially Mortimer Plano, who had met the Emperor in Ethiopia before welcoming him—or *Him*—at the Kingston airport in 1966. Plano saw Rasta as *the strangest man on Earth*, to quote the title of his book. But at the end of his life, he didn't appear that glorious. Sheltered on the campus of the University of the West Indies in Kingston, weakened by diabetes, disfigured, and using a wheelchair, he was negotiating his interviews. The producer Bunny Lee who knew the Wailers very well, tells a strange story about Planno. The Wailers, he says, had heard that their mentor had raped some guys in prison. Disgusted, Bob Marley allegedly shaved his head and drifted away from Rasta, declaring himself a *soul rebel*—the title of one of his albums for Lee Perry. But Bunny Lee is a cunning fox. In the song *Soul Rebel*, Bob sings: *I'm a rebel, soul rebel / That's what they say...* The last sentence seems to express the helplessness of a man unjustly ostracized. On the other hand, Bob has always blurred his messages. Anyway, what Bunny Lee tells next is interesting. He adds that Bob came back to Rasta in 1972 because of Chris Blackwell. Blackwell, the rich and white producer of *Island Records*, was the lifeline that Bob had been longing for, a passport for international recognition, and the way out of frustration. When the Wailers signed with Blackwell, *Island* was an established company. Blackwell, who was born in Jamaica, had always been a good investor—at least, he had the money to start. When he gave 4,000 dollars to these dubious guys from Trench Town, his friends laughed at him: "*These guys are going to buy 4,000 dollars worth of ganja, and you'll never see them again.*" According to international standards, the money he gave them wasn't enough to produce a single song. But the Wailers soon came back with a full album, *Catch A Fire*. Blackwell still tells around how surprised he was—should we believe him? He knew what Rastas could do. As a kid living on the North Coast, he used to fear them. But he wrecked his boat one day, and was saved by some Rastas who took care of him and sheltered him for a while—so his official biography reads, at least. That's how Blackwell allegedly learnt to love Rastas. Did he intend to turn their faith into a marketing tool? Bunny Lee claims he signed Bob Marley to replace Jimmy Cliff, the then star of the label, who had untimely converted to Islam—just as locks and *ganja* were growing popular among the western youths who bought records! Was Bob Marley an opportunist? Did the *soul rebel* compromised, as Yabby You (see portrait) thought? This sounds quite unfair. Indeed, Bob questioned his faith through subtle lines inserted in his texts—some are hurting the Rasta orthodoxy—but he has always appeared as a genuine Rasta. Don Taylor reported that when a *gunman* opened fire at him in 1976, Bob's last words were: "*Haile Selassie Jah Rastafari!*" Could hypocrisy prevail in such moment? Bob became a defender of the faith, not only because his interviews were published all over the world, but also because he rescued Rasta in the worst time of its existence, the passing of Haile Selassie. In 1975, the Ethiopian Negus was overthrown by a communist *coup*, and put to death by General Mengitsu. Mengitsu feared the unusual power of the Negus and kept his dead body for years in a room beside his office, to make sure he *remained* dead. The remains of the Emperor were nowhere to be found for dozens of years—burnt, scattered? No one knew. But no doubt, the Negus was no more. The news traumatized the Rasta fraternity. How could the living God die? Without Him, the whole Rasta doctrine was falling apart. A lot of Rastas lost faith, and shaved their heads out of shame and resentment. *Since the wicked them say Selassie I dead*, sang the artist Cornell Campbell, *nuff ah-them* (a lot of them) *turn back to baldhead*—a *baldhead* is a non-Rasta, a man with no dreadlocks. Bob Marley went to check Lee Perry—as usual. Together they penned a melancholic but hopeful song, *Jah Live: Jah live, children / Fools say in their hearts, Rasta your God is dead / But the foolish dog bark at a flying bird, and I & I know Jah live.* Disembodying Haile Selassie to focus on His spiritual manifestation, they launched Rasta on the way to eternity. After *Jah Live*, the mockeries couldn't attain Rasta anymore. Thus was the Rasta faith delivered, by the word of its most eminent prophet.

Night Shift

Bob was from Rema, the bottom part of Trench Town; the first seven streets of JLP obedience. In the song *Natty Dread*, he takes a walk in his community: 1st Street, 2nd Street, and so on. But he carefully avoids crossing 7th Street, the invisible frontier with the upper part of Trench Town—Concrete Jungle, a PNP stronghold. Yet, Bob has always more or less sided the party of Michael Manley, the PNP. The 1970s witnessed the rise of Rasta in the political arena thanks to Manley, who exploited it politically.

Furthermore, socialism was far more attractive to a rebellious teenager of West Kingston than the conservative policies of the JLP. Not to mention that the street has always blamed the JLP for the wave of violence that started at the time. In 1971, the Wailers partook in the PNP Bandwagon, a tour put together by Clancy Eccles for the sake of the party. But they were just a group among many others, and only sang their songs on stage. The artists drove around the island in a mini-bus; they had no means but they worked wonders—dozens of thousands of people came to enjoy the show all over the island. Bob & the Wailers left the tour before it came to an end—but not for political reasons. The skirmishes with JLP supporters were quite rare, and of little consequences— Clancy's gun gently settled most of them.

Some artists like Max Romeo or Ken Boothe were openly supporting the PNP. Others just seized the opportunity of a national tour—which was probably the case with the Wailers. Apparently, nobody held a grudge against them when they left; but the political wars hadn't yet come to maturity, and The Wailers were still a rather insignificant local group—they hadn't met Chris Blackwell yet. But people have a good memory in Jamaica. And when Bob, now an international star, lost his neutrality on the eve of the 1976 general election, it was another story.

Smile Jamaica

1976, the year of chaos. The economical situation was disastrous; the social programs had become empty shells, and were mainly used to enrol the youths in the PNP militias. The leader of the opposition Edward Seaga made sure things would get from bad to worse. Some divide to conquer; he destroyed to build his dream on the remains of his country. Michael Manley and his inconsequent administration panicked as the election drew closer and declared the state of emergency to keep the situation under control. The island became even more prostrated. The police and the army spread in Kingston, looking for any individual suspicious of stirring up social unrest—they went for

Claudie Massop, the JLP Don of Tivoli Gardens, as well as for several JLP politicians linked to gangs—Seaga cried *coup d'état!*

Tension rose to its maximum—people remained at home, terrified. The previous year had cost the lives of 400 people, and the current one looked even bloodier. So Bob Marley suddenly sang: *Smile, you're in Jamaica!*, everybody thought they had misheard him. Was the author of uncompromised songs such as *Burnin' and Lootin'* and *Get Up, Stand Up* urging the *sufferers* trapped in the middle of a civil war to—smile?

In fact, *Smile Jamaica* was a command of the Ministry of Tourism to counteract Seaga's propaganda—it was aiming at the American tourists who refused to visit a soon-to-be-socialist country. *Smile Jamaica* was a political song, which seemed to indicate that the *soul rebel* was now openly supporting the PNP. He put out two different versions of the song, including a darker and speeder one, recorded with Lee Perry, of course. *Smile Jamaica* made people frown as far as England. The black activist Linton Kwesi Johnson commented: *"Bob begs the listener to smile because he's in Jamaica; be happy, he says, because everything is all right, the sun is shining. But the song leaves certain questions without answers. Who are we when he sings we are going to help our people? Surely not himself and his Wailers who don't live in Jamaica anymore, nor the JLP, which lost the 1976 elections."* There was no doubt left, Bob had just taken side. Everything is suspicious in this story, up to the artwork of the label. *Smile Jamaica* didn't come out on the usual label of Bob, *Tuff Gong*; well, it did, in fact. But the name itself is mentioned in small characters while the title of the song, on the contrary, is written across the record in big letters. The background also differs from the regular one, and its orange rays spreading like sunrays over a yellow sky is an obvious reference to the logo of the PNP. *Smile Jamaica* was never featured on any album. *Island Records* (who owned the international rights for Bob's songs) put it out, though, as a maxi 45, in 1976—it has become extremely rare. The record company repressed it two years later, in 1978—a very unlikely coincidence, as this was the year of the Peace Treaty, another main political event.

    Bob Marley swept away the critics, and claimed he wasn't into politics. Music soothes the mind, and feeling the helplessness of his people, he had decided to give a free concert in Kingston, the *Smile Jamaica Concert*. He just wanted his *children*—as he used to call his listeners—to forget their trouble and dance. Marley was then the most influential Jamaican personality in the world. Within five years' time, he had exploded on the international scene. The first two albums of The Wailers were successful but everything accelerated after Eric Clapton's cover version of *I Shot The Sheriff*. The biggest stars started to pack up at Bob's shows to see the Jamaican phenomenon, and to listen to his songs of redemption. The Wailers had now become *Bob Marley & The Wailers*. Bunny had calmly stepped back, as he never liked the pop rock direction taken by the group since the signature with *Island*—it didn't prevent him from signing with the same label to pursue a brilliant career as a solo artist. Bunny didn't like travelling; he feared plane. Furthermore, he was an anxious mind, and usually stuck to himself. The separation was more difficult for Peter Tosh; it left him a bitter taste. An outspoken man, he resented the fact that Blackwell had put Bob forward, and stated that it was because of his lighter complexion—more attractive, he said, to the white audience. He used to call the producer Chris *White-worse*. Eventually, he had no choice but to slip into Bob's shadow. The name Wailers now referred to Bob's backing band, which consisted of the Barrett brothers, the horn section of Zap-Pow, the I-Three—the female backing vocals composed of Rita Marley, Marcia Griffiths and Judy Mowatt—, and a few complementary musicians. Bob's success generated envy. His music was criticized; some said it was drifting away from the Jamaican reality. But it made no sense. His *Natty Dread* album of 1974 was deeply rooted in reality—and the sound remained as upright as ever. Bob Marley was an adept of sharp and clean rhythm tracks. Far from the local musical fashions, he stuck to the straightforward, hypnotic and abyssal *one drop* style. His music stood sovereign, and his influence spread way beyond Jamaica. In this context, siding a political party was dangerous. In the *Smile Jamaica* case, Bob's behaviour was suspicious to say the least. He later claimed he hadn't understood the political dimension of it, and shouted *manipulation*! Which wasn't convincing at all, mostly for a guy who grew up in Trench Town. Let's be clear, Bob hadn't turned a PNP representative; he always watched politics from a distance. He probably liked the progressive policy of Michael Manley, and the movement of racial pride instigated by the PNP; but it was a different thing to openly support Manley. Did he knowingly take the initiative of the *Smile Jamaica* concert? Some say he did.

When Michael Manley heard about the show, he was so excited that he invited Bob to his official residence. The singer later claimed that he had insisted on the non-political dimension of his project. Really? Did Marley and Manley, whose names only differ from one letter, privately evoke the tribulations of the politician, and the policy of terror orchestrated by Seaga? The *blind man with a pistol* (see Seaga portrait) was portraying Jamaica as a communist nest ready to lapse into state terrorism, and scared the hell out of American tourists; they went to smile somewhere else. Isolated, trapped into a spiral of violence, Jamaica was on the eve of despair. It seemed logical for Bob Marley to oppose political violence—after all, that's what he had always been doing. But he who sang *we no have no friends in the high society* had so far succeeded in keeping away the political adders. He defined himself as a non-political artist. Of course, he was a Rasta; and as he put it: *Rasta no work for no CIA*—but not a word about the KGB.

Leaving the Prime Minister's office, Bob went to his colonial mansion of Hope Road—Chris Blackwell's former childhood house—, and officially announced the *Smile Jamaica* concert. Right away, Michael Manley called a press conference, and announced the next general election date—fifteen days after the show. Who, in this Jamaica, believed in coincidences?

Ambush in the night
Ambush in the night, all guns aiming at me, sang Bob Marley in *Ambush In The Night* (1978). This autobiographical title was directly inspired by the assassination attempt he survived just before the *Smile Jamaica* concert. The JLP's opportunities to win the general election were growing thinner with every new low blow; and Bob's show was obviously perceived as such. Claudie Massop warned him: the JLP didn't want this concert to take place. This was as good as an open threat—the Tuff Gong premises were put under police watch. Judy Mowatt from the I-Three obstinately refused to appear on stage while Marcia Griffiths, another I-Three, told Bob of a morbid vision she had had, involving the singer's death. Meanwhile, Chris Blackwell came to Jamaica and stayed at the Sheraton Hotel in Kingston. After a few hesitations, it was decided that the concert would take place at the National Heroes Circle, in the heart of downtown Kingston. At Tuff Gong, the musicians started to rehearse.

On November 5, 1976, as the policemen from the Echo Squad who supposedly watched the place had mysteriously vanished, four *gunmen* entered the 56 Hope Road. Bob Marley was then in a room at the back of the house, talking to his manager Don Taylor. The first gunshots, those fired at Rita Marley while she tried to run away, made the two men frown. Bob grimaced: "*Who is playing with fireworks in..?*" He didn't finish his sentence—all of a sudden, a *gunman* stood before him, and opened fire. Placed between Bob and the shooter, the body of Don Taylor acted as a protective screen—hit several times, he was considered as dead for a short while. Miraculously, Bob was only hit once—in the elbow.

At Tuff Gong, panic was at its peak. The musicians left the rehearsing room and jumped into the bathtub to escape stray bullets. Aston Barrett the bass player arrived first and David

Madden, the trumpeter, Glen DaCosta the saxophonist and the trombonist Vin Gordon all piled on him. Once the dust had settled, Rita Marley was found in her car, leaning on the steer with a bullet between her scalp and her skull—a minor injury. Bob was injured and Don Taylor was lying in a pool of blood—he unexpectedly survived. The hit men left no signature, leaving everyone guessing. Probably a JLP commando recruited among the most zealous warriors of Tivoli Gardens; or the retaliation of some crooks over a swindle orchestrated by Bob's friend, Allan Skill Cole?

It was said at one point that Claudie Massop himself had the offenders caught and punished. Two were allegedly hanged and a next one beheaded. Don Taylor related in his memoirs a disturbing scene he located near the McGregor Gully, in Kingston—a notorious gang turf. Tek Life, one of Massop's cronies, asked Don Taylor and Marley to join him there one day. They were introduced to a youth who had allegedly partaken in the raid. Bob was offered a gun, and the opportunity to retaliate. He refused, wrote Don Taylor, and the youth was drawn to a nearby yard, and executed. How does the song go? Smile, *you're in Jamaica*.

A striking scene, indeed; and a credible story. But could four petty crooks set up such an operation without their Don's consent? And what for, if the orders weren't coming from above? Unless they had *another* boss. In his book, Don Taylor also wrote that Bob identified the fourth man, one day, hanging out at Tuff Gong. He called his manager, asking for the guy's identity. "*He?*" said Don Taylor. "*A youth from Tivoli, named Jim Brown.*"

When Claudie Massop was shot to death in 1978, the said Jim Brown became the most notorious Don of Jamaica. Did he personally shoot at Bob Marley? He might have gone behind Massop's back, then—for a few weeks, the ambitious criminal had been at work in the underworld of crime. His advancement meant Massop's death—sooner or later. He could have taken orders directly from Edward Seaga, then. But if it was the case, how did he escape his Don's retaliation? Unless the trial reported by Don

Taylor was nothing but a morbid and cynical pretence, and the victims mere scapegoats—they would be neither the first, nor the last. Up till today, the responsibility for the shooting has never been clearly established. But the message was clear—not even Bob Marley was safe from the political warfare. He appeared on stage at the *Smile Jamaica* concert with his arm in a sling, in front of 50,000 people, adding a chapter to his legend. "*When I decided to give this show two months ago,*" he said that evening. "*I was told it was not political; I just wanted to sing for my people.*" Then he started to sing *War*, an adaptation of Haile Selassie's speech he had subtlety adapted to the Jamaican situation. Bob was supposed to sing one song only, he remained on stage for one hour and a half, delivering what is considered to be his best performance ever. He didn't sing *Smile Jamaica*, but Michael Manley joined him on stage for a handshake. Right after the show, as Jamaica celebrated his courage, Bob left the island for several years. The PNP officially communicated on the event:

> When Bob Marley, renowned for his anti-capitalistic songs was shot at the eve of his FREE concert opened to ALL Jamaicans, who benefits the crime?

The PNP politicians made sure it would at least partly benefit them. Bob triumphed, but ran away with all his relatives and his musicians; far from Trench Town, the Tivolites and their machines of destruction. The *Exodus* album, the darkest of his work, came out soon after—it talks about heathens, guiltiness and repatriation; but the following opus, the most consensual of his work entitled *Kaya*, featured a disturbing autobiographic song, *Running Away*. The broken voice of Marley is here but a coarse complaint as he sings: *You're running and you're running and you're running away/ But you can't run away from yourself.* The end of the song vaguely evokes a love story but one can't help linking it to his exile. Although it features a few classic songs like *Kaya*—the original cut for Lee Perry is far better—or *Is This Love?*, this is Bob's weakest album.

The exile of Marley was a consecration for Seaga; so Michael Manley flew to London to urge the star to come back—in vain. To welcome him to Jamaica, he had to wait for the One Love Peace Concert of 1978. Meanwhile, Bob lived a life of luxury, staying at expensive hotels; a life of lust, too—dating dozens of beautiful women. His wife Rita Marley later described these ephemeral relationships as a spiritual wreck. She remained by his side as his official wife despite his numerous conquests, his illegitimate children, and daily humiliations. He got upset when she suggested divorce. He was a violent husband, she said, who regularly beat her; but she stayed, and inherited the kingdom when the King died.

Bob was paying astronomic bills in top-class palaces, driving B(ob) M(arley and the) W(ailers)s, and dancing in the hippest nightclubs. But he never lost his focus. The kid from Trench Town could never be caught off-guard. The way he used to dress betrayed his lack of interest for luxurious gaudery, as he usually wore a pair of baskets, a tracksuit or a pair of jean's—an unusual superstar look. The tabloids related his love affairs, asked him about Rasta, *ganja*, Haile Selassie or his revolutionary statements. Bob Marley bore the whole Trench Town on his shoulders, the dreams and the fears of its people—his advancement in life looked like a Way of the cross. Exhaustion fell on him one day; during a football match against a team of French journalists, he injured his big toe. The wound became infected; he underwent some medical tests and was diagnosed with cancer in 1977. He died four years later.

The One Love Peace Concert

The *Exodus* album came out in 1977, one year before *Kaya*. It was a brutal mixture of light and darkness. Some sensual love songs, a tribute to his *three little birds*—the I-Three—, but also the dark *Heathen* or the desperate *Guiltiness*, where Bob cast a spell on all the wicked—a beautiful but derisory last resort. The arrangements were limpid, furious, and gave an incredible magnitude to this *one drop* reggae album. The song starts like in the middle of a cloudy dream; some notes rise from the bottom of nothingness, slow but intense—just like a hypnotic call from ancient times; and then explode! *Natural Mystic*, another recut of a composition from the days of Lee Perry: *Though I tried to find the answers to all the questions they ask, now I know it's impossible to go living through the past, don't tell no lie.* A strange verse left without a clear explanation—like many others. There's always a part of doubt in Bob's songs, some sort of poetical blur. Notwithstanding the concessions he made to be a bankable singer, his songs remained prayers; trying to hit *the top one hundred*, he still jammed *in the name of the Lord*. And when he described the migration of the African diaspora to the Promised Land on *Exodus*, it sounds like a hypnotic stampede, a blind and chaotic march—almost unbearable.

The following year, Bob put out the disappointing *Kaya* and the second live album of his career, *Babylon By Bus*. The latter was recorded during his American tour, and reminded that he was first and foremost a great performer; a sort of musical gladiator, who conquered the world on stage, wearing his dreadlocks like a crown. Thirty years after his death, Marcia Griffiths was still ecstatic when evoking Bob's aura. "*On stage,*» she said, «*he wasn't playing his music, he* was *his music*." She remembered one specific show when he entered the stage, dancing on the rhythm of *Jamming*: "*We were there, staring at him, and we couldn't take our eyes off him; we forgot to sing our part, the three of us, until he opened his eyes and inquiringly looked at us.*" His shows were professional. He was a hard-working man, always rehearsing, always singing. You don't become Bob Marley by chance.

At the end of the day, his shows were both unique and alike. He often linked songs like *Roots Rock Reggae* and *Running Away*, for example; and *Lively Up Yourself* was crossed by a series of *Yeah, yeaaaaah.... Hey ho!*, aimed at warming the audience. But sermon after sermon, reggae music was growing; and Bob was its prophet.

RIP Peace

In 1978, the gangs of Kingston suddenly realized what it had come to, and put down the guns. The unbelievable truce exploded like a bomb. Former deadly foes embraced each other in the middle of the battlefield, started to smoke together while dreaming of a better tomorrow. Behind the scenes, the politicians growled; and eventually smiled. "*Peace?*" asked Peter Tosh on the stage of the One Love Peace Concert that celebrated the peace truce. "*It's the diploma you get when you enter the cemetery: here lies John, rest in peace.*" All didn't give into cynicism, though. Some believed in the truce; they really thought they could put an end to the blood bath. The triumph of reason called upon by Bob and all the Rasta artists for years had turned into a reality. It wasn't coming from the politicians, or from the intellectuals—but from the black sheep of Jamaica, the *gunmen*. But it remained fragile, and music was its sole cement. Should Bob Marley come back from exile, the credibility of these former warlords and new princes of peace would be reinforced. Bob hesitated. There were still a lot of Jim Browns in the lanes of Trench Town. Whom could he trust? *They stab you in the back,* he sang, *and they claim that you're not looking.* Claudie Massop gave him his word that he could safely come back—an implicit confession? Anyway, it wasn't enough. To convince Bob, the mentor of the 12 Tribes of Israel, Prophet Gad, was sent to England.

Gad was another incredible man from Trench Town. His story started in the 1960s, as he was walking up and down his community, speaking to flowers and stones. The kids mocked him, and sometimes threw stones at him. Then people got used to him; some even started to wonder what he was up to. They approached him, they listened to him, and they grew fascinated. A few years later, Gad was ruling the most powerful Rasta organisation of all times. According to the month of his or her birth, each member was affiliated to one of the twelve biblical tribes of Israel, thus inheriting special attributes and functions. Bob Marley, born in February, was from the tribe of Joseph. People who were born in October were from the tribe of Dan, etc. As an open organisation preaching a Rasta doctrine very close to Christianity, the 12 Tribes attracted numerous members from all over the world. Bob joined Gad's troops in the 1970s, and he even bought a piece of land in Kingston, upon which the organization built its headquarters. Gad disliked taxes, and did his best to avoid them—as a consequence, the 12 Tribes remained a nebulous and elusive body. He was ready to chop off a whole branch to quiet down his tormented soul, or purse—that's what happened to the yet promising musical branch of the 12 Tribes. Gad's growing influence dragged him into politics; he was said to be close to the PNP.

Edward Seaga from the JLP wasn't the only one who loved war—some influent members of the PNP were also displeased with the truce. Nevertheless, the come back of Bob Marley was a victory for the PNP. His arrival was made a national event, and people crowded the airport to welcome him. He didn't disappoint his people, and went beyond all expectations, having—almost forcing—Manley and Seaga to shake hands on stage in front of the delighted crowd of the One Love Peace concert. A farce! A few months later, asked about this historical moment, a disillusioned Bob said about the two politicians: *"I should have killed them both."* Even his music couldn't stop the downfall of the nation. In fact, despite the truce, war never stopped gaining ground in Jamaica—and many peacemakers soon passed their death exam, thus getting their *peace* diploma.

Exodus

Rastas identified with the Jewish people enslaved by the Babylonians. They sang *King Alpha songs in a strange land*, waiting to return to the Promised Land—Africa. *Exodus! Movement of Jah people,* sang Marley. His *Exodus* song is a straightforward composition, almost brutal—a victory song. He went to Africa himself. And not as a tourist. In 1980, he was officially invited by Robert Mugabe to celebrate the liberation of former Rhodesia, renamed Zimbabwe. From Jamaica, it looked like a revolutionary army overthrowing *an unhappy regime* close to the devilish Apartheid system of South Africa. Bob was enthusiastic and celebrated in the song *Zimbabwe*. His designer Neville Garrick built up a sleeve jacket for the 45 record. On the photograph, Mugabe raised his clinched fist. *Majority rules!* reads the caption. *Brother you're right, you're right you're so right!* sang Bob Marley with a genuine intensity. But Trench Town had taught him about politics. He added: *Soon we'll find out who is the revolutionary cause I don't want my people to do tricked by mercenaries.* The day he performed in front of the officers of the revolutionary army in Zimbabwe, some soldiers who hadn't been granted access to the stadium forced the door, firing their machine gun in the air. Bob turned towards his musicians: "*Now we know who are the real revolutionaries.*"

Africa offered Bob one of his most ready albums, the flawless *Survival*. Once again, the design of Neville Garrick didn't simply illustrate his music, but it gave it a complementary dimension. The artist juxtaposed several African flags on a black background, and added the cut-off profile of a slave ship. *Survival*. On the drawing, small characters line up in the ship's holds by the hundred, like flour bags—slaves! They have no space, no intimacy—and no dignity. *Survival* came out in 1979, two years before Bob's passing. And the Wailers sounded more powerful than ever. The sound is intense, rumbling like a storm, containing its strength and fury—ready to burst. The Barrett brothers rule the rhythms like two authoritarian generals leading their troops in good order into battle—a masterpiece.

What Bob saw in Africa was different from what Peter Tosh saw. The latter went there after his inner darkness, following terrifying visions and witnessing sorcerers transforming themselves into birds. Peter was different from Bob—tougher?

More raw, more cynical too. His words were like swords plunged into the hearts of the listeners—he accused people; he attacked Babylon and its ideologies without any apology—unrestrainedly. He burnt himself to the flames of the furnace, and ended up in a pool of blood—murdered at home in 1989. Bob Marley showed more empathy, calling his listeners *children*. His texts were less brutal, and when it hit your conscience, you felt no pain. Peter Tosh was blaming the sinner; Bob Marley only blamed the sin. *The greatest man you've ever seen was once a baby*, he reminded. He cast a spell on the oppressors but at the end of the day, he questioned humanity at large. *Where did it start and when will it end? Seems like total destruction is the only solution.* For Marley, Man is responsible—but he's also ruled by his passions that haunt him like a bunch of restless devils.

Bob knew the end was near, and he left a musical testimony on the *Uprising* album, *Redemption Song*—*'cause all I ever had, redemption songs*. Bob was on a crusade and music was his weapon. But he had doubts, too—and expressed them; that's why his lyrics are so powerful. *How long shall they kill our prophets while we stand aside and look?* he asked, before adding: *Some say it's just a part of it, we have to fulfil the book. Some* say? A touch of heresy, as usual. *Redemption Song* is a melancholic song but it remains a message of hope, the last call to arms from a falling soldier—*none but ourselves can free our minds*.

Uprising
Till his very last breath, Bob raised his fist, calling to upheaval on the cover of his last album *Uprising*—the last one to come out during his lifetime. Once again, the design outraged the politicians from the JLP, who saw a tribute to the PNP in the orange rising sun—but this time, the filiation was less obvious. This isn't Bob's best album, even though it features some classic like *Could You Be Loved*, which covers very dark lyrics under a joyful—almost idiotic—rhythm. Once again, Bob questioned mankind.

In 1980, he collapsed during a footing in Central Park, New York. This was a serious warning. He gave several concerts during the following months, including at Le Bourget, in France, in front of 50,000 people. But he soon had to fight the most important fight of all. And he tried everything: he started to eat meat; he drank carrot juice in a German clinic, and even broke his Nazarene vow by shaving his head. "*You look like a rude boy,*" laughed one of his friends. "*Don't be rude,*" he answered.

Unlike Augustus Pablo, a deeply committed Rasta producer from the 1970s, who died refusing the assistance of the Babylonian medicine, Bob complied with his doctors' orders. Even Christ doubted on the cross. And Bob was just a man, with his strength and his weakness—as he had always sung. A lot of rats gathered round his deathbed, waiting for his *ship to turn to dark*. The inheritance was at stake—millions of dollars. People started to fight over it as Bob wasn't even dead yet—*could you be loved?* Don Taylor, the manager who was more or less left aside after the Zimbabwe swindle, wrote that some tape recorders were found under Bob's bed, that some people including Rita Marley—whom he accused of having murdered Bob—tried to take advantage of the singer's weakness. That's how superstars die—celebrated worldwide, and desperately lonely. Bob died; and flew away to a hypothetical home. Rita suggested carrying his body to Ethiopia. Fortunately, we were spared this jester. As a Rasta, Bob defined himself as an African. But he was a Jamaican from birth; he was the symbol of the local culture. Everyone there is proud of this kid from the parish of St Ann, of the local music he represented, and of his endemic Rasta faith. No politician has ever turned him into a national hero, though. He almost made it to a bank note, once—some saw the project as a devilish attempt to belittle his message; others, including genuine Rastas, as a well-deserved honour. Every now and then, Jamaica questions Bob's place—Rita Marley put out a book a few years ago, and said she would maybe take his remains to Africa. It created a national debate. The book of Rita was exposed, and the idea quickly abandoned.

When Bob Marley died, on May 11, 1981, the JLP had been in power for a few months; the militant reggae Bob had always stood for was on the decline. The national funeral brought the whole island to the street—in the crowd, the hypocrites mingled with the good people. The ceremony was broadcast on TV and Edward Seaga spat *Jah Rastafari!* on the star's coffin—Bob didn't belong to himself anymore. Legend warmly welcomed him. He died as a young man, only 36—he never grew old, and the youth of the world can still identify to him.

Bob Marley's posthumous career is as much important as his living one—*Confrontation* came out in 1983 with some interesting songs; but the sound was less intense, less *roots*. We may wonder about the input of Bob in this work. There was also the rat race for the inheritance of the Marley kingdom: the trials, the suspicious deaths, the doggedly dealings around Rita Marley who triumphed after a life of humiliation. To her went Tuff Gong, the bank accounts, as well as the royalties. The abused musicians signed some agreements with the widow or with *Island*—they cashed in the money, then changed their minds, asked for more, and sued again. Hazy projects saw the light—techno remixes of Bob's songs, posthumous duets with some Rap stars, clothes—they even put out a shampoo named *Exodus*. The Marley family needed no one to ridicule, or at least to belittle, the prophet's works. Nevertheless, it seems like nothing can alter his message—not even the low quality compilations sold in supermarkets, or the annoying and consensual biographies and other mediocre unreleased tracks celebrated as masterpieces by some covetous producers. Bob's music keeps on spreading, as strong as ever. Solid as a rock, it stands; and Bob Marley remains, as the best artist who ever came out of Jamaica.

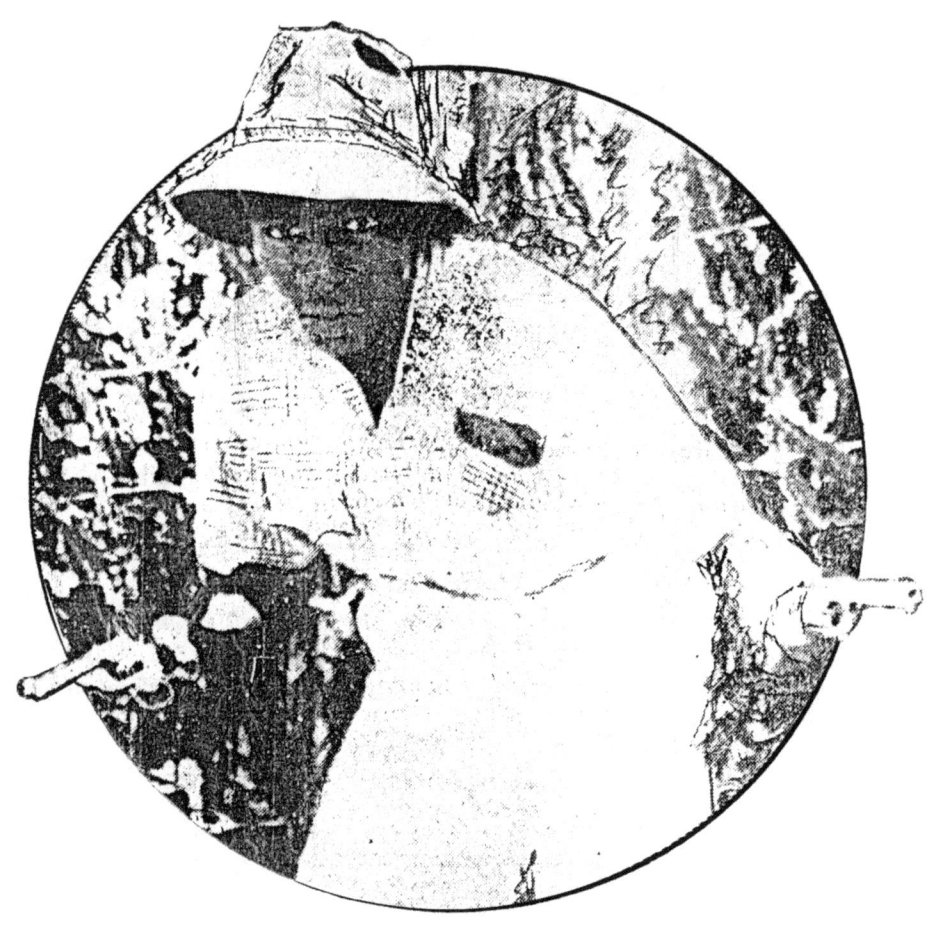

The two-gun killer, fiercely posing in front of the camera while on the run.
These photographs greatly contributed to the birth of his legend
as well as the movie *The Harder They Come* (1972)
in which Jimmy Cliff played his part.

Martin, Vincent
aka Ryghin
(1924-1948)
The Two-gun Killer

Vincent "Ivanohe" Martin was one of those numerous country boys who had come to Kingston in search of fame and fortune, and who eventually turned to crime. In the 1930s, he was still the *nice boy* later described by his mother when he jumped on the back of a truck in Linstead; the driver dropped him in West Kingston where he disappeared. What did he do then? Apparently, he became a blacksmith. Aged 14, he was convicted a first time for wounding—the Judge ordered him to receive twelve strokes of the tamarind switch. Hanging with the bad boys of his community, the young Ivanohe slowly went wild; he was only five feet three inches tall but his blacksmith's fists hit hard. In the dirty lanes alongside Spanish Town Road, he lost a few upper teeth and took the stand of a hunted animal—the journalists later described him as permanently looking over his shoulder, and spitting all over. Two years after his first conviction, he ran into trouble again—a fine settled it down. At 19, the country boy had made a name for himself, or rather a nickname, *Ryghin'*—a slang word meaning *always on top*. He became a burglar, and was caught again. This time, he spent six months in jail. Right after this, he picked up a gun and was charged for illegal possession of firearm—back to General Penitentiary for five years. At this precise moment, Ryghin' was just an ordinary petty thief treading the broad road of crime. But a series of incredible actions were about to turn him into an urban legend. It all started when he escaped from General Penitentiary in April 1948. With the help of another inmate, he slipped through a window and ran away—as simple as that. Began a manhunt that ended up six months later in a cloud of smoke and a pool of blood.

I am a Legend

"*I have made a record in crime history,*" boasted Ryghin' in a letter sent to *The Gleaner*. "*I know my grave is dug already. I have nothing to look back for. (...) I have ten rounds of ammunition left and I'll make at least nine of them count.*" Ryghin' had something of a movie star. He had charisma. A bold man with a flexible and determined walk, he loved to show off with a girl on each arm; he also spent hours watching Charlie Chan movies at the cinema. There were many bad guys in Kingston in the 1940s. One of them, the notorious George Brown, was shot dead by the police in Trench Town in 1941, right in the middle of the street. Nobody really cared. But Ryghin' didn't intend to go down in silence—and he didn't. He made it several times to the front page of *The Gleaner*, an exploit partly due to some wonderful, almost unbelievable pictures—a journalist's dream. Indeed, the arrogant fugitive posed in front of the camera, wearing a hat, and ready to bounce like a wildcat. He had a threatening look, too; and last but not least, he held a gun in each hand—a real movie poster! What made these photographs even more striking is that they were taken while Ryghin' was on the run. He went to a professional photographer in Kingston, Mr Brown, who later sent some copies to *The Gleaner*. A decision that gave him cold sweat: "*You can tell your mother to put up the money to bury you. It is only time,*" warned the two-gun killer in the aforementioned letter sent to newspaper. Yet, Ryghin' owed him a lot. Thanks to him, he indeed wrote his name—and printed his face—in the history of crime. But Ryghin' didn't rely upon his art of directing only—he had talent in his domain, crime. To start with, he had become the leader of a small gang that supported him while on the run, providing him with food and warning him about the police any time they closed in. Then, when required, he became a formidable fighter, as proven during the Carib Hotel gun battle—the real starting point of his legend. The event matched the most thrilling gun battles of cowboy movies.

The Carib Gun Battle

The Carib Hotel stood right outside of Kingston, on the corner of Spanish Town Road and Regent Street. On the evening of August 30, 1948, Ryghin' entered with a girl, and rented a room on the first floor. He paid with the booty of his latest robbery—he had broken in the White Horse Inn on Rousseau Road, knocking down the watchman before peacefully walking out. Around 10 p.m., he was lying naked on the bed when he saw a ray of light from the other room over the gabling. He stood up: "*Ah-who dat?*" A sound answered him, like a gunshot; he caught his 38 H&R Defender on the bedside table. "*Ah-who dat?*" he asked again. The same sound answered him so he opened the door, peeped outside—nothing. Then came a gunshot. All of a sudden several silhouettes bounced up and down the corridor—the cops! He hurled into the corridor, where shower of bullets greeted him—one hit him in the shoulder, but he instantly fired back, deadly wounding Detective Lewis. Ryghin' reached the staircase where more policemen were waiting, some dressed as women— the proof that the operation had been carefully planned. A bullet hit the butt of his gun, but he aimed back and hit Corporal Earl. At last, he shot his way out of the hotel. In the street, he shot again, hitting another policeman, Sargent Gallimore from the Criminal Investigation Department (C.I.D). *A running gun battle reminiscent of Chicago gangster days*, summed up *The Gleaner*. Ryghin' jumped a fence and plunged into a nearby slum. Breathless and wounded, he had to stop shortly afterwards. He leaned against a tree in a yard while the whistles resounded all around.

The police cordoned the block between Regent Street, Trinity Lane, Blunt Street and Dumfries Street. They started to search, yard-to-yard and house-to-house—the rat was trapped.

In the darkness, Ryghin' waited for several minutes, dazed—if only he had his clothes on. All of a sudden, he heard someone close by. His heart raced in his chest, his arms became heavy as lead. "*It's over*," he thought. "*This is the end of the road.*" Hidden behind a bush, he realized he had only two shots left. The yard was now crowded with policemen—they had literally swarmed the place. Ryghin' decided to let them come as close as possible. He didn't want to miss a single shot. In a handful of seconds he would stand up, aim his gun with his two hands—his wounded arm wouldn't respond—, and kill—twice—, and then die. He closed his eyes tightly: "*Come on, man! N—!*" Suddenly, a strident whistle reverberated. The policemen froze, and then walked back. It was too risky to go after such a dangerous fugitive by night; the operation was postponed until dawn. Ryghin' pulled himself together and slipped through the net. It was written he wouldn't die tonight—but on October 9, 1948.

Rampage Business

Who was Ryghin'? A twenty-four, twenty-five year-old man, a narcissist as indicated by the photographs published in *The Gleaner*, but mainly a tough boy. After the incident of the Carib Hotel, he was wounded, and supposedly scared and desperate. But on the contrary, he was actually meditating revenge.

He sought refuge at Elfreda Myrie's home, on Matthew Lane. She gave him something to eat, provided him with clothes and even money—she was later charged for complicity. The killer was thinking. Only one man could have informed the police on him, Eric "Mosspan" Goldson. Earlier in the day, around 7 p.m., Ryghin' had come across this little freak on Spanish Town Road. "*He asked me: What's happening?*" later told Mosspan to a journalist. "*I told him: "Nothing." And then I asked him: "Where* are you coming from?" He said: "Spanish Town." That was all. We spoke no more. We parted and I went East." Mosspan's position in the whole case was quite ambiguous. He publicly denied having informed the police on Ryghin', but there was tension between the two of them. A few months earlier, Ryghin' had had some words with his girlfriend Tiny, and the scared girl had run to the house of her friend Ilcida Tibby Young—who happened to be Mosspan's girlfriend. Did the two-gun killer come after his girl? And did Mosspan block him on the doorstep as he later stated? "*I told him not to come to my home for I didn't want the police coming after him to my place*," he told *The Gleaner*.

Nursing his fresh wound, Ryghin' also remembered his meeting Iris in the afternoon, a girl from the community. What if she had told Icilda, who, in turn, had informed Mosspan? Then Mosspan had probably followed him to the Carib Hotel before calling the cops. There was no room left for doubt in the killer's mind—and, apparently, he liked revenge very hot. A couple of hours after his deadly encounter with the detectives from the C.I.D, he hit back the road. In the middle of the night, he walked up Spanish Town Road and reached the Greenwich Farm community. It was 1:30 a.m. when he rushed inside Mosspan's place, holding his gun. The traitor wasn't here, only Ilcida, Iris, and a girl by the name of Estella Brown. "*If I can't get him*," said Ryghin', "*then I'll get you*." Ilcida was deadly wounded, and the two other girls ran under the bed; he hit one of them before she reached, then bent to hit the second one. They were both seriously injured but reached the hospital on time, and recovered. The gunshots had awakened the whole community and Ryghin' ran away on Spanish Town Road—*with dogs barking at him*, stated *The Gleaner*, which makes it sound like a scene from a thriller. Challenged, the police launched the biggest manhunt ever. On September 2, *The Gleaner* read: "*The Radio and the Press were drawn into service, and every citizen of this island was asked to be on the "look-out" for a man, and malevolent, described as follow:*

Aged, 29. Height, 5 feet, 3 inches; medium built; colour, black; eyes and hair black; several front teeth in upper jaw missing. When last seen was wearing trousers and light brown check shirt; will probably be in possession of a revolver. Any information should be given to C.I.D. Telephone 3634, or to any Police Station. As this man is believed wounded, the special attention of hospital staffs, doctors and druggists is requested, as he may ask for medical attention."

The Hunted

The more a fugitive is exposed, the more he tends to remain quiet—not Ryghin, who revealed himself once all the projectors had focused on him. On September 2, the whole nation was mourning Corporal Edgar Lewis whom he had shot at the Carib Hotel. Prime Minister Alexander Bustamante himself attended the funeral. The politician, who ruled the workers' unions with a fist of iron, wasn't easy to impress. Yet, this very day, several policemen in plain-clothes mingled with the crowd to ensure his safety. They were looking for Ryghin', and Mosspan went with them. The two-gun killer had phoned the Mayor of Kingston to let him know he would attend the funeral too, and that he would kill Bustamante *if he* (didn't) *find work for the people by* (the) *week-end*. This weird claim owed Ryghin' the reputation of a modern Robin Hood. The letter wasn't taken seriously at once— but another one was sent to *The Gleaner*, featuring a morbid list of the killer's future victims. It was kept secret, but the list included Mosspan, Brown—the photographer—, or the girl who was with him at the Carib Hotel, as Ryghin' suspected she was also a police informer—he promised her a full cylinder. An irrational fear got a hold on everyone. From a desperate outlaw, Ryghin' had become a dangerous predator on the loose. He didn't show himself during the funeral, but on September 3, he killed again.

Jonathan Thomas was a *higgler*—or street hawker—from Waltham Park Road. On that day, a man came up to him, who introduced himself as *the murderer of Corporal Lewis* before asking for money. Things didn't go smooth and the aggressor eventually shot Thomas in the belly, leaving him bleeding to death before his woman's eyes. During the incident, another man escaped death by fighting with Ryghin'. His name was Selvyn Maxwell, and he was 59. As he was struggling with the two-gun killer, the latter's gun fell on the ground—Selvyn took his chance and ran away as fast as possible. It has never been clearly established whether Ryghin' was actually responsible for the killing—any petty thief might have usurped his identity.

From his part, Mosspan was worried. He knew his enemy well, and took him seriously. Ever since Ilcida had been killed, he hadn't slept twice at the same place. A journalist interviewed him. Sitting on his bicycle, the young man made quite an impression. He was handsome, and had a charming smile with a golden tooth. He was also well built and wore his trousers *à la française*. Furthermore, he expressed himself with confidence. Scared? He giggled: "*Of course not. I can outshoot Ryghing. Give me a gun and I'll go and get him.*" The traitor boasted. Yet he had asked for police protection, but was turned down. He was alone in West Kingston with an armed devil on his heels—a devil that read the press. *The Gleaner* soon received a new letter from Ryghin'. It was more of a pamphlet, or a list of curses cast upon his enemies, beginning with Mosspan: "*I have seen where Mosspan is asking for 2 guns. I can tell him this: if it were not for people who I would not like to injure, I would pin him long time (...) I am now asking the head of the Police Department to give him 4 guns and 500 shots and tell him that he must not hid*(e), *he must walk free like me. (...) Mosspan, (...) one of the nights when you are on the Spanish Town Road I will catch up with you. That's why you are looking police friend to keep them eyes on you. Be good until I met.*" As far as the so-called *exemplary policeman* he had shot at the Carib Hotel, he only had one regret, not to have killed him before. "*From around 1943 he would always like to make a case of me and this is the end.*"

Ryghin' Mania

The Great Manhunt stirred everyone's imagination and *The Gleaner* talked about a *Rigin' Mania*. The police were now offering a 200-pound reward for his capture—a small fortune. Furthermore, the fugitive was known for walking in the open, in broad daylight. On September 4, he was spotted on East King Street—the heart of downtown! He was then seen wearing his famous sunglasses in East Kingston. Afterwards, he was allegedly driving a black Sedan V8 in Saint Thomas with two girls in the back. He remained uncatchable, mainly because various witnesses reported him at several places at the same time. In Western Kingston, a bold barmaid broke a bottle of water over the head of a client who had inappropriately ordered a glass of Punto-Pruno—Ryghin's favourite drink according to the newspapers. She knocked him down, but didn't get the reward—"*No, Not Ryghing*", lamented *The Gleaner*. Lamented? In fact, the newspaper probably rejoiced at Ryghin's long run. The day before this short article was published, the Montego Bay selling point was swarmed by a mob of curious readers anxious to get their copy. The police had to intervene. Meanwhile, fear spread like a plague among the Haves of Jamaica. Ivanohe "Ryghin'" Martin was spotted near the house of a policeman whose name was on the desperado's death list—someone had tried to break into the officer's home before leaving a note, *You're dead*. The policemen were given brand new Webster handguns!

A few days later, a fisherman in Hunt's Bay found a corpse. The police rushed there to take the body's fingerprints, only to discover they didn't match with the two-gun killer's.

Ryghin' was both everywhere and nowhere. *I was here*, read the walls in Kingston like a provocation... *but I disappeared*. Who wrote these graffiti? Maybe the same kids who sang the bold exploits of their rebellious hero—or the killer himself? Ryghin' had probably something else to do. Protected by his little gang, celebrated by a whole nation, he had lost control over his destiny—every new gunshot propelled him further into the urban legend of Jamaica. Only his brutal death was yet missing—and it was just a matter of time.

Pestilence by Night

In the 1940s, Perry Henzell was a blond kid from the society of Jamaica whose parent owned a property in Kingston that stretched as far as the swamp of Ferry Pen. Sometimes, the little Perry boldly rode there on his horse, nervously looking around as Ryghin' was said to hide nearby. Little did he know then, that he would one day make a legend out of the outlaw. Indeed, in 1972, he shot a movie entitled *The Harder They Come* directly inspired by Ryghin's story. The international star Jimmy Cliff played the Two-gun killer's part, and the movie became at once a cornerstone of the Jamaican culture. A dream come true for this petty bad boy frow West Kingston, who had spent so many hours watching thrillers! If fact, this movie has become the true guarantor of the bad boy's legend over the years.

Ryghin' was indeed hiding in the swamp, near Leleta Shallow, where he fished by throwing batons of dynamite into the Ferry River. In his small camp, an old lady cooked for him while a few cronies looked after him. But on October 8, several dozens of policemen surreptitiously cordoned the area and started to close in towards the fugitive's hideout—some informer had given him away. All of a sudden, a strident cry reverberated from the top of a nearby tree: "*Police!*" A kid came out of nowhere in front of the policemen, and hurled himself into the swamp to warn the wanted man. The desperado jumped to his feet, threw away his bottle of Porto-Puno, his beer and a bunch of keys, and then ran towards the nearby Ferry Hill. The muddy soil slowed down the police—one of them dislocated his knee, and was evacuated on a stretcher. Powerless, they saw their prey crossing Duhaney Bridge in the distance. Once on the other side, he jumped into the luxurious vegetation. *I was here... but I disappeared.*

The next day, the police sent some marksmen after him in the hills of Ferry and Marshes—in vain. Yet they were closing in. Ryghin' had some reliable friends, indeed; but also some determined enemies. It was time to leave the island, and he considered the neighbouring Cuba to start a new criminal life. A few days later, he met two friends in Greenwich Farm, a small fishermen's community in Kingston. He was nervous, and kept on looking over his shoulder. Before he boarded the *Gloria Again*—a small fisherman's boat—, he sent a kid for a bottle of Coke, looking nervously around him. He had a disturbing feeling—as if someone was spying on him. Actually, someone was. Three policemen and a journalist from *The Gleaner* were hiding in the shadow nearby. But no one doubted now that Ryghin' was a dangerous man, and that it wasn't safe to try to arrest him at night-time. The Detectives let him sail off. Seven hours later, dozens of men led by Inspectors Long and Wellington—both laid on the death list of the two-gun killer—went after him. And he hadn't gone far.

Lime Cay

The last scene of Ivanohe "Ryghin" Martin's tragedy—his death—matched any Hollywood movie. First, the scenery was sumptuous: the killer had crossed Kingston Bay, sailed alongside Port Royal and reached Lime Cay, one of these uninhabited nearby sandy islands. Standing on the beach of white sand, Ryghin' was looking at the three US warships that were then heading to the bay, when the man who was with him suddenly shouted "*Cops!*" and ran to a canoe. Ryghin' plunged behind a bush where he remained breathless, holding his gun. Twelve policemen disembarked on the cay on cordoned the place. It was 7:30 a.m., Ryghin' stood up and shot—twice. Then there was a silence. The policemen crawled nearer—then came another gunshot from the bush. Two bursts of machine gun answered, then four teargases were thrown at Ryghin. "*Quick shooting* started and went on for ten minutes," read the *Jamaica Daily Express*. "And then came a shout, and Ryghing was dead. He had eight holes in his body." Ryghin' had sworn he wouldn't be caught alive—he was a man of his word. Just like in a thriller, the desperado stood firm until the end, bravely falling under the bullets of the police—one hit him in the right eye, another suspicious one went through his neck, and several hit him in the legs. *"Crime-Does-Not-Pay" Lesson At Lime Cay*, wrote *The Gleaner* below two pictures of Ryghin' on October 10. On the first one, the killer arrogantly held his two guns, looking dreadful and invincible. On the second one, he was lying on the beach at Lime Cay, his arms stretched out wide. The caption insisted on his wretched aspect, mentioning his *erstwhile natty clothes*. Thus came to an end six weeks of a manhunt, the greatest ever—and it ended up just like it had started at the Carib Hotel, in a cloud of smoke and a pool of blood.

Duppy Gunman

Ryghin's corpse was brought to Kingston Mortuary where he was photographed. Laid on the back, his clothes half-torn, he looked quiet—apart from his fingers clenched in death, he could have been asleep. Leaning over his body, Mosspan who claimed he had never been afraid of him, felt relieved when he made out his former friend's face. Upon hearing the news of his death, he had jumped on his bicycle and pedalled to the Mortuary where he had waited all night long before he could glance at his dead enemy. He came out smiling, and the *Daily Gleaner* reported that he was heard muttering: *"The race is not for the swift."* A huge crowd had gathered in front of the building—others were already waiting for the coffin at the cemetery. Someone recognized Mosspan and asked him if it was Ryghin' lying in there. "*Yes*," he answered. "*It's Ryghing.*" Then he disappeared in West Kingston to spend his first night of rest in six weeks' time.

The journalists grew partial, calling Ryghin' a *rat* after they had participated in creating his myth. This man, they wrote, *lived*

like a rat, and died like a rat. They wrote about his criminal life, enumerating his criminal records at length. His little gang on Spanish Town Road was evoked as his outraged men had sworn to kill the informer who had given their boss away. But these barking dogs could hardly bite, and the successive raids of the police in West Kingston kept them quiet. Thirty years later, with the help of the most influent politicians of the country, far-West Kingston was turned into a no man's land where throve the most vicious criminals of all times; compared to them, Ryghin' was an amateur—or a pioneer. Indeed, from the bottom of his grave, he who was *always on top* slept the villainous' sleep, unaware that one day, he would become the main character of
one of these thrillers he had loved so much.
The little rascal could rest in
peace—his destiny
was at work.

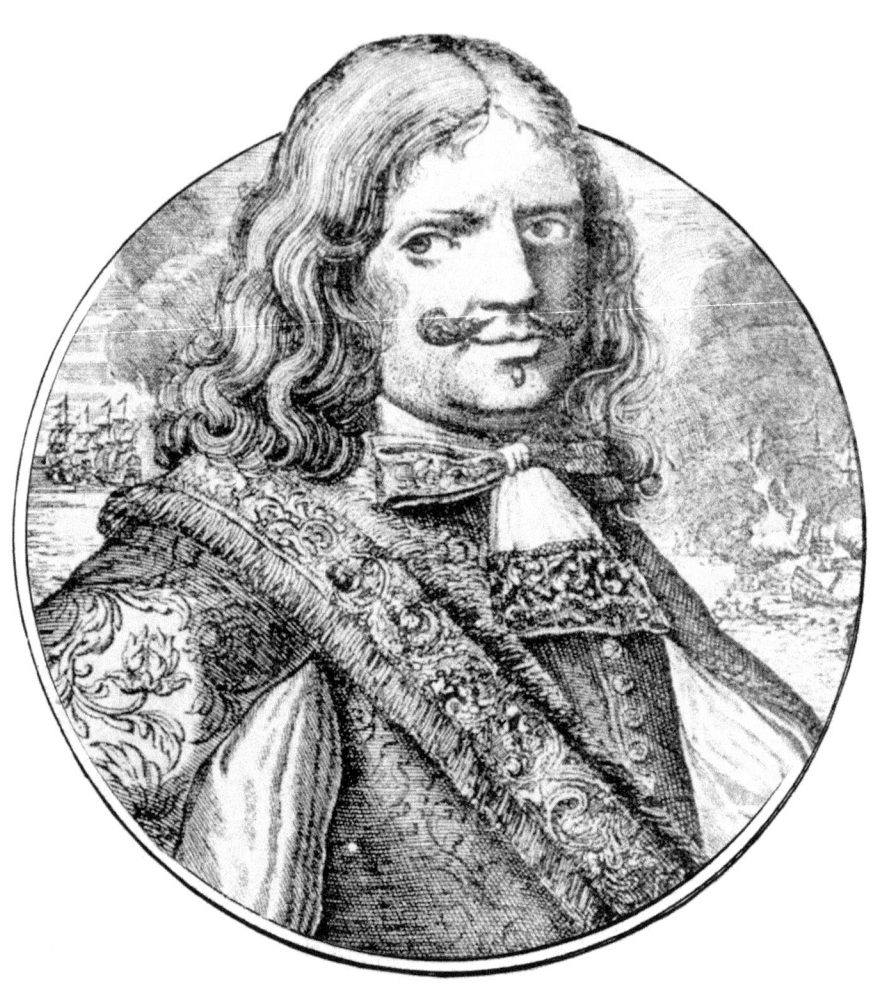

Sir Henry.
(DREAD Archives)

Morgan, Henry
(1635-1688)

Sir Ain't No Saint

Edward Long was the typical English historian from the 18th century. Deeply concerned about the glory of his country and its colonies, and especially of Jamaica where he spent twelve years of his life from 1757 to 1769, he did his best to legitimate the official existence of the island. A planter and a Member of Parliament himself, he had no intention to apology neither for slavery—God, he said, had placed black people in the hands of the Whites for their own good—nor for privateering. Before writing about the Jamaican buccaneers, or privateers, in his *History of Jamaica* (1774), he made it clear that he only intended to vindicate these people so unjustly misrepresented by other historians such as Charles Leslie *. According to the latter, the fame of these modern Hercules *might have equalled the glory of any, either of ancient or modern heroes; but the indelible stain of piracy sullies their great actions and make them looked upon as disturbers of mankind and villains, who are only famous for murder and robbery.* And Henry Morgan was the most notorious of all. But he was no pirate like Blackbeard and his likes, underlined Edward Long. Indeed, he only looted and sacked under legal

---

* *A New and Exact Account of Jamaica* (Edinburgh, 1740).

commissions given to him by the Governor of Jamaica. Morgan, he wrote, was a *gentleman* who acted for the good of Jamaica. "*It is to the Bucaniers that we owe the possession of Jamaica at this hour,*" concluded the historian. He was right—and it's probably the reason why he tried to erase all their sins, going as far as turning vice into virtue. Should we believe him, a Sir would be a Saint.

Terrible People

"*He trained to shoot, and was quite good at it. He was bold and determined; nothing ever surprised him as he always expected everything; his boldness insured him success in every action he took.*" Thus was depicted the controversial Henry Morgan by Oliver-Alexander Esquemeling, an obscure and celebrated author also known as the privateers' surgeon. Esquemeling was said to be French, but he first published his *History of the Bucaniers* in Dutch, in 1682. A Protestant, he had probably fled from his country because of religious harassment. As he couldn't pay for his travel to the New World, he engaged in front of a solicitor to freely serve some unknown Good Samaritan in the New World ready to pay for his passage—he engaged for 36 months' time. The position of *servant* was probably the worst in the New World—even slaves were treated better. Some had been offered a drink in a Scottish tavern where they had been knocked down, and then embarked by force. They had woken up in chains, en route to a tropical ordeal. Servants were left to the good care of their masters, the famous buccaneers—who were nothing but boors. These nomad hermits lived amidst their hound of dogs, working miracles with their notorious rifles, and hunting the savage cows so numerous in these parts. They skinned them, and then smoked their meat on a *boucan*; a sort of rack set above the fire borrowed from the Indians—hence the name *boucanier*, bucanier or buccaneer. When the Spaniards chased them from Saint Christopher where they had first settled, the buccaneers scattered all over the West Indies—it became very hard to dislodge them as they lived in the bush like savages. Said to have no religious belief, and to be reluctant to social life, they usually went by two, like seamen. In fact, they were little more than beasts sleeping in the open. What could an educated man reduced to the rank of servant like Esquemeling expect from such masters? Furthermore, being quite cheap, servants had no real value. When one of them displeased his master, he was beaten on the head. Had the buccaneer's hand been too heavy, the victim was buried on the spot, and no one ever mentioned his name again. Describing the horrible condition of these poor wretches, Esquemeling knew what he was talking about as he almost perished himself in the hands of a tyrannical master.

Little by little, the buccaneers became legions. Freed from servitude, many servants joined their ranks alongside disillusioned adventurers or people running away from trouble. They organized by creating a brotherhood: *the brothers of the coast*. Tasks were shared out. The inhabitants were in charge of the settlements; the buccaneers had to supply them with meat, and to fight the Spanish guard when necessary; others embarked in makeshift boats to board the Spanish ships—they were called the flibustiers in French (privateers), and they started what Edward Long called *a sort of predatory Tropical war*. They were so bold, they triumphed over impressive preys; they emboldened themselves even more, organized, looted and brought back fortunes. The governors of the West Indian colonies first feared them, and then courted them. Indeed, to shelter them was the best way to avoid their terrible fury. So they issued official commissions, or letters of marque, that gave them the right to attack the enemies of the colony—a licence to loot.

The privateers—the vast majority being French, English or Dutch—followed the currents that favoured their enterprises. At the end of the 16th century, Jamaica was the place where they could most easily get a commission. Port Royal, located at the end of the spit of land that protected the future bay of Kingston, became the headquarters of these terrible people animated by the thirst of gold and the sight of blood. There they dilapidated their ill-gotten fortunes in infamous taverns, spent their fiery nights in the arms of prostitutes, and lived every day as if it were the last. Welcome to the tropical Sodom, home of Henry Morgan.

Mr Governor
People love heroes who started from scratch; thus Morgan was said to have sprung from the Scottish rabble when he was actually born in a family of good quality in 1635—well, for what we know. In fact, little is known about his early life—historians still wonder about his first years in privateering for instance. Some say he was kidnapped in a tavern of Edinburgh before being sold as a servant in Barbados in 1660. He would have fled to Jamaica to embrace a career in privateering, taking the lead of a small bunch of adventurers within a few years' time. The tale is charming, but it sounds like a fairy tale. Morgan went to Barbados, indeed; probably to join his influent and potbellied uncle, Colonel Edward Morgan, the right hand of the influent Sir Thomas Modyford. The latter hadn't always been in odour of sanctity, though. A former royalist, he had sought refuge to the New World in 1642, after fighting the victorious troops of Cromwell in England. He had many enemies in Barbados, but a mighty friend in England in the person of the famous Duke of Albermale. When Charles II recovered his throne thanks to the same Duke in 1660, the table turned—Modyford was appointed Governor of Jamaica. He went there from Barbados with his trusted friend Colonel Morgan and 1,000 colonists, in June 1664. A man of network, Modyford took care of his relatives, whom he appointed to various influent positions—not less than 80 of them came along to Jamaica with him.

Oliver Cromwell is a controversial figure in the history of England. He fought Charles I for several years, triumphed and had the King beheaded—and regicides were hardly forgiven at the time. He was a tyrant, a religious man, but also a charismatic leader who put his country back on its feet, creating a period of growth reminiscent of the days of Elizabeth. *"Other nations thought England buried under its own ruins until it suddenly became more formidable than ever under the yoke of Cromwell, who subjugated it with the Scriptures in hand and behind the mask of religion; in his administration, he covered the qualities of a great King under the deeds of an usurper,"* wrote Voltaire. As long as he was ruling the Commonwealth, historians called him Lord Protector; when his exhumed remains were exposed on the London Bridge, they called him *the usurper*. But if Jamaica had been taken to the Spaniards in 1655, meaning under the government of a usurper, how could it legitimately belong to England? The case was delicate. Charles II felt uneasy with his new Spanish friends. Furthermore, the evil deeds of the privateers of Jamaica outraged the Catholic Monarchs, who officially complained about it. For a while, Charles II seriously thought of returning Jamaica; after all, the lucrative trade of the Spanish Americas was at stake. But he changed his mind—and blamed the Governor of Jamaica instead. His successor, Thomas Modyford, was sent to the island with the order to eradicate privateering. Upon his arrival, he portrayed the scapegoat governor as *a weak creature under influence*. No one knew by then that the same Modyford would soon become the most zealous protector of privateering ever—not even himself.

As soon as he reached Jamaica, Modyford moved the Governor's residence from The Point—or Port Royal—to Spanish Town. He wrote respectful letters to the Spanish Governors of the neighbouring islands, and even sent fourteen privateers to the gallows in February 1665. Yet, Modyford started to wonder. Within a few months' time, he had outraged the privateers—*a fatal error*, he wrote to the Secretary of State in England, Lord Arlington. The once protectors of the island, now its resentful enemies, left Port Royal for the nearby island of Saint-Domingue—a French dominion always at war with Jamaica. Of Jamaica, the privateers knew all the secrets and weaknesses. What if they suddenly decided to plunder it? Who could oppose them since they were the only ones who could fight? One month after the execution of the fourteen pirates, England went to war with Holland—the second Anglo-Dutch War. Modyford knew the conflict would soon reach the New World, and he was worried, as he feared a raid from the nearby Dutch islands. *Alea jacta est*, he called back the privateers to Jamaica by giving his Deputy Governor, Colonel Edward Morgan, a commission to attack the Dutch islands of Saint Eustache, Saba and Curacao. The Governor was a cautious man; he wrote to England asking for the official support of the cold and distant Lord Arlington—who didn't answer. But the Duke of Albermale sent the requested written authorisation.

The operation was far from a regular military raid—of the 650 men who embarked upon the ten vessels that reached Saint Eustache, the vast majority were privateers recruited in the taverns of The Point. Their rebellious inclination surfaced after the death of Colonel Morgan, which took place during the first assault. On November 16, 1665, Modyford wrote to England: *"Colonel Morgan with 319 men landed, and after a small opposition took the place; the good Colonel leaping out of the boat, and being a corpulent man got a strain, and his spirit being great he pursued over earnestly the enemy on a hot day, so that he surfeited and suddenly died."* The Colonel died a poor man, leaving his family in need. Fortunately, his eldest daughter was married to Sergeant Major Byndloss—a good alliance. Modyford expressed his sympathy for Morgan in the official State Papers, urging the King not to replace him, as he would never again meet with one *so useful, so complacent, and loving as Col. Morgan*.

After Morgan's death, Colonel Carey took the lead of the expedition, and sent a party to Saba three weeks later. But after they had hidden their booty in the nearby cays and creeks, the privateers never felt that enthusiastic about attacking the fortified island of Curacao. They sent some emissaries to Jamaica to inform Modyford. The Governor was outraged; he ordered them to attack their main target. The confused privateers asserted that they would comply, of course—but a next time. "*Some of the privateers are well bred,*" wrote Modyford to Lord Arlington, "*and (I) hope with good handling to bring them to more humanity and good order.*" But the Governor was a realistic man: these privateers were no soldiers marching in good order. The only wise attitude was to go with it, and to use them for what they were, mercenaries.

Ol' pirate

Richard Brown, a companion of Henry Morgan, asserted that his friend had come to the West Indies in 1658, aged 23—maybe. His first deeds in the New World remain uncertain and some even said he had come to Jamaica aboard the fleet of the Western Design that captured Jamaica in 1655—most unlikely. When did he reach Jamaica? What did he go there for? It might not be romantic enough to say he joined his uncle, but it looks quite logical. As a matter of fact, he married his cousin Mary Elizabeth, daughter of the said Colonel Morgan, in 1665, thus integrating a powerful familial network. This union made him the brother-in-law of Colonel Byndloss and Henry Archbould, both influent Members of the Council—the embryo of the notorious *Morgan's clique*. In 1666, the *honourable* Henry Morgan became the captain of a ship in the small fleet commissioned by Modyford to attack the Dutch islands—an obsession. This was the sign of a rapid social advancement. Morgan's boldness, it was said, had impressed Edward Mansfield, *an ol' pirate* (Esquemeling) made Admiral by the privateers of Port Royal in January 1666 to succeed the late Colonel Morgan—he appointed his predecessor's nephew Vice-Admiral for the raid on Curacao.

According to Esquemeling, Morgan had no relatives in Jamaica, and had to build his reputation from scratch. He was a tough man who used to hang out in the smoky taverns of The Point where he made good money as a gambler. He soon invested in a boat, and sailed with two or three villains to the Bay of Campeche to cut wood and to take ships. Is it how he eventually attracted Mansfield's attention? Or did he become close to the influent people of Jamaica thanks to his familial network? Morgan sued Esquemeling's book when it came out in England in 1684. The incriminated passage related this period of his life; Morgan said it was calumnious; indeed, if he had taken ships without commission, then he wasn't a privateer but a petty pirate, and as such, he deserved the gallows. Yet Morgan never went as far as *openly* breaking the law. He knew of the importance of acting within the bounds of an official commission, and sailed all his life on thin ice. The work of Esquemeling does contain a few incorrect facts—as well as some additions from successive printers that make it even more delicate a reading. As a consequence, historians have frequently criticized it. Edward Long or Franck Cundall—the renowned 20th century historian—for instance, had come to the conclusion that his book was nothing but a libel designed to discriminate one of their worthy fellowmen. What Esquemeling wrote about the beginnings of Morgan as a privateer is second-hand information, as the author was then serving a tyrannical master in Saint-Domingue. He wasn't there—but didn't pretend either. On contrast, he was with Morgan when he plundered Panama, and he spent a lot of time with the privateer and his men at The Point. He witnessed their debauches, and the barbarous treatment suffered by the Spaniards. Esquemeling embarked with them as a surgeon, which supposes a certain level of education, especially in the 17th century. Of course, many so-called surgeons who joined the privateers knew little about surgery. But Esquemeling was obviously a learnt man who knew how to write—his book speaks for itself on that matter, and also proves he had a global vision of events. Some passages might be perfectible, but the whole work remains a serious historical source—furthermore, it doesn't require a lot to imagine Morgan taking certain liberty with the law.

Esquemeling gave a lot of details regarding the first official expedition of the privateer—the one he did alongside Mansfield to capture the island of Providence (now Santa Catalina) off Costa Rica. They had no commission, but there's no evidence that

Morgan was present. Mansfield (or Mansvelt) was there, on contrast, and he hadn't chosen Providence at random. He knew the Spaniards usually brought their prisoners to this island, and he expected to find one who could show him the way to Nata, a Spanish settlement located on the other shore of the Panama Isthmus—his true target.

Providence was well fortified, luxurious and a very convenient place for privateers. Mansfield decided to turn it into a sanctuary, just like Tortuga, the island off Saint-Domingue; he left a man of confidence there—a French named Saint-Simon—, and then set sail for Nata and Carthagena. But internal feuds forced the privateers to abort their successive plans; they came back to Jamaica. Mansfield was anxious to face Modyford. Once again, the priority target Curacao had only been used as a decoy by the privateers. The *ol' pirate* still pretended to have good news for the Governor: *"The old fellow was resolved (as he told me) never to see my face until he had done some service to his Majesty,"* wrote Modyford to Lord Arlington in June 1666, *"and therefore with 200 men which were all (that) left him and about 80 of them French, he resolved to attempt the island of Providence."* Mansfield asked for a retroactive commission for his take. The Governor rejected his propositions, fearing to displease the King. *"Besides that, giving him the men he desired, and necessaries, he must of necessity diminish the forces of that island, whereof his was governor,"* wrote Esquemeling. Modyford acted cautiously, and waited for official instructions—when he eventually sent a ship full of supply to Providence, it was too late. Saint-Simon who felt he had been forsaken, had surrendered the island to Juan Perez de Gusman, the new Governor of Costa Rica, on the condition of safely sailing off with his men.

According to Esquemeling, Mansfield died in Tortuga shortly before returning to Providence. But our author was wrong. The Spaniards captured Mansfield under unknown circumstances, and his name popped up in the English State Papers a few years later. In 1688, the Spaniards arrested an English Commandant by the name of Henry Wasey for accosting Puerto Bello in wartime. They sent him to jail and he reportedly came across Mansfield, chained in the hold of a Spanish vessel bound to Havana, Cuba. In 1673, an official order arrived from Spain: "*Mansfield, alias Manco, an English pirate having committed great exactions and killed more than 200 Spaniards whom he cruelly treated, must be put to death.*" Thus ended the *ol' pirate*.

June 1668

In 1667, fearing an alliance between France and Holland, England and Spain came together, ratifying their alliance by some commercial agreements that included the lucrative West Indies trade. But they didn't settle their disagreement over the New World, where the blurry legal situation seemed to justify every manoeuvre. As far as the Spaniards were concerned, Jamaica was an illegal war prize they intended to recapture. For the English part, Spain had no right to prevent them from trading in this part of the world—and they were too aware of the advantages of commissions to ban them. Modyford was standing between the rock and a hard place; he cautiously asked Lord Arlington about the position of England. The Secretary of State was a cautious man too, who disliked Modyford—he sent him to the Duke of Albermale. The latter explicitly told Modyford to *serve his Majesty's interests the best he could*. And who could serve the royal interests better than the new Admiral of the privateers, Henry Morgan?

In early 1668, an alleged rumour urged Modyford to give a commission to Morgan—the Spaniards of Cuba were said to plot against Jamaica. It was necessary, of course, to find out about this matter; all the West Indian villains were asked to meet Morgan off the South Coast of Cuba, where he revealed his project: the plundering of Puerto Principe. Being far from the sea, this wealthy Cuban settlement was ill fortified—an easy prey. But the booty didn't match the privateers' expectations, and tension rose between the French from Tortuga and the English from Port Royal. Quarrelling over the narrow-bone of an ox, a French and an English challenged one another. *"Being on the place of duel,"* reads the English version of the book—these details are absent from the French edition of 1688—*"the Englishman stabbed the Frenchman in the back* (the French version mentions a gunshot) *whereby he fell down dead."* The French and English versions of Esquemeling's book also differ over the following scene. For Oexmelin—the French orthography of his name—, Morgan *broke the head* of the English buccaneer to settle the score. For Esquemeling, the wise English Admiral put the criminal in chains, and sent it to Jamaica to be judged. Of course, the second version is most unlikely—how could the French let the criminal get away with it? Anyway, after the sack of Puerto Principe, the French and the English went their separate ways.

Puerto Bello shone like a jewel on the North Coast of the Panama Isthmus, as the last American receptacle of the Peruvian riches on their way to Spain. Indeed, once a year, a fleet loaded with the riches of the Americas left for the Old Continent; of course, the privateers knew its maritime road by heart, and on due time, cohorts of villains waited in ambush in the cays of Cuba for the powerful fleet to pass, and then followed it at a distance, hoping for a tempest or some unexpected event to isolate one of the vessels. Sometimes, they went as far as the ports of Spain!

Once a year, Puerto Bello's fair drove the quiet city into a frenzy. Thirty years earlier, the English traveller Thomas Gage* gave the following description of the event: *"What I most wondred* (sic) *at was to see the requa's of mules which came thither from Panama, laden with wedges of silver; in one day I told* (counted) *two hundred mules, laden with nothing else, which were unladen in*

---

* In the 17th century, he was the first non-Spaniard to give an insight into the Spanish empire of the Americas. His relation inspired Cromwell to attack the Spaniards. This expedition resulted in the capture of Jamaica.

the publick (sic) *market place, so that there the heaps of silver wedges lay like heaps of stone in the street without any fear or suspicion of being lost."* Gage also wrote: *"I dare boldly and avouch, that in the world there is no greater fair than that of Portobel* (sic)." Did he embellish his description on purpose? After all, his book was used as a political tool by Cromwell to excite cupidity in the hearts of the English at a time when he was about to launch an attack on the Spanish settlements in America—he wanted to motivate his troops. Anyway, should have reality happened to be ten times less beautiful, it was still enough to stir the imagination of any privateer.

Morgan's raid was a bloody one. In the official relation he later gave to the Council of Jamaica, he portrayed himself as an angelic conqueror trying to protect the virginity of those he had endeavoured to turn widows and orphans—O brave privateer! Esquemeling told another story, though—the story of a dreadful warlord forcing the Spanish women and religious who had sought refuge in the churches to assault the ramparts of their own fortresses. These unusual assailants perished under a *friendly* rain of bullets and arrows, imploring their own people in vain. The buccaneers soon took the place; what happened next was far from pastoral poetry. They put the Spaniards to the question—or torture—to learn about their secret hiding places. Those who had nothing to hide were the most miserable, claimed the surgeon, as *many died on the rack, or presently after.* As the privateers committed debauchery and excess of all kinds, the Spanish prisoners starved to death among the ruins of their broken dream. Disease spread among the invaders, as the corpses were so ill buried than some arms and legs were still showing. Furthermore, the food was insane and the debauchery exhausting.

From Panama, President Don Juan Perez de Gusman sent 1,500 men to rescue Puerto Bello, that the privateers threatened to set afire shouldn't a ransom be promptly paid. But the negotiations took time, and the chivalric De Gusman sent some refreshment to Morgan; he even wrote him a letter, casually asking about the type of rifles used by the buccaneers. Morgan sent him back a pair of those formidable rifles made in Dieppe, France, which worked miracles when properly handled. Gusman was in a talkative mood; he answered, deploring that a man of such value should live such a horrible life. Morgan lost patience, and told De Gusman he would soon see him in Panama, where he would concretely show him how these famous rifles worked. And he was a man of his word.

The buccaneers plundered Puerto Bello for two weeks, and left it in ruins. Once the booty shared, Morgan and his men returned to Jamaica, where *being arrived they passed here some time in all sorts of vices and debaucheries, according to their custom* (Esquemeling). Very soon, though, a new watchword circulated in Port Royal. Morgan had been given a new commission, and he was asking all privateers to meet him at l'Isle Avache—or the Isle of Ash, as the English called it—, off Saint-Domingue. Soon afterwards, they sacked the South Coast of Cuba.

In January, the Spaniards almost lived a miracle. While anchoring off L'Isle Avache, Morgan called a council with all the top privateers to agree over their next target. Then *this resolution being taken, they began abroad the great ship* (*Oxford*, Morgan's frigate) *to feast one another for joy of their new voyage (...). Most of the men being drank, by what accident is not known, the ship suddenly was blown up, with three hundred and fifty Englishmen.* Morgan was thrown into the air and ended up in the middle of the bay, among bits of wood, corpses and panicked sailors—only fifty people were spared, but Morgan was one of them. A few days later, he ordered the bodies floating in the bay to be searched for, *not to afford them Christian burial, but for their clothes and attire,* underlined Esquemeling. *And if any had gold ring on their fingers, those were cut off*—the kind of details that makes Esquemeling's book a must-read. The surgeon also said that Pierre Le Picard, a French sailor, then suggested attacking Maracaibo where he had already been with L'Olonnais, another notorious privateer. The expedition was of a rare violence. Morgan triumphed again, brilliantly overcoming some Spanish vessels that tried to capture him. The privateer proved he was as bold a warrior as any Admiral of the Royal Navy—it reinforced the respect his troops had for him. Yet, when he returned to Port Royal, the mood wasn't that jovial.

Port Royal's Pit

In 1699, one John Style wrote from his Jamaican jail to a former classmate in England, Secretary of State Lord Arlington! Style had come to Jamaica in July 1665 where had he enjoyed two years of prosperity as a planter until the Anglo-Dutch Wars, when martial law was proclaimed. The old soldiers *who call themselves the conquerors of the land* (Style) then took advantage of the situation, imposing some tyrannical measures on the small planters. Every Christian being compelled to keep guard, some found themselves unable to take care of their plantations, and were forced to sell them at a vile price, or to abandon it. Corruption had spread to the law officers, whom Style denounced as *illiterate ex-convicts and drunkards*. Not to mention the unavoidable fund raisings organized by the churches. "*More than 500 l. raised in the parish of Saint John under various pretences,*" complained Style, "*of which the poor never had 5 pounds.*" As he refused to give in what he called *extortion*, Style was tried and convicted over false testimonies. He also pretended to be marked for death, and the victim of a plot orchestrated by the buccaneers against the honest planters and tradesmen. Jamaica was supposedly a wealthy trade place but in January 1699, Style gave a dull insight into its commercial exchanges—plates, he said, a few jewels and other stuffs of little value; all stolen by the buccaneers, who sold it at vile price to the merchants of Port Royal, who themselves sent them to New England or Madeira. In return they got some Brandy and some provisions—not that exciting. According to the latest estimations, there were then 2,400 white Christians in the island—including 800 buccaneers. The latter didn't really care about Jamaica. Could the law-abiding inhabitants count on them in case the island would come under attack? Style wondered. They were no patriots, and gladly sailed under French commissions to avoid paying taxes on their booty.

The buccaneers, as the last sentence of the French edition of Esquemeling's work reminds us, were *terrible people*. John Style confirmed. He met with a few of those who had tortured some Spaniards at Puerto Bello. They had slowly burnt them with matches, then cut them into pieces—first a piece of flesh, then a finger, an ear or a lip, etc. They passed a noose around the neck of others, and then tightened it until the eyes of their victims burst out—they called it *woolding*. They once tied a naked woman to a burning stone and roasted her to death. Most of them proudly revealed their misdeeds, laughing at the memories—only one was sick with remorse. According to Esquemeling, the privateers also exercised terrible tortures upon the Spaniards in Maracaibo: "*Some were hanged up by the testicles, or privy members, and left till they fell to the ground, these parts being torn from their bodies. If with this they minded to show mercy to those wretches, thus lacerated in their most tender parts, their mercy was to run them through with their swords; otherwise they used to lie four or five days under the agonies of death, before they died. Others were crucified by these tyrants, and with kindled matches burnt between the joints of their fingers and toes; others had their feet put into the fire, and thus were left to be roasted alive.*" Morgan himself ordered to put a Portuguese to the question. The victim was over sixty, according to the French edition—only fifty, reads the English one: "*They stretched him with cords, breaking both his arms behind his shoulders. This cruelty went not alone; for not being able or willing to make any other declaration, they put him to another sort of torment more barbarous: they tied him with small cords by his two thumbs and great toes to four stakes fixed in the ground at a convenient distance the whole weight of his body hanging on those cords. Not satisfied yet with this cruel torture, they took a stone of above two hundred pounds, and laid it upon his belly, as if they intended to press him to death; they also kindled palm-leaves, and applied the flames to the face of this unfortunate Portuguese, burning with them the whole skin, beard and hair."* Such were the games the children of Port Royal played.

Style described the Point as a tropical Sodom full of vermin and whores; a place soiled by blasphemy and adultery, where *the most savage heathens (...) might learn cruelty and oppression; the worst of Sodom or the Jews that crucified our Saviour might here behold themselves matched, if not outdone, in all evil and wickedness by those who call themselves Christians.* This is quite a dark description. Let's bear in mind that Style hated the buccaneers. To him, they poorly benefited the island—a point of view shared by more and more people. According to Style, the island needed Christian servants willing to work honestly, and to lead the little Negroes to the God of love. He also deplored the abundance of alcohol in Port Royal: *"The number of tippling houses is now doubly increased, so that there is not now resident upon this place ten men to every house that selleth strong liquors."* Historians have repeated this figure for centuries, but it is considered today as exaggerated. Nevertheless, alcohol was obviously at the root of Port Royal. As the Royal Brandy imported from England earned the King considerable sums of money, the Council complacently granted forty licences in the first two months of existence of Port Royal! After defying death at sea, the buccaneers needed the adrenalin; nothing really mattered to them. They drank, and spent their money with prostitutes in the middle of fiery nights. *"They are an uncommon type of men,"* wrote the French philosopher Guillaume-Thomas Raynal (1780). *"They had nothing in Europe but their swords and their boldness, and they made good use of both in the New World. Enemies of all, feared by all, always exposed to extreme perils, they lived everyday as the last one, and dissipated fortunes as easily as they wan them; they gave themselves to all excesses linked to debauchery and profusion; back from fighting, the feasted and drank the wine of victory; they embraced their mistresses in their blood-stained arms; they fell asleep in the bosom of sensual delight, and only woke up to run to* new massacres. *Indifferent to where their dead body would lie, on the land or at sea, they coldly considered both life and death. With their fierce hearts and their lost consciences, with no relatives, no friends, no fellow citizens, no country, no shelter, no material consideration to cool down their boldness, they blindly attempted the most perilous projects. They were unable to stand poverty or idleness, and too proud to find an ordinary work. Had they not become the plague of the New World, they would have subdued the old one.*" Raynal had style, and a natural eloquence, but the buccaneers he portrayed here were the taverns' rats, the purse-robbers—not Henry Morgan, who was close to the Governor and to several Members of the Council; he was more a gentleman villain than a petty thief. Yet, he spent nights drinking with his men in the taverns of The Point, where all indiscriminately mingled. There were also some psychopaths among privateers, who gave way to their deadly passions. According to Esquemeling, the dreadful L'Olonnais once pulled a Spaniard's heart out of his chest and forced a friend of his, who had witnessed the whole scene, to bite into it. Roc the Brazilian hung there too, loved when sober and hated when drunk—then he strolled about Port Royal with his drawn sword, cutting asunder the first man who displeased him.

* * *

The name of Morgan had become notorious all through the New World. The sermons of the Spanish priests in America described him as a monster rushing innocence, a devil with a sulphuric breath, swollen with vices and sated with blood. His exploits were so unbelievable they had to be the devil's work. Preceded by such a reputation, the buccaneer restlessly triumphed over terrified and resigned enemies. And if his men were devils, Port Royal had to be hell. It is said, notwithstanding Style's testimony, that there was proportionally more money in circulation in Port Royal than in London at the time. Rents were as high as in the most luxurious quarters of the English capital. Such splendour arose jealousy in Europe, and in August 1669 Modyford felt the need to justify the privateers to Lord Arlington: *"We'll say something of the unreasonable rumours of the great wealth these privateers are said to get: the Puerto Bello business cleared them 60l. per head, and the fight (...) in Maracaibo 30l.; this the common sort spent immediately in arms, clothes and drink, and the owners of the ships in refitting, and some of the officers and civiler sort are settling plantations (...) so that they are from hand to mouth and have little or nothing left."* Far from romantic novels, Port Royal was first of all a trading post. Stores full of goods were aligned alongside the quays, and dozens of ships from all over daily disembarked their cargos and their hairy sailors. Slave drivers sold their disgusting merchandise, then stayed weeks in Port Royal where they spent their finest gold. There weren't less than two thousand buildings in the city and three daily markets. It was also an ecumenical place where Quakers, Jews and Christians lived together, peacefully attending their respective places of cult.

Port Royal was an allegory of the New World, oscillating between fantasy and reality, vices and splendour; it shed its mighty but dirty light on the West Indies. But God eventually *heard the cry* of Port Royal just like He had heard Sodom's; disgusted by so much corruption, He decided to chastise this nest of devils. But Morgan escaped the wrath of his creator and the perdition of his sweet inferno. Indeed, when The Point partly sank into the sea in 1692, Morgan was already dead.

Meet me at l'Isle Avache

Privateering had become a diplomatic burning issue in Europe. Back to Jamaica from a new Iliad against Maracaibo in 1668, Morgan found a worried Modyford. The governor had given his friend a commission to attack the Spaniards at sea, not to plunder cities. Modyford cautiously explained the situation to Lord Arlington in August 1669, saying he had to issue commissions so that the privateers wouldn't leave for Saint-Domingue. He admitted that Morgan's commissions didn't authorize inland attacks, and he condemned the plundering of Puerto Bello and Maracaibo. He reminded the Secretary of State that he had demanded the privateers an explanation, and put their testimonies on paper—sent to London, these relations were never heard of again. Meanwhile, said the Governor, it was wiser to postpone any sanction and to adjourn all commissions—thus the Spanish galleons could peacefully sail off the West Indies this year. He added that many privateers had already joined their French companions in Tortuga, hoping to intercept the Spanish fleet.

From his part, Morgan bought some land, and claimed he had become farmer. But Spain didn't buy it, and official complaints kept on reaching the Court of England. After a while, England casually retorted: *"The English subjects know no peace in the Indies."* This was too much to bear. Order was given by the Queen of Spain to her subjects to seize all English ships, ports and settlements in America. In January 1670, the Jamaica privateer Thomas Rogers was consequently assaulted in the Bay of Campeche by a Spanish man-of-war. But after a short fight, Rogers boarded and took the Spanish boat. On board, he found an English traitor named Edward Browne, who confirmed that war had been proclaimed in Cartagena by beat of drum.

Meanwhile, the Spaniards multiplied their raids on the North Coast of Jamaica. The commission given to Morgan in 1670 to attack Panama read: " *The Governor of St Iago de Cuba (...) lately in a most hostile manner landed his men in three several places of the north side of this island (...) burning all the houses they came at, killing and taking prisoner all the inhabitants they could meet with."* A suspicious Spanish fleet was spotted off the South Coast, and all planters were called to arms—a petty militia, to tell the truth. As usual when it came under threat, Jamaica had to call upon its protectors, the privateers. On June 29, 1670, the Council assembled in Spanish Town, and gave Morgan a commission, urging him to constitute an armed fleet. His mission was to *attack, seize and destroy all the enemy's vessels that come within his reach (...), and finally to do all manner of exploits, which may tend to the preservation and quiet of this land, being his Majesty's chief interest in the Indies.* The privateer found himself at the head of 28 ships—plus eight taken to the French. He sailed from Bluefield. "*Morgan was mounting a Malouin ship with 24 guns called Le Cerf-volant (...). She had been seized by the Governor of Jamaica to her Captain who was glad enough to have got off lightly and to keep his life,*" read the French edition of Esquemeling. But this time, the enemy was more determined than ever. A Spanish officer accosted on the West Coast of Jamaica, and pinned the following letter on a tree:

> "I, Captain Manuel Rivero Padral, to the chief of the squadron of privateers in Jamaica. I am he who this year have done that which follows: —I went on shore at Caimanos, and burnt twenty houses, and fought with Captain Ary and took from him a catch laden with provisions and a canoa (sic). And I am he who took Captain Baines, and did carry the prize to Carthagena, and now am arrived to this coast, and have burnt it. And I am come to seek General Morgan, with two ships of twenty guns, and having seen this, I crave he would come out upon the coast and seek me, that he might see the valour of the Spaniards. And because I had no time I did not come to the mouth of Port Royal to speak by word of mouth in the name of my King, whom God preserve.—Dated the 5th of July, 1670."

Morgan didn't even bother going for Padral—he sent John Morrice, one of his captains, who soon joined the arrogant Spaniard in a cove West of Cuba. Morrice put an end to the Padral's bragging by piercing his throat with a bullet.

After multiplying small expeditions from L'Isle Avache, Morgan eventually called a council with his 37 captains on December 2. The privateers agreed that *for the safety of the English* and more especially *for the security of His Majesty's island of Jamaica*, they should attack a place of consequence; they opted for Panama, the masterpiece of Morgan's career.

The Jewell of the West Indies

Morgan sent Vice-Admiral Collier with six vessels to reconnoitre. For months, privateers had been gathering at L'Isle Avache. On September 30, the aforementioned Captain John Morrice triumphantly joined them on board of the ship he had just taken to the late Padral. In October, three French ships arrived, themselves followed by six Jamaican ones. The troops were almost complete and Collier came back from his mission with two more ships and 38 prisoners, who informed the privateers that Panama was on its guard—the Spaniards had been fortifying the place, and evacuating their riches for two months. To weaken his enemies, the President of Panama was issuing commission on commission against the English. A few months earlier, Morgan had promised to pay him a visit, but De Gusman didn't seem that impatient.

To reach the beautiful Panama that stood on the shore of the Pacific Ocean, the privateers didn't round the dreaded Cape Horn, but walked across the Isthmus of Panama instead. It wasn't that broad; mainly as they could sail the River of Chagres on a few miles. Of this incredible West Indian epic march, Morgan left an official account of eight pages that he read in front of the Council in Spanish Town, on June 10, 1671. This exceptional document is to be read with care. *"Having called the captains again on board to consult of the manner of carrying on the attempt, and whereby to find prisoners to be our guides for Pennama* (sic)*, it was noted that Providence being the King's ancient propriety and most of the people there being from Pennama* (sic)*, that no place could be so fit."* Six days later, Morgan's troops took possession of this island—so dear to the *ol' pirate* Mansfield—without resistance. The Spanish prisoners were sent on the continent excepted four soldiers, enrolled as guides. "*By them* (we) *underst*(ood) *the castle of Chagraw* (sic) *blocked our way.*" The privateers sent Captain Bradley and 470 men to assault it. "*They fired a volley at the castle, and fell into the trench, which was 12 foot* (sic) *deep,*" continued Wm. Fogg, another eyewitness of the raid on Panama—he was a privateer from Saint-Domingue. At eight o'clock the following morning, the fight was still raging. The Spaniards happened to be determined. But suddenly, a grenade set afire a guardhouse leaning against the fortress, *which caused a breach, where our men courageously stormed,* concluded Morgan. The Spaniards refused to surrender or to suffer their enemies' mercy; the 370 of them were thus put to the sword—the fate of heroes. "*Of our side,*" kept on Morgan who arrived after the fight, "*was lost thirty out right one captain and one lieutenant, and 76 wounded, whereof the brave Bradley was one with two lieutenants, who died within ten days after of their wounds to the great grief of myself and all in general.*"

The privateers anxiously started to sail the said river, knowing that the Spaniards had erected breastworks all along—but they found out that the enemies had deserted all their positions. Some privateers were on board of the ships, but the majority were walking on the banks, making their way through the luxurious vegetation with machetes. It required intense efforts, especially under the tropical sun, and this long march that Morgan summed up in a single line was a real ordeal. The fleeing Spaniards made sure to leave no provision behind, and he assailants were starving. These terrible people didn't usually carry food with them, as they ate on their preys. This time, they had to eat tree leaves and leathern bags—or *canastres*, as Esquemeling called them in French. They grated the leather, boiled it, and ate it up. "*Some who were never out of their mother's kitchens, may ask how these pirates could eat and digest those pieces of leather, so hard and dry. Whom I answer, that could they once experiment what hunger, or rather famine, is, they would find the way as the pirates did.*" The French edition added:

"*I can testify that a man can live out of it, but I doubt he will become very fat.*" When anger is the game, deceived hope is worse than hardship. Reaching Venta Cruze, *a very fine village (...) where they land and embark all the goods that comes and goes to Pennama* (sic), said Morgan, the privateers could already smell the cooking meat. But their enemies had left nothing behind. The privateers chased down a handful of cats and dogs, though; they also found a large quantity of wine from Peru that Morgan claimed was poisoned, as he feared his men would get drunk before the fight.

The next morning he found himself at the head of 1,500 men. Two hundred were sent to reconnoitre the most risky part of the journey, the path leading from Venta Cruz to Panama—ever since the *very fine village*, the Chagres River wasn't navigable, and everybody had to walk. But this part of the road was very narrow; four men only could walk abreast, and Morgan feared the invisible Indians who floated in the forest around them. At one time, a shower of arrows fell from nowhere on the privateers, killing ten. Some insults uttered in broken Spanish were heard in the remote, but the rare skirmishes turned to the advantage of the privateers— just like mosquitos, the Indians upset more than they harmed. "*The 17th*," continued Morgan, "(...) *about nine o'clock in the morning* (we) *saw that desired place, the South Seas and likewise a good parcel of cattle and horses.*" Esquemeling continued: "*While some killed and slayed cows, horses, bulls and chiefly asses, of which there were most, others kindled fires and got wood to roast them: then cutting the flesh into convenient pieces, or gobbets, they threw them into the fire, and half-carbonated or roasted, they devoured them, with incredible haste an appetite; such was their anger that they more resembled cannibals than Europeans, the blood many times running down from their beards to their waists.*" Once fed, the privateers camped in front of Panama. The drums and trumpets resounded and the unfold banners floated in the wind— fury was about to swarm Panama.

In the morning, Morgan parted his troops in three. Major John Morrice led the first set, Colonel Edward Collyer the second, and Morgan took the lead of the last one. In front of them, the Spanish soldiers of President De Gusman were waiting for the West Indian devils in battle array. The Spaniards had elaborated a curious stratagem, gathering a herd of bulls to trample the buccaneers—or at least to break through their lines. According to the English edition of Esquemeling, on sight of the numerous enemies, the pirates were *surprised with fear,* and *even doubted the fortune of the day.* But according to the French edition, they were just impatient, and shouted three dreadful war cries, to which the Spaniards responded: *Viva el Rey!* One Francisco de Harro, an officer from Panama, desperately gave the charge on his horse, *so furiously that he came upon us full speed,* marvelled Morgan. He entered eternity full speed too.

The Spanish cavalry was soon scattered, so were the bulls. Frightened with all the noise, the cattle panicked, and partly turned back against the Spaniards. Amid the general chaos, men and beasts mingled in a desperate run toward Panama. Some complementary troops were waiting there for the privateers, behind two strong fortresses—but panic had the better of the soldiers, and their officers blew up the fortifications *in such a hurry they killed forty of their men in the process,* underlined Esquemeling. The French and the English editions of the book here quoted differ a lot in the relation of the battle. The first one describes the capture of Panama as a swift and easy enterprise that cost the lives of 200 privateers only: *"It might sound like a lie, I can assure anyone it is not, as I saw it for myself."* The English one tells of a ferocious battle fought against a determined and dangerous enemy, and that lasted several hours. Morgan, it reads, made a review of his men just before the final assault and found *both killed and wounded a considerable number, and much greater than had been believed.* In the ranks of the bold assailants, friends dropped continually because of the Spaniards *who never ceased to fire.*

Both editions agree on one thing: Morgan and his men took Panama. Esquemeling depicted Morgan as an American Nero, who set fire to the city for reasons unknown to this day. For his part, the Admiral claimed he had fought in vain a fire of unknown origin. "*Thus was consumed the famous and ancient city of Pennama* (sic)," said Morgan in front of the Council of Jamaica. But the fire destroyed the heart of the city only, not the suburbs. When the smoke cleared, two churches and 300 houses were still standing. "*Herein this city, we remain 28 days,*" said Morgan. The privateers made daily incursions in the Gulf of Panama and in the nearby woods and creeks, tracking down the runaway Spaniards. As usual, they tortured, raped, killed and gave in all sorts of debauchery—the privateers' routine. Esquemeling reported Morgan's love affair with a beautiful and virtuous gentlewoman of quality, *who had been designed for (...) pleasure.* Failing to conquer her through mildness, he tried rigor. The lady then took up a knife, almost stabbed her aggressor and then threatened to kill herself. At the end of the day, she escaped Morgan's lust; he let her go once her ransom paid. This tropical affair sounds quite unlikely.

The privateers shared the booty on their way back to Jamaica, at the castle of Chagres. The Spaniards had evacuated the major part of their wealth before the enemy could reach Panama; nevertheless, the remains were impressive—the richest booty in Morgan's career. His share became even more important once he had double-crossed his accomplices, hastily sailing back to Jamaica. Upon learning about his hasty departure, some privateers swore they would catch up with him in Port Royal—a privateers' promise. Let's say that many of his men, mainly the French, complained about the share of the spoil. But the law of the jungle prevails among wolves. While in Panama, Morgan uncovered a plot aiming at depriving him from his share of the loot—it's hard to cross a double crosser.

In Port Royal, Modyford warmly welcomed his old companion—he got ten per cent of all spoils—, but he was worried. In Europe, England and Spain had signed a peace treaty just before the privateers left for Panama—a diplomatic thunderstorm was brewing.

From disgrace to grace

News took time to reach the West Indies, but the sack of Panama could cause Modyford and Morgan serious problems. As a matter of fact, in June 1671, the King of England sent a new governor to Jamaica, Thomas Lynch—Modyford welcomed him with apprehension. Lynch knew Jamaica quite well, and had been sent to publish the Treaty of Madrid signed with Spain, and to restore a good relationship with the Spaniards—in other words, to eradicate privateering.

England needed to send a positive signal to its new commercial partners—Modyford was made a scapegoat, and removed. In August, he was sent home a prisoner. But it wasn't enough for the Spaniards who asked for the head of the devil himself, Henry Morgan. Lynch was quite embarrassed. He wrote to Lord Arlington: "*And was afraid the sending home Morgan might make all the privateers apprehend they should be so dealt with, notwithstanding the King's proclamation of pardon. However shall send him home so as he shall not be much disgusted, yet the order obeyed, and the Spaniards satisfied. Could not do it now for he is sick and there is no opportunity, but hopes the Welcome will be ready to bring him in six weeks. To speak the truth of him, he's an honest brave fellow, and had both Sir T(homas) M(odyford) and the Council's commission and instructions, which they thought he obeyed and followed so well that they gave him public thanks (...). However it must be confessed that the privateers did divers barbarous acts, which they lay to his Vice-Admiral's charge.*" The historian Edward Long talked about a shameful and unjustified disgrace that fell upon *this gallant man*—he meant Morgan. But although sent to England, he was never sent to the Tower of London, unlike Modyford. The latter, though comfortable in his cell, did remain two years behind bars. Morgan, wrote Long, *without being charged with any crime* (was) *forcibly kept there three years at his own great expense to the ruin of his fortune and his health*—poor Henry! In fact, a folkloric figure and an excellent drinking bud, he wasn't without friends in London where he became close to Christopher Monck, the son of the Duke of Albermale. Ever since the death of his father, who had so dearly supported Modyford in Jamaica, the young Duke had been drinking his life away in the smoky nights of London. Morgan had a few toasts with him—vices are said to bring men together more rapidly than even interest. No magistrate ever heard Morgan, who wasn't legally accused of anything—though probably forced to stay in England. The looter of Panama freely roamed the streets of London while his influent friends were at work, trying to have him rehabilitated. They eventually went through in 1674, turning disgrace into honour. Appointed Deputy-Governor of Jamaica, the privateer became Sir Henry, and was sent back to his dear island. The news spread at once in the New World; the Spaniards armed several vessels with dozens of guns, and started to patrol the Caribbean Sea. In the meantime, they fortified several cities. Such was the power of Sir Henry. One may easily understand the Spaniards, as Morgan came home with his old fellow Thomas Modyford, who had just been released. Triumphant, Sir Henry left behind the vessel of the new Governor of Jamaica, Lord Vaughan, who had set sail with him. He was at home, and he let it be known. Worst, before reaching Jamaica, he anchored at his favourite spot, L'Isle Avache—the rallying point for the sack of Panama. What a bad omen to the Spaniards! But the Spanish Americas had no reason to worry; Morgan, who had left as their worst enemy, came back as their best ally—or almost.

On March 7, 1675, Lynch demitted office and Lord Vaughan assumed the government. In Port Royal, no one had forgotten Morgan, and the Council awarded him a 600 l. rent for what he had done for the colony. But Vaughan didn't like him. In May, he suggested to His Majesty to replace this *useless officer* and to appoint Lynch in his stead. But his letter received no answer, and Lynch soon left the island. In September, Vaughan complained about Morgan again, who, he said, *made himself so cheap at Port (Royal) drinking and gambling in the taverns.* A leopard can't change its spots, even when appointed Lieutenant Governor. Lord Vaughan decided to live in Spanish Town, far from the sinful Point—a matter of honour. The animosity between the two grew to such proportions that Secretary of State Sir Joseph Williamson intervened, exhorting Vaughan to find a common ground with Morgan. But the Governor was upset. How could he ever get along with a man who *contrary to his duty and trust, endeavours to set up privateering, and has obstructed all* (his) *designs and purposes for the reducing of those that do use that curse of life?* He officially accused Morgan and Byndloss to set up illegal privateering expeditions, urging their fellow privateers to sail under the commissions given by the French governor of Saint-Domingue. The Council questioned them on the matter, and they mumbled some explanations that were sent to England. Once again, commissions were at the heart of a hypocritical system. Indeed, in December 1676, England asked Lord Vaughan to issue commissions against the Spaniards, who had captured several English vessels in the West Indies—they remained valid for two years' time. Furthermore, said to be covetous and selfish, Vaughan wasn't liked in Jamaica. He confronted the Council several times—especially Samuel Long, the historian's ancestor. One of these disagreements regarded Captain James Brown, a Scottish privateer, who had taken a Dutch slave ship under a French commission. Since it was forbidden for any British subject to sail under foreign commissions, the culprit was condemned to death. Samuel Long pleaded the cause of the Scottish captain, but Vaughan wasn't into forgiveness anymore, he had Captain Brown hanged.

Following a dreadful slave rebellion in St Mary, Lord Vaughan then decreed the martial law and decided to rigorously apply the laws regarding slaves ownership. But the Negroes were the wealth of the 3,000 planters of Jamaica, who expected to import as many as possible—they teamed to fight Vaughan's decision. This new economical development played a key role in the ending of privateering. Despite a few last expeditions, the occupation was on the decline. Jamaica was becoming a giant plantation, and privateering was hurting the interest of the planters. It was bound to disappear.

The sycophants

In Jamaica, Morgan lived among his *clique*, composed of a handful of faithful companions such as Byndloss, Archbould or Captain Charles Morgan. They were influent both in the Council and in the taverns of the Point, and they planned various illegal expeditions of privateering. Yet, Morgan showed a lot of respect to Charles II in his official correspondence—we might even talk of deference. When the King ordered him to get rid of his former friends and associates, the privateers, he complied; and he became their worst enemy.

After *a short and ineffectual term in office* (Cundall), Lord Vaughan was replaced by Lord Carlisle in 1678. When the latter left in May 1680, Henry Morgan was appointed Lieutenant Governor again. And he was worried about the privateers of Saint-Domingue who raided the coasts of Jamaica to kidnap some slaves and servants. Using small fisherman boats, they were hard to spot, and hid in the mangroves; Morgan asked for some smaller vessels in England, and soon caught Everson, a notorious privateer, whom he put to death. "*Such is the encouragement which privateers receive from my favour,*" boasted Morgan. A few months later, after he had sent more privateers to the gallows, he added: "*I abhor bloodshed, and I am greatly dissatisfied that in my short government I have been so often compelled to punish criminals with death.*" As a humble servant of his Majesty, Sir Henry wrote some letters full of deference and self-satisfaction to the King. He obviously enjoyed his position, and did everything he could to keep it, including uselessly trying to procure permanent revenue to the King—a burning issue in Jamaica. Nonetheless, he learnt in May 1682 that Sir Thomas Lynch was sent to replace him. Morgan and his clique were ready and waiting.

Morgan coveted Lynch's position, and decided to bring him down. Consequently, he enrolled his clique—described by Lynch as *a peculiar Club of five or six little sycophants*. They all met at nightfall in the taverns of the Point to curse the Assembly and to plot against their enemy. To confound Morgan's ambitions, the Governor obtained from England a dormant commission of Lieutenant Governor in favour of Colonel Hender Molesworth, an influent merchant and a close friend of his. The Governor feared the island might fall into the hands of Morgan, should he suddenly die. He could foresee the damages such an event would cause to the colony. But it wasn't to be.

Everything collapsed for Morgan and his clique on October 2, 1683. In England, King Charles II and his brother the Duke of York had just escaped the Rye House Plot, allegedly set up by some Protestants from the Whigs party, who suspected the King of promoting Catholicism. When the news reached Jamaica, a zealous subject of Charles II named Edward Halo decided to celebrate; he headed to Charles and Mary Barnes' Tavern in Port Royal, knowing them as fervent subjects of the King. Around 10 p.m., he was drinking on the first floor balcony with Charles Morgan, Henry Archbould and the owners, when one Charles Sadler arrived, loudly asking for a drink to celebrate the King's good fortune. Some of his friends joined him, including a Negroe boy, who inconsiderately threw a firecracker on the balcony where it violently exploded, breaking a window, and leaving everyone stunned—all were left with holes in their clothes and buzzing ears. After a few seconds, Charles Morgan jumped back on his feet and rushed down the stairs with his drawn pistols, yelling after *the Whig son of a bitch* who had thrown the projectile. Push came to shove. The fight that followed was violent and almost turned to drama. Edward Harlo was badly beaten, one guy ended up with a broken jaw and several others were left unconscious on the ground. The incident made a lot of noise in the island, and Lynch seized the opportunity to eradicate Morgan's clique. The Council met and grievances started to rain on Morgan and his creatures. Some witnesses testified that unlike his victims Charles Morgan wasn't sober this evening—he was dismissed from the Captaincy of the Fort at Port Royal. Byndloss, who wasn't present at Barre's Tavern, was nevertheless turned out of the Council—he had accumulated other grievances against him. Henry Morgan, who was also absent during the incriminated evening, was condemned for various mischiefs—he was notably overheard one evening shouting *God damn the Assembly!* in the street. The privateer didn't vehemently fight back, and offered his dismissal instead. On October 12, 1683, his troublesome career came to an end—without glory or booty.

Morgan's Death

In 1684, Lynch deceased, leaving his position to Molesworth. Jamaica had to face new problems. The privateers from Petit Goâve, in Saint-Domingue, harassed the fishermen from Jamaica, while the Spaniards from Cuba seized every English ship they came across, taking their goods and sentencing the crews to hard labour. Diplomatic tension arose, and the trade of turtles with Cuba was cut off—2,000 people in Port Royal lived on this trade, another proof of the new commercial direction taken by the growing colony. The sugar economy developed and slowly forced the privateers to become honest—or to turn pirates. Privateering had become a threat to trade, so it had to stop.

Henry Morgan retired in his property near Port Maria, where he received his friends and former associates. At that time, he sued Theo. Malthus, the English publisher of Esquemeling's book, and received 210 l. in damages. But he stayed far from politics until his old good fellow Sir Christopher Monck, second Duke of Albermale—with whom he had spent so many nights in London—arrived in Jamaica. The son of Modyford's former protector had been appointed Governor in 1686, but took his time to take office. Having spent the entire familial fortune over his licentious way of life, he resorted to come to Jamaica only because he had invested money in a lucrative expedition. Indeed, the Commissioner of

Marine was retrieving the valuable cargo of a Spanish galleon that had sunken off Saint-Domingue forty-three years earlier—the expedition was successful, and the Duke went to collect his dividends in December 1687. The Duchess who came along with him, suffered from mental disorder. She was under the care of a young and promising physician, Hans Sloane—the collection of plants he gathered in Jamaica later became the embryo of the British Museum collection.

The young Duke of Albermale hadn't forgotten his friend Morgan, whom he endeavoured to have re-admitted to the Council. The case was delicate; but Sir Henry was eventually rehabilitated in July 1668. He didn't enjoy his new position very long, as he fell ill two months later. To recover, Sir Henry called upon every one, including a Negroe medicine man who covered him with mud from head to toes—*this only aggravat*(ed) *his coughing*, said Sloane who also attended the sick, describing him as *lean, swallow-coloured, his eyes a little yellowish, and belly a little jutting out or prominent (...) much given to drinking and sitting up late*. When Morgan eventually died, he was fifty-three. Though he hadn't officially plundered any Spanish colony in the Americas for years, his passing was celebrated all through the New World. Meanwhile, Jamaica buried him with full honours. On August 28, 1688, his body was carried to Port Royal for a funeral Mass, and then his coffin was taken to the Palisadoes, not far from the Point. The forts of the bay fired their guns, and their martial salute was followed by another one, fired by the war ships, and then by a last one coming from the merchant ships. This was the last noise of the terror of the Caribbean. His benefactor, Duke of Albermale, soon joined him in the grave. A jovial fellow, he didn't listened to his friends who kept on warning him about the wine of Madeira he drank so profusely—much stronger than the French one, it was, they said, leading him to death.

Privateering was already in decline when Morgan died. Jamaica was now engaged on the way of sugar trade, and the days of Sir Henry and his peers were over. Morgan remains a controversial figure, but those like Edward Long who praised him unconditionally never had a place to pay him a tribute. Indeed, his grave sank into the bay of Kingston during the dreadful earthquake of 1692. This natural disaster destroyed a good part of the Point and is often compared to Judgement Day—but could Port Royal redeem itself? After all, the privateers were seen by some as the exterminators sent by God to punish the Spaniards for what they had done to the Indians. In this New World one evil chased the other, and although men beseeched honours to their fellowmen, history teaches us that there's often a long way from a Sir to a Saint.

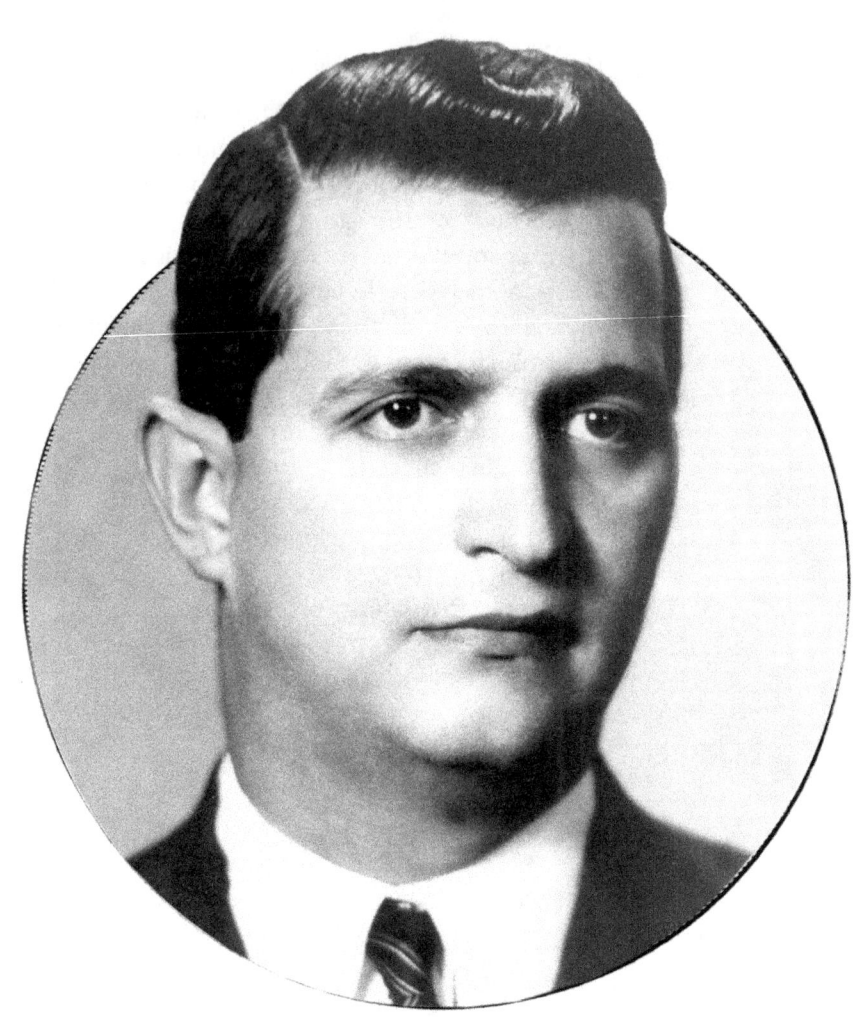

Eddie.
(DREAD Archives)

Seaga, Edward
(1930)
Blind Man With A Pistol

In the nearby Haiti was Baron Samedi. This voodoo creature wore a top hat and a coat tails, and shone its pale skull in the moonlight while roaming cemeteries on Saturday nights. People feared its laughing imprecations and its deadly curses that came from the darkest regions. In Jamaica was the mysterious Mr Brown *who rode from town to town in a coffin*, skinning his teeth and scaring the little children—and the grown-ups as well. In the 1950s, Mr Brown was mostly spotted in the little community of Buxton Town, where he drove a black Vauxhall car that looked just like a hearse. He was going under the earthly name of Edward Seaga, and the kids were instinctively afraid of him. They called him the *black-heart-man*—a traditional figure said to take the little children away and to devour them. But who was Mr Seaga? The offspring of a comfortable Jamaican family, Edward Seaga—Eddie, to friends—was born in Boston, U.S.A, and bred in the island. After some mediocre studies at Harvard, Eddie came back to Jamaica to study *obeah*, the local voodoo. Revolving around obscure rites, *obeah* was the cradle of nocturnal terrors inherited from black Africa, the dark side of slaves that had remained beyond the masters' power. *Obeah* scared the most sensitive—it fascinated Eddie. He rapidly got interested in the revivalist movement born around 1890 in Manchester, and that later gave birth to two distinct branches: the Pukkumania and the Zion. To capture the spirit of revivalism, Eddie went to the slum of Dungle, in West Kingston—almost an open dump. He rented a little room nearby the revivalist church he attended tirelessly. But at the same time, he was regularly seen with the most influential politician of the time, Alexander Bustamante—Busta, as he asked Eddie to call him during their first meeting orchestrated by *daddy Seaga*, in 1957. Busta wasn't originally from the high society, but his political course and his determination forced the admiration and the respect of the young man. He was an old fashioned politician, a short-tempered orator more into the emotional impact of his speeches than into syntax. A man *larger than life*, as Jamaicans love them—they brought him to the head of the Jamaican Labour Party (JLP). The legend goes that Seaga was first attracted to the rival People's National Party (PNP) led by Busta's cousin, Norman Manley; but that he was turned down. In his memoirs, Seaga evoked his relationship with Bustamante only, who rapidly took the young man under his wing—"*I was drawn to him instantly,*" he wrote. He became his devoted creature, the most promising recruit of the party at the dawn of Independence, achieved in 1962. With Busta as his mentor in the political sphere, Seaga still needed a street mentor, as required by the silent codes of Jamaica. He knew a man, powerful and feared—Malachi "Kapo" Reynolds, Captain of a Zion group. This reputed *obeahman* was said to have great powers but introduced himself as a faith healer.

Eddie used to capture ritual ceremonies in Trench Town with a portable recorder. They were uninterrupted chants in *bailo*—Jamaican—or in *country*—Kumina, a dialect reminiscent of the Angolan language. These recordings awoke the interest of *Folkways Inc.,* which pressed them without authorization. Eddie felt no way—he was just glad for the opportunity, and started to tour the record shops in Kingston to advertise them. But he found out that sellers weren't that interested in his records, and that they rather asked for the latest American hit records—as required by their costumers. Their request didn't fall on deaf ears, and Eddie engaged himself in the music business. He was 27.

WIRL Records

In the 1950s, Kingston became the battlefield of a new kind of war, a sound war. At sunset, gigantic speakers were dropped on the sidewalks, turntables connected, and musical missiles sent all through the night by sound system owners. Crowds of connoisseurs built up their reputation within a couple of days—and destroyed it just as fast. On this merciless battlefield, victory was sometimes one song away—the rare one, that no one else could play, often imported from America. The best sound system owners were crowned, carried in triumph by the crowd—and their enemies mocked and humiliated. It was just a game, at first; a serious one, though—business was a stake. The race for originality forced everyone to excellence. The rarest American records were jealously kept secret; sound system owners scratched the labels of their records to delay their identification by the rival factions. Young and ambitious producers like Clement "Coxsone" Dodd entered the musical arena, going to and fro between Kingston and America to find some rarities.

Meanwhile, Edward Seaga imported the latest American hit songs to Jamaica. When the government decided to tax those imports to sustain the burgeoning musical industry of the island, Eddie wasn't put off business; he opened a pressing plant in Kingston, licensed some songs from US record companies like Columbia or Atlantic, and then pressed the records in the island, thus escaping taxes. West Indies Records Limited (WIRL) was born—a major step in the musical industry of Jamaica. In the mean time, sound soldiers kept on fighting. To attract more people, and to sell more drinks, creativity was the key. America was far, and the records easier to identify; it was just a matter of time before sound system owners realized that the best way to get original songs was to record some local artists. The first trials were convincing, but were pressed at a unique copy on raw acetates, and then sold at very high prices to sound system owners from the countryside. Eddie changed the rules with *Nanny Oh*, a duet sang by (Joe) Higgs & (Roy) Wilson that he produced and pressed like an ordinary vinyl—designed to last in time. Joe Higgs was a young singer from Trench Town, the vocal mentor of all the kids from West Kingston. On the veranda of his little house on 3rd Street, he taught harmonies to the most talented generation of Jamaican singers; the Wailers were among his numerous pupils.

Edward Seaga was thus at the root of the Jamaican musical industry. But he was also very active during the 1958 federal election. The following year, the JLP lost the general election but Busta wasn't demoralized—in politics, fortune is often whimsical, and defeat nothing but a temporarily state of affairs. The Chief, as he was affectionately called, was already preparing the next election—one sunny afternoon, he met Seaga on his veranda to inform him that he had appointed him to the Legislative Council. "*A new life was beginning for me,*" said Eddie. And the nightmare began.

Guns & Obeah

No one has ever proved anything. It has been said, yet—repeated; even written, though implicitly; shouted sometimes, but never sung: Edward Seaga is to be blamed for political violence in Jamaica—he allegedly organized massive imports of firearms to the island, allegedly developed a powerful gang in his constituency of Tivoli Gardens, and allegedly did all he could to generate chaos with the help of the C.I.A. To fight the socialist government of the PNP, he allegedly armed an entire community of sufferers whom he allegedly enrolled in his political army. He allegedly used murder, destabilization, set up a criminal system and orchestrated the impunity of his most zealous generals—or Dons—, played with fire and burnt several generations, excitingly drove his country on the edge of civil war to serve his personal interest—a notorious criminal, the Don of all Dons, the *eminence grise* of Jamaica, the cancer of this once tropical paradise.

Allegedly, as no evidence has ever been given. And until that day, you're dealing with hearsay. Let's also remember that it takes two to make a fight; Eddie had some responding adversaries in the PNP, especially Dudley Thompson who keenly went to war. The PNP youths were given sweepers to clean the ghetto sidewalks and to sweep away 400 years of colonialism, but their sweepers soon turned into rifles. Edward Seaga and Thompson—*allegedly*—plunged the nation into madness and made the 1970s the most traumatizing decade of the history of Jamaica. As *civil blood made civil hands unclean*, corruption settled in Jamaica. Evil was inoculated to the country that started its slow agony under the sun. And these were the nicest years in Eddie's life, a challenging era when a man had to stand up for what he believes in. He trampled the socialist beast and tore it to pieces, laughing behind his eternal sunglasses—he was called *the blind man* because of them. But come on! Away with these Anancy stories—or fairy tales—, my friends! Seaga has always wiped them out disdainfully. His reputed links with the CIA? *Political destabilization*, he retorts—even his nemesis Michael Manley admitted it, the CIA has never been at work in Jamaica. The escape tunnels in Tivoli Gardens where hundreds of firearms would be stored? Anancy stories for *gunmen*! Drugs trafficking to finance the guns, his acquaintances with the most notorious criminals of the country? Where are the evidences? And what do *you* call a criminal? Edward Seaga has received full honours in his country, he is an honest law-abiding citizen, a humble servant of Jamaica—and he has a clear conscience. If you're not happy about it, then prove he's not was he's saying. Meanwhile, Eddie bids you good-bye!

Everything went wrong in the 1960s, as little Eddie climbed the steps to power. A bold and determined man, quite clear-sighted, he stepped into the forefront during the 1961 Referendum. He modernized the JLP's view on budget and supported Bustamante from St Thomas to Westmoreland. Elected politician of the year by the journalists, he triumphed in the shadow of his master while the opposition got stuck in a campaign in favour of the West Indies Federation—a boring topic to most Jamaicans. Seaga was appointed to a special constituency, West Kingston. It scared everyone, but it galvanized Eddie. Like a pike, he jumped into the political waters, overflowing with ideas and energy. One day, during a meeting in Coronation Market, in Kingston, he took a small bell out of his pocket and frantically rang it above his head: *the bell of freedom is ringing!* The crowd went wild, and the bell became the symbol of the party—during the following election, it rang the defeat of the PNP, and the end of the West Indies Federation from which Jamaica withdrew to march toward independence. This campaign was Eddie's baptism of fire—and he plunged at once into the hottest furnace, West Kingston. The veterans from the party had advised him not to play with fire, fearing he might get burnt. But Busta could feel people. To him, Seaga had all it took to gain the hearts of the residents of West Kingston. He had lived among them, he didn't fear them like most others, he understood them—he was one of them. The PNP decided to oppose him a serious contender, Dudley Thompson, also known as the *Burning Spear*—in Africa, he had been the lawyer of Jomo Kenyata, the Kenyan revolutionary from whom he had borrowed his *nom de guerre*. This was a strong political symbol: Dudley was a black man, and a respected lawyer who had stood for the African cause. Even Seaga had to confess he was a tough opponent. Their rivalry went on for ten years, and cost many lives. They were like two mad dogs facing each other, and coveting the same bone; growling, barking and biting.

Dudley wasn't supposed to lose. West Kingston had always been an unsettled community, but it dictated the rest of the island. And West Kingston vomited the lukewarm. Down there, you were loved or hated—and Eddie made himself worshipped! While the over-confident PNP led a classical campaign, Seaga knocked on every door, and gave many meetings that always ended up with music.

With Eddie, the honest residents would take control of their destiny. In his memoirs, the politician remembered how these poor people used to live in fear of the PNP-related gangs of the neighbouring slum of Back O' Wall, where the PNP recruited its soldiers, and made the dead vote to kept the nearby streets under control. *"Back o' Wall had no roads, only dirt tracks; no lights, only oil lamps; no sanitary conveniences at all, only a jungle of bushes offering dubious privacy; no houses, only lean-to shacks of discarded pieces of cardboard, wood and rusty old corrugated zinc sheets. It was accessible only on foot, an option that not even the police would take. (...) But it was worse than a slum,"* continued Seaga. *"It was also the most notorious criminal den of the country."* Seaga will never forget the day he tried to enter the slum with a few friends to gently give away gifts to the kids—a wonderful act of generosity. Unfortunately, and most unexpectedly, a dozen of *badmen* led by the notorious Bing Crosby fell on them with machetes. The politician had to run away—but he swore he would be back. During the counting of votes in a poll station close by, he was physically assaulted by a PNP supporter who cut his scalp and made him bleed. The culprit was caught up by a JLP supporter and stabbed in the belly. Seaga made good use of this incident: he went to the hospital where his wound was stitched and his head bandaged, only to rush back to the heart of the action. There he climbed on the roof of a car, and crossed the community, exhibiting his injury. What a triumphant hero! His admirers shouted his name in awe, jumping and dancing all around the vehicle. The bleeding politician exulted: *"At that point I knew my election was won."*

Negus 66

1962. Jamaica became independent, and Busta danced with Princess Margaret. The new flag waved at the top of the pole, bearing the three symbolic colours of the island, and Eddie was appointed Minister of Development and Welfare—a peculiar ministry that became a rare opportunity in his career. Seaga gave up his American nationality and heartedly plunged into the Jamaican culture. He was of all cultural events—supporting the revivalists from West Kingston, arranging the creation of a folkloric group, The Jamaican Folk Singers, and making some instruments available for the kids of his constituency. The birth of a new endemic music, *ska*, couldn't pass him by. As soon as 1965, he took a dream team of singers, including Jimmy Cliff and Toots & The Maytals, to the International Fair of New York to promote *ska*. This striking cultural embassy was broadcast on television, and the images are still regularly exploited in documentaries about Jamaican music—only a few from this period are available. The same year, Eddie had a love affair with the beautiful, and brown, Misty Constantine who had just become Miss Jamaica— the beauty and the beast. Seaga wasn't a romantic male lead, and didn't even enjoy the dark charisma of his old days yet. Nevertheless he had an energetic attitude, and the behaviour of a well-educated bad boy. A picture taken with his wife at the Kingston airport while they were both waiting for the eminent arrival of Haile Selassie's plane in April 1966 tells more about Seaga than a full book. It is a low-angle shot. Seaga is wearing a dark suit and his eternal dark sunglasses. He's holding his elegant wife's arm. Is he chewing gum or is it just a general impression given by his attitude? We can almost see his shoulders rolling under his expensive vest, and his jaws moving with a touch of vulgarity—we also make out his arrogant look behind his darkers. Eddie looks like a tropical petty king—there's some Busta in him.

In the 1960s, Seaga was at the heart of the cultural life of his country. Aware of the music, the beliefs and desires of his now compatriots, he actively partook in the repatriation of Marcus Garvey's body (see portrait), buried in England in 1940. Garvey's organization, the UNIA, had hardly survived the passing of its creator. There were still some activists in Jamaica, though; and they were more than sceptical about the motivations of pale Seaga. People knew him by then, and apparently suspected he could have repatriated an empty coffin. Garvey's family refused to expose the body—Garvey was embalmed when he died, but he had been at rest for a few years now. What could his legend gain from a spoilt image? Seaga couldn't help it, though. And when Munroe Scarlett, an early leader of the Garveyites, closed in the coffin during the official ceremony, Eddie took a screwdriver from his back pocket and opened the coffin in front of the stunned relatives of Garvey, discovering the particularly well-preserved face of the father of self-determination. That's how Eddie put an end to the rumour, without any consideration—a blind man with a screwdriver. Garvey's destiny thus took another bizarre turn: the prophet of the *Back-to-Africa* movement who had been buried in England eventually came back home—to Jamaica that is—, where he had sworn he would never go back. But who could fight Seaga's will? The politician even appointed Marcus Garvey first National Hero of Jamaica. Rastas were grateful, but not taken in. The JLP and Seaga had never been their friends. Neither had Manley and the PNP, as a matter of fact—but this was about to change.

The JLP totally overlooked the Rasta cultural revolution at the turn of the 1970s. And while the party stuck to its conservative values, the PNP jumped on the train of social change, capitalizing on the aspirations of the turbulent youth. Rasta attracted the deprived in need of social help and spiritual salvation; it charmed the intellectuals who saw it as the local reverberation of the American Civil Rights movement; but it upset a part of the middle-class—embodied by an allegorical *Mr Brown*—who rejected their African roots in favour of the western model. Mr Brown was more inclined to vote JLP; he shared the traditional views of the party; he was a good Christian; he considered the white and wealthy England as the ultimate model; and he believed hard work and business were the keys to a sane economy. When the JLP welcomed the Ethiopian Negus in April 1966, it was reluctantly; but too many cultural organizations had pressured the government to add Jamaica on the calendar of the Negus to be ignored—the Emperor was then visiting the West Indies. The JLP decided to make the best of the bad deal. After all, it was the dreamt opportunity to humiliate Rasta once and for all. How could the movement survive the Emperor publicly stating that he was no living God? That's when all their idiotic theories would fall down like a house of cards—the sect would be discredited. Everyone remembered how Rastas had put the nation upside down when six of them had murdered a poor gasoline intendant in Coral Gardens with machetes, shouting *Burn Babylon!* Then they had set the station on fire. Busta had reacted like a cowboy, sending the army, and having all Rastas arrested nationwide—even those who lived at the other end of the island. The police had raided their houses, beat them, and jailed them. Some had been tied to a chair and shaved before being sent back home with a kick in the ass. They have never forgotten, and they gather every year in Montego Bay to commemorate the event—some Rasta elders testify on stage of what they went through at the time. Though it apparently tried to integrate them to the rest of society, the JLP saw Rastas as troublemakers, and it longed to hear what the respectable Emperor of Ethiopia had to say about them. These bearded men had been creating disturbances for too long: from the scary Leonard Howell to the mad Bedward, to the traitor Henry, people had grown suspicious toward their insane theories and claims. To ease the tension, and in an attempt to assimilate them, the government had sent a couple of searchers from the University of the West Indies to study the various sects of the movement. It gave birth to a quickly written report, the *University Report*, that depicted Rastas as *peaceful citizens* and recommended to send cultural missions to Ethiopia. Some Rastas went there, and met the Emperor at the magnificent Court of Addis-Ababa—but they only reported what they wanted to.

    Seaga went to the airport to welcome Haile Selassie. He stood for a while on the tarmac, holding his beauty by the arm, wearing his sunglasses, not far from the red carpet that had been unrolled for the Ethiopian Emperor—that's when the aforementioned picture was taken (see page 164). Rastas by the hundreds had rushed the place, playing drums and chanting traditional liturgies under a rainy sky. As soon as the Negus' plane landed, they rushed the tarmac, broke the security lines, trampled the red carpet and lit their chalices under the wings of the plane in the middle of the vapours of gasoline—a disaster was miraculously avoided. In the middle of fury, the Emperor took time to come out of the plane. Mortimer Planno, one of the bredren sent by the Jamaican government to Ethiopia, was asked. Planno was a key figure of the Rasta movement, one of the first preachers of Trench Town where he taught Rasta to many youths, including Bob Marley. He talked to the Emperor who finally came out of the plane by his side. The ecstatic audience roared, and the photographer of *The Gleaner* did his job. The photograph appeared on the front page of the newspaper: Haile Selassie surrounded by the official members of the government and Planno! Rasta had officially taken over an event that no one else could have claimed.

For a few days, Haile Selassie visited the island. The government expected his firm rejection of the Rasta doctrines. But nothing came. A verbatim speech is sometimes evoked that was supposedly printed in *The Gleaner*, quoting the Emperor denying his divine character—but no trace was found in the archives. On the contrary, he received the heads of the various Rasta congregations in front of the photographers. One picture features Prince Emmanuel, the leader of the Bobo Ashantis, leaning his tall and skinny body in front of the very small Emperor whose charisma transcends the scene. Once the photograph published, the legend of Emmanuel was on a good track. Eventually, Selassie left. And Rasta triumphed. Rastas weren't refuted, and a rumour spread about a secret interview between the Negus and the leaders of the movement. Surrounded by the wicked and standing on sinking sand, the Negus couldn't publicly reveal his true identity, or openly chastise the devil. He left a message for the brothers in Jamaica instead, *liberation before repatriation*. The struggle took a new turn, and the Rasta movement implanted itself deeper into the Jamaican society. About the coming of Haile Selassie, Seaga wrote two laconic lines in his memoirs—as if the victory of Rasta was still a painful memory.

TG 67

Jamaica went through the 1960s like a tornado, rushing towards a new era. Eddie had visions. Everywhere he went, he foresaw luxurious hotels, lines of tourists in short pants buying souvenirs. He spoilt the looks of Bloody Bay, which beauties were secretly sprouting, far from the cupidity of Man. On the blood of the buccaneers, he had a complex erected; then he bought the plots alongside the sumptuous Dunn River, on the North Coast—the historical site where Christopher Columbus wrecked his ships in 1504, and where the first Spanish colony was established five years later. Eddie turned it into a tourists' haven, a promoters' dream, and a meeting point to all the gigantic cruising ships in the Caribbean. While the nearby Cuba had become a refuge for gangsters, Jamaica was swearing allegiance to tourism. As governmental contracts grew more numerous, politicians got ready for the fray. The JLP had always accused the PNP to make dead people vote. For the 1967 election, voters had to present their photograph and fingerprints. As a result, thousands of dead quietly remained in their graves on election day—the number of voters went down for a third!

For the first time, the founder of the nation, the holy monster, the Chief, wasn't running—over eighty, he had decided to retire. The PNP rejoiced—not for long: the JLP was re-elected, and Donald Sangster became Prime Minister after fifteen years of loyal service to his party. But two months after the achievement of his life, aged 55, he died from brain haemorrhage. Rastas weren't surprised. Stepping on Lulu's foot during the official visit of Haile Selassie, the politician had sealed his fate. Lulu was the Emperor's Chihuahua. The late journalist Kapuscinski once described it as follow: *"He was a small dog, a Japanese dog. He was named Lulu. He had the right to sleep in the big imperial bed. During the official ceremonies he would often leap from the*

Emperor's knees to urinate on the dignitaries' feet. These august people couldn't blink or give the hint of a gesture while their feet were getting wet." The insult of Sangster, though involuntary, was a crime of lease majesty.

Once Sangster buried, Hugh Shearer took the lead. During the intern election, Seaga had supported Shearer's opponent, his friend Clem Tavares. Together, they controlled West Kingston. But the devilish duet never lasted—after his defeat, Tavares changed and slowly perished, joining Sangster in the grave a few months later. Edward Seaga, now Minister of Finance, elaborated a powerful war machine, the Urban Development Corporation (UDC). Beyond the touristic sites, he started the most important project of his life, the building of Tivoli Gardens. He decided to erect this model community, daughter of his most ambitious dreams, on the ashes of Back o' Wall—a symbol. But first, he laid a claim on downtown Kingston, another historical PNP stronghold. He launched several ambitious building sites on the seafront, including Newport West—a new wharf he would later make good use of. He also built huge buildings to attract businessmen and stores owners. But the waterfront project was the first dream of Eddie to sink into a pool of blood. "*Sadly,*" he wrote in his memoirs, "*many of the dreams of the development halted after the first stage. The adjoining areas had become part of an urban zone blighted by the onset of crime wave, creating a shadow of fear which blunted further investment.*" Ever since, the waterfront has remained a no man's land, a dangerous place to walk, especially at night—anyway, the huge desert avenues sided by big and almost empty buildings create a morbid atmosphere that hardly fits romantic walks.

Eddie's masterpiece would then be Tivoli Gardens. And Eddie's dream inevitably looked like the nightmare of everyone else. The removal of Back o' Wall residents didn't go without trouble. The slum erupted in 1966. All public meetings were banned, barbed wire was strung to prevent anybody's entering the community while the police and the army cordoned and searched the place, looking for arms and homemade bombs. The State of Emergency was decreed in this notorious and filthy PNP turf. *"There was absolutely no way this situation could be allowed to continue,"* wrote Seaga who eventually had the slum bulldozed in front of the residents—he had come back, as promised to Bing Crosby and his cronies. Eddie's project was a 4,000 residents community scattered over 40 acres of land and sheltered in bungalows or short buildings—a football playground, parks to spend some quality time, or a cultural centre with the capacity for 1,000 people. From Kindergartens to golden age houses, Eddie thought about everything. The name Tivoli Gardens, taken from the former movie theatre of the community, was the last link between the new township and the old slum. Leaning against the dump of Dungle and the biggest cemetery of the island, Tivoli Gardens had style. Here we were—heads, the dream; tails, the nightmare. Tivoli was designed as a political fortress from the start, sheltering Seaga's most fervent supporters to weaken the PNP's influence in the area, and to insure Seaga a seat for life in Parliament. Tivoli's residents were poor, and needed everything. Eddie became their only hope—because of his powerful position in society, first; then because of his strong ties to this so often discriminated part of Kingston. Eddie had an aggressive attitude and a bad boy behaviour that people in West Kingston understood and respected. He was the only one who could speak in their names.

In the late 1960s, politics took a new turn. Supporters weren't enough anymore, politicians now needed enforcers. With Newport West, Tivoli Gardens had a direct access to the sea, a convenient situation to import and export goods. According to a contemporary witness, the first cargo of arms came to Jamaica through this port just before the 1967 election—the guns were stuck inside the bellies of some Teddy Bears. Edward Seaga had invited an American circus to Kingston. Among the attractions offered at George VI Memorial Park was a shooting range with prizes: Teddy Bears for the kids, bearing deadly fruits. These were the days of amateurism, and this story is somewhat humorous—in fact, it isn't. In the streets of West Kingston, soldiers were recruited among criminals—those who refused were shot—, guns were handed to the kids who wanted to earn of few bucks, or to make a name for themselves. Soon they were left with a sole choice, sink or swim. Each community abode by a political party; they were divided and opposed; they spied at each other and eventually fought one another for the sake of their respective Member of Parliament (MP). If the latter was elected, money would reach the community; well, let's say that a few jobs at a minimum wage would be available for a handful of youths—but a starving man feasts with crumbs. The MP rubbed elbows with the leader of the community, soon known, respected and feared as the *Don*. As the right arm of the MP, the Don obtained governmental building contracts. If asked to build a 150 meter-long road, he hired a few kids of the community to build a 50-meter long road, and kept the rest of the money. Everyone was happy, no one complained. Later, money would run both ways. When the sums involved became important because of international drug trafficking—favoured by politicians—, part of the money would go back to the party, so that the Don could keep his position—the lion's share.

In recent years, a Jamaican journalist found the perfect name to describe these armed and partisan communities, *garrisons*. And these garrisons have always been at war. Tivoli Gardens became the mother of all—many flourished in its wake, on both sides of the fence. Tivoli Gardens (TG) has always been regarded as the toughest one, the most heavily armed—its residents repelled the police and the army twice in ten years' time before it was taken in 2010. The community was no slum. Kindergartens, renowned maternities, nice little stores, loans with the lowest interest rates in the country, social order. But behind the mask hid the nasty face of TG. Some horrible rumours circulated about the Tivolites who were even said to skin people alive. As soon as

1967, the turbulent Dudley Thompson—the PNP counterpart to Seaga, or his political reflection—openly accused his opponents to murder PNP activists in broad daylight. On the front page of *The Gleaner*, he accused some military groups of firing at the PNP headquarters on Regent Street—and he called Edward Seaga's name. *Fantasies!*, retorted Seaga. The PNP were the nasty ones, and everybody knew that!

Before the 2010 downfall of Christopher "Dudus" Coke, the Don of TG, everything from coke to crack, to guns, was allegedly going through the community. It sheltered the most important criminal organization of the country, and it was supported by one of the most powerful and feared politicians. This was Eddie's dream, a trap for the poorest, an army of ragamuffin soldiers—the West Indian stray children. Ghetto youths usually killed each other over business; sometimes out of pure fun—such places are hardly short of psychopaths. All day long, reggae songs—including Bob Marley's—were repeating it was necessary to love one another, to stop the tribal wars (read the *political wars*), and to live in harmony (read *at peace*). The western audience of the 1970s misunderstood this coded message, and identified it with the claims of the hippies—reggae music became a *peace and love* music. But the artists were actually singing about the few streets around their places, where people cut each other's throat over politics. They believed in the Bible, of course; but if they quoted the Holy Book so extensively in their songs, it's also because they lived among the *devils* they criticized. And only Biblical warnings were tolerated in this environment. Singers were relatively safe, as long as they took no side but God's side.

1972, the I-Election

The topic is a taboo, but Rastas have always more or less been on the PNP side. Well, things appear to be more complex. Let's say that the social aspirations and the dream of equality of Rastas naturally drew them closer to this party—especially in the early 1970s. Actually, Rasta preaches a theocracy, a religious system of divine right, a black empire. But in the ghettoes of Kingston, where Rastas mingled with the turbulent youth of the country, the socialist party of the young and dynamic Michael "Joshua" Manley was far more seducing than the conservative JLP. Michael Manley took notice, and adapted Marcus Garvey's theories for his program; he also used *I-words*—words in which the pronoun *I* replaces, or stands in front of the first syllable, as a symbol of purity and togetherness. "*Who say so?*" shouted the crowd at Manley's rallies. "*I-man say so!*" answered the politician, abiding by the patois syntax. Reggae music exploded in Kingston and kids started to wear knotty dread locks —or *natty dreadlocks*—, a peculiar haircut resulting from the Nazarene vow. A symbol of Africanism and of a pure and incorruptible faith, *dreadlocks* fascinated the intellectuals and disgusted the conservative, who had always done their best to match the respectful standards of the English culture—including a sharp and clean haircut, as *cleanliness is godliness*. All these craps about the Ethiopian Negus being the returned Christ, about the end of the world and the use of *ganja*, deeply irritated the Jamaicans who looked up to the European excellence to take their country out of ignorance. These illiterate living in the slums of West Kingston gave a terrible image of their nation, and they didn't represent Jamaica. Jamaica was a proud nation of people who worked hard to attain the standards that England seemed to unconsciously expect from them. Nevertheless, supported by an almost orgasmic uprising of a worldwide contesting subculture, Rasta took the Jamaican society hostage. The movement wasn't strictly religious or sectarian anymore, but had become cultural. Michael Manley got in touch with Claudius Henry (see portrait), who informed him of the value of the rod the politician had received as a gift from Haile Selassie during an official visit to Ethiopia. This was a sceptre just like the one Moses had used to lead his people out of Egypt—it captured the imagination of Jamaicans at once.

Artists musically commented this apocryphal Exodus, identifying the JLP candidate Hugh Shearer as *Pharaoh*, and

Michael Manley as *Joshua*—Moses' brother and successor. About the rod, Seaga had to admit that Manley used a powerful symbol—how could he deny it? Beaten on his own ground—the occult forces—, the young politician was outraged. He did try to beat the power of the rod, brandishing a replica in the newspapers while pretending he had it stolen from Joshua—it only strengthened the power of the rod. Nevertheless, Seaga is still very proud today of this obviously inefficient trick: *"The JLP had reduced some of the magical power in the PNP campaign,"* read his memoirs. Is he serious? Probably. But he admits that at the time, *the JLP was just not able psychologically to deal with the mushrooming PNP gasp of the political psyche of the Jamaican electorate.* What an euphemism! In fact, the JLP was totally swept away by this social movement. Producers and singers kept on recording *Joshua tunes* to celebrate Manley. Banned from radio, these songs were mostly played on the jukeboxes all around the island.

Invited to a PNP rally, the singer Clancy Eccles glorified Michael Manley in a song. As the crowd went wild, Beverley Anderson, Manley's wife, had a genius idea. After the show, she approached the young and streetwise producer. Nobody officially asked him to record the partisan song *The Rod of Correction*—at least, that's what he said—but it came out on his own label to the politician's greatest joy. Beverley Anderson then asked Clancy Eccles to organize a PNP musical tour of the island. It only took him a few days to gather the most extraordinary reggae line-up of all times: Bob Marley & the Wailers, Max Romeo, Ken Boothe, Inner Circle, The Gaylads, Scotty—the cream of the crop. The producer turned promoter even published his impressive posters in *The Gleaner*, at his own expense—at least, that's what he said. In some remote villages where nothing ever happened, the show attracted up to 10,000 people. The band was playing from the back of a truck, and one evening the vehicle gave way under the weight of the musicians, who ended up upside down among the material. They only had two small amplifiers and the people who stood more than 30 feet away probably couldn't hear a thing. But everybody came to enjoy the show, and to see the stars. "*Hail that man!*" shouted Clancy Eccles to introduce Michael Manley who attended the most important dates. Without a word, the charismatic politician would step forward, sententiously grabbing the rod before brandishing it over his head. Then the crowd started to sing: *Chase them Joshua, chase them with your rod of correction!* No doubt, Joshua had it. He even recorded a few lines of his program over a reggae rhythm produced by Clancy Eccles—ironically, the song was recorded at Seaga's studio. The *Joshua mania* spread all over Jamaica, and music became its vehicle. Max Romeo, known for his lewd songs, reinvented himself as an advocate of black people rights, and recorded several tributes to Manley. A lucky strike—times were political. His complacency seduced in high places, and his song *Let The Power Fall On I* became one of the official PNP hymns for the 1971 campaign, alongside *Better Must Come* by Delroy Wilson (see Trevor Wilson portrait).

Michael "Joshua" Manley believed in what he called Democratic Socialism, a confused political program he hardly ever defined—apparently, it wasn't clear to him either. He asked his friend Max Romeo to express it in simple words for the masses, and the singer recorded the song *Socialism is Love: You're asking what is socialism and what it really means / It's equal rights for every man regardless of his strength / So don't let no one fools you, Joshua say, (...) socialism is love between man and man*. Rapidly, people in Jamaica were divided between the socialists (PNP) and the capitalists (JLP)—just as Seaga had planned it, the Cold War had set a foot in the island.

Apparently, no song was voluntarily recorded in favour of the JLP at the time. Worst, some songs more or less openly denounced the party of Seaga. The deejay Prince Jazzbo, for instance, sang: *They take the guns and kill their own sons / Move capitalists, I & I want socialists!* This is one of the most direct accusations ever sung against the JLP—unfortunately, the singers never went any farther, always shying from straight denunciations. The JLP's defeat reflected its poor campaign. In February 1972, Michael Manley was elected Prime Minister by a landside. Meanwhile, Seaga was re-elected Member of Parliament in his West Kingston constituency; his third victory in a row—he never lost once in his long career.

Manley exulted in the newspapers, and Rastas rejoiced in the open while the singer Ernie Smith enjoyed a hit song with *Hail That Man!* But Edward Seaga and the JLP were already planning to retaliate. And while people danced on *Better Must Come*, the worst was actually on its way.

Of Rhetoric

"*The loss of election upset me greatly,*" confessed Edward Seaga in his recent memoirs. "*I decided to withdraw from active politics for two years.*" He was then 42, and the father of two. The regrets he expressed about his family are a recurrent point in Seaga's rhetoric. He said he neglected his beloved ones to serve his nation, wasting his time in useless political considerations—he talks about *the bitter cup of leadership*. Concretely, he was thrown out of Val Royal, the official residence of the Minister of Finance. He then bought a property at 19 Temple Meads, where he received various celebrities such as Muhammad Ali or the Jackson Five. For a while, his biggest problem consisted in ruling the whimsical cow of his kids that created a lot of disturbances in the neighbourhood. But don't you worry; Eddie remained active in his constituency. Besides writing speeches for Hugh Shearer, he registered a few finance companies and got closer to the UNESCO and several influent people in the Caribbean Zone. He said he was offered a lucrative job in Barbados, but that the call of Jamaica was too strong—he turned it down. Meanwhile, the PNP government launched its first social programs. One of them, the *Crash Program*, consisted in giving the youths a sweep to clean the ghetto streets. A few gossipers claimed the party used the program to recruit soldiers. But Joshua and Jamaica were on honeymoon, and the politician's determination invigorated the country.

The JLP was assessing the situation. Hugh Shearer, described by Seaga like a *gentle, likable giant*, was blamed for the loss of the election. Isolated inside a party described as *a headless corpse* by one of its influent members, Pharaoh resigned as the leader of the opposition. Backstage, the young and ambitious wolves got ready, including the bold Edward Seaga, who was urged to apply for the position. But just like Pope Sixtus V in his time, the politician pretended not to be interested. Too much stress, not enough consideration—and what about his tender and loving family longing for his paternal attention? The suspense was almost unbearable, but Eddie had already dipped his lips into *the bitter cup*, and on November 5, 1972, he officially announced that he was running for the position in front of a relieved crowd in South Parade. The bitterness of power, you see, couldn't distract him from his duty, as he was a humble servant, and blah blah. The vote itself was a pure formality. Appointed head of the opposition, Edward Seaga now faced the most serious opponent of his life, the charismatic Michael Manley. That's when he realized that *an unseen hand* had guided his decision not to accept the job in Barbados. As it was *unseen*, nobody knows whether it was good or evil.

Eddie was ambitious and passionate, but his first speeches were too close to Joshua's, and far less inhabited. He repeated his mistake of 1972, fighting on the enemy's field where he stood unbeatable. Even in the name of his first official campaign of 1975 reflected it, *Turn Them Back*. But Eddie was a quick learner, and he soon realized that only a head-on attack could destabilize Manley. He started to look for the weak part of the PNP fortress, and he found it in the word socialism. "*Socialist programs have weak links which could be exploited,*" he wrote. "*One such weakness was the strong similarities between socialism, which was unknown to the people of Jamaica, and communism, which the people were aware of and feared because of knowledge of the great difficulties experienced in Cuba.*" Manley was no communist; he preached moderate socialism according to the historical line of the PNP that had always featured the redistribution of lands on its agenda. Concretely, it manifested through various social programs like *Jamal*—to fight against illiteracy—, the *Labour Day*—one day of solidary work—, etc. Nevertheless, Manley struggled to give a satisfying definition of Democratic Socialism; a far too complex concept for the masses, anyway. But even the supposedly magic slogan *Socialism Is Love* didn't strike any chord in the street. Rapidly, Manley's discourse hardened. According to Eddie, he suffered from *the messianic complex*, and eagerly gave into grandiloquence. But the more he got close to his Cuban friend Fidel Castro, the more he mingled Biblical idioms with communist patois, describing businessmen as avid imperialists, answering *We are not for sale!* to the International Monetary Fund (IMF) in 1977, and even evoking *a march toward the mountain top* while standing beside Castro. In fact, Manley believed in cooperation between the private and public sectors only as long as the latter could impose its condition to the former, as it derived its power from the people. He set up a curious, and quite suspicious, cultural exchange program with Cuba. A few hundred Cubans came to Jamaica to share their building *savoir-faire*—but couldn't Jamaicans build their own houses? As a counterpart, many Jamaican youths were sent to Cuba to learn masonry—there they learnt how to handle a towel, but also a Kalashnikov. The United States were very touchy about Cuba, and they started to watch Jamaica, mostly after Prime Minister appeared at the convention of the non-aligned countries. The CIA sent some agents in the island, who probably got in touch with Manley's antidote, Eddie. On the walls of Kingston appeared some slogans featuring his name, spelt *CIA-ga*. *Propaganda as usual*, he said. The CIA in Jamaica was a pure fantasy, the fruit of romantic-minded people who read too many spy novels. Indeed, who could seriously imagine the CIA trying to destabilize a regime in the Americas? The real question is to know whether the secret services of Uncle Sam furnished the JLP with weapons. Once again, nothing has ever surfaced that could let us consider such a novelistic situation. But as the politicians fought each other with words, blood was running in the streets. Violence spread like a poison; mainly in Kingston, aka *Kill-some City*, where each community picked up its colour—orange for the PNP, green for the JLP. Eddie's creatures drank nothing but Heineken—in green bottles. Joshua's supporters stuck to the red bottles of the local Red Stripe beer. Some rang their little bells while others wanted to *sweep* their opponents clean. Never had the mood been that political before. Raising taxes on bauxite—the first natural resource of the island—, Manley forced the powerful and rich companies to cough up. It was the end of the *friendly arrangements* that had ruled this sector for so long. But Manley wasn't clear sighted enough—bullying the industrials, he scared them, and forced them to fight back. His decisions brought down commercial exchanges, the investors started to flee with their capitals and Jamaica soon drained out of blood—then the oil crisis of 1974 brought social programs to an abrupt end. There was only one option left for Manley, communism. A *coup*? That's what many feared when the State of Emergency was called in 1976.

Emergency 76

The first campaign of Seaga against Manley was a failure. The times were socialist. Yet, the first disillusions were expressed through the most trustful social poll of Jamaica, music. Several artists wondered about the direction taken by Manley, and eventually asked the thorny question: when will better come? Max Romeo, the yet unconditional supporter of Manley, informed his *friend* in the song *No Joshua No: Since you are my friend Joshua, I think you should know, Joshua: Rasta is watching and blaming you / You took them out of bondage and they thank you for it but now (...) they think they are forsaken, they think they have been used (...) / They say you must forward and start anew.* Manley was a cool guy—he invited Max Romeo to his office, made a few promises and sent him back with a slap on the back. A few months later, the singer recorded *Socialism Is Love*, and officially presented the record to the Prime Minister, in front of the press and the photographers.

Meanwhile, the *gunmen* from the PNP and the JLP enthusiastically played at communists and capitalists in the streets—and the skirmishes led to a blood bath. The inhabitants of Trench Town, where reggae music was born, were surrounded by violence and madness—they were the deprived, or the *sufferers*, those who couldn't afford to leave the place when things got out of hands. Enrolled in the political armies of their respective communities, the kids learnt how to make guns with bicycle handles rather than to read and write. Each kid had to take a stand for his community, no matter what—a quitter was a traitor. Tivoli Gardens, Eddie's turf, had the most powerful guns, and regularly raided the nearby PNP community of Concrete Jungle. In order to reach it, the Tivolites crossed the southern part of Trench Town, Rema—seven streets affiliated to the JLP, where the *gunmen* from TG behaved like beasts, raping, killing and robbing. Once they had raided Concrete Jungle, they hastily returned to TG, leaving a defenceless Rema to cope with the deadly retaliation of their enemies. It became necessary to fight in order to survive—and it wasn't a priority then to define Democratic Socialism.

In the meantime, the MPs rubbed shoulders with the Dons of their respective constituencies. And as the struggle intensified, these self-made *Generals* grew more powerful. They behaved with complete impunity in their communities—and sometimes like dogs. But respect was due; these men were dangerous, they controlled your life and the lives of your relatives. Without them, you were helpless, defenceless, and most of the time jobless. To be part of the community, you had to get involved in the political warfare. In Trench Town, entire streets were bulldozed because of the ambition of a politician; it created a no man's land between the rival communities of Rema and Concrete Jungle. The then Minister of Housing said he wanted to have a view on the sea from his PNP stronghold of Concrete Jungle. He dreamt of bulldozing the remaining seven streets of Rema. Such were the aspirations of this generation of political wolves.

Institutionalized violence was at the heart of the 1975 campaign. The State of Emergency was declared following an upsurge of violence in Trench Town. Some *gunmen* from the JLP fired at the police who were trying to enter their turf. Edward Seaga never disapproved his guys; to him, this was a natural reaction to previous PNP attacks on various neighbouring JLP communities—the policy of terror implemented by the PNP forced the JLP inhabitants to run away from their communities, thus giving way to PNP supporters. Then came the terrible events of May 1976, when several hundreds of JLP houses were burnt down on Orange Lane. When the firemen reached the place, unidentified *gunmen* opened fire at them, forcing them to retreat. Eleven persons perished in the flames that day, right in front of their rejoicing executioners. A mother running away from the fire was stopped, her child taken from her and thrown it into the furnace—evil at work.

In 1974, the government opened a penitentiary painted red, Gun Court. Anyone involved in a gun related case was sent there for indefinite detention—even those caught with a simple round of ammunition. At the same time, the churches were opened to repentant *gunmen. Bring in the guns, no questions asked*, read the official posters. But most people like the singer Dr Alimantado remained practical: "*If a badman back me up round the corner and the police and soldiers no deh deh* (are not there), *whey me ah-go use to defend I-self* (what will I use to defend myself)? *Gimme my gun, say me want mi gun cause I no run / Gimme my gun cause my life can't done.*" Only an idiot would run naked in a field of thorny bushes.

Fearing the blood bath, Michael Manley declared the State of Emergency and put the whole island under martial law. Seaga was infuriated. The PNP now had the power to arrest people without justification, and to detain them as long as they wished—

right in the middle of the general election! He feared a *coup d'état*—or, at least, a rigged election. Expecting the police to come for him at any time, he gave instructions to his wife Misty and planned to start a hunger strike. Several influent members of the JLP were indeed arrested, mostly those supposedly connected with gang activities, but not Seaga. His arrest would have probably set the country afire.

The campaign got off to an inauspicious start. The artists were less enthusiastic about Joshua by then; except Neville Martin who was probably paid by the party to sing about the race issue. Manley had tried to abolish the on-going racial segregation in the island. His campaign of cultural and racial pride might be one of his greatest achievements. As a matter of fact, black pride was all over the place. The *I'm-black-and-I'm-proud* movement had finally reached Jamaica. Neville Martin's song entitled *My Leader Born Ya'* (*Ya'* for *here*) was still dubious, and indirectly referred to Seaga's American origins—born in Boston, he had already been tagged as *a foreign voice in Jamaica* by Norman Manley.

But the JLP couldn't get rid of its negative image. It was perceived as a conservative party working for the Haves, and as such, outraged by the social ambitions of Michael "Robin Hood" Manley. A bad loser, Eddie contested the results of the 1976 election for months, adding confusion to this confused period. Champing at the bit, the Tivolites enraged at those damned communists who monopolized all the riches. At the end of the day, the JLP had to bow, but the militants were roused by this episode, the mad dogs started to pull on their leads, willing to bite. The following years were tainted with rare violence—and were probably the most exciting of Eddie's career.

Red 80

Seaga never liked Manley, and apparently considered him with a mixture of disgust and admiration, being both irritated and charmed by his insolence and his natural charisma. Eddie was full of contradictions: stating that only a man with *a heart of gold and a stomach of iron* could rule the community of Tivoli Gardens, he also disliked mavericks—when elected in 1980, he surrounded himself with women whom he found more pragmatic, and less self-centred. Eddie saw Michael Manley as enslaved to his passions, and he had little respect for that type of men. He blamed his populist and dangerous flights of poetry, but couldn't help being fascinated by some of his shock statements like *We are not for sale*—aimed at the IMF—or *To anyone who* (wants) *to be a billionaire in Jamaica, my advice to them is to remember that five flights depart five times daily to Miami.* Manley was the romantic male lead; handsome, witty, and definitely elegant, he was a Jamaican JFK. Seaga, behind his sunglasses, looked more like an upstart. As a matter of fact, he was no better at containing his feelings—and probably worst. His career is riddled with unhappy statements uttered with the voice of anger. No one has forgotten his prophetic promise of violence thrown at an unfriendly PNP crowd in the late 1960s: he threatened to send them some Tivolites, and then added that from that day on, it would be *blood for blood, fire for fire*—and Eddie has always been a man of his word. He never feared to wet his shirt either, another lesson learnt from Bustamante. As a matter of fact, the Chief died in 1977, the shadow of his former self—but Seaga stayed true to his teachings and stuck to old fashioned politics. No wonder most of the artists—apart from a few grateful mouths—didn't side him in the early 1970s. How many spontaneous songs were then recorded to celebrate the JLP? Almost none. As a matter of fact, Tivoli Gardens grew few major artists—maybe because *Rasta reggae* was the order of the day, and that Seaga had no special affection for these bearded men whose degenerated concepts were shamefully spreading through the entire society. He realized with obvious resentment that, *in the late 1970s, the political intellectuals cultivated eccentricities to identify with ordinary people. Sometimes, at house meetings, some would sit on the floor and pick their toenails while making profound points. (...) The emergence of a renegade sub-culture of wide-scale indiscipline began at this time.*

The politician clearly identified Bob Marley as the head of the *renegades*, and if he doesn't openly criticise the artist in his memoirs, he does it restlessly. During his funeral in 1981, he shouted out *Jah Rastafari!* over his coffin—probably one the most hypocritical obituary—, then announced on TV that there was no more room for false prophets. In other words, militant reggae had gone out of fashion. Reggae music bowed to the new lord of Jamaica. Fourteen years after Selassie's visit, Eddie got his revenge. Truly enough, Bob Marley had always sided the PNP—that's probably why Seaga thought he was a very bad example for the youth. Yet, during the funeral of Lester "Jim Brown" Coke, the Don of Tivoli Gardens, Eddie was suddenly more understanding. He blamed the dirty journalists who dared questioning the dead man's probity. They saw nothing but evil, and they never took into consideration the voice of the people! he raged. Dons were loved, even worshipped, by their communities. So they *had* to be men of good—QED. These were the good examples Eddie had in mind for the youth, not Bob Marley.

In May 1978, the microphone of the House of Representative overheard one of Eddie's legendary furies—the politician threatened the Leader of Government Business who had tried to reduce his speaking time. The rabble of TG rejoiced at their master's ferocity: *no one diss* (disrespects) *Eddie, man!* One might reproach a lot of things to Michael Manley such as his political blindness, his radicalism at a time when the economy of the island was sinking, his detachment from reality and also his violent entourage—like Dudley Thompson or Anthony Spaulding, or even worst, the two PNP enforcers Winston "Burry Boy" Blake and George "Feathermop" Spence. But he wasn't bloodthirsty. For his part, Edward Seaga never backed down, as promised. As the next general elections were closing in, he feared another manipulation from the PNP—like another State of Emergency. He went to the US to add red oil to the political fire. "*On 22 October 1979, while on a visit to the US, I drew attention to the* build-up of Cuban-type militant units—the Home Guards, patterned after the Cuban Peoples Militia, and the Cuban-trained brigadistas—as signs of militarization, and voiced my concern that Jamaica was becoming the subversion capital of the region." By subversion, he meant communist agitation. Such was acting this cold-blooded politician; but he had mitigating circumstances, including the ruthless butch of PNP gangsters he faced. Let's take Roy McGann, for example, *a terror to JLP supporters who in a manner of speaking, lived by the gun*, wrote Seaga; a dangerous man, who had taken an active part in the Heroes Park gun battle in 1979, and who was eventually gunned down by his own bodyguard during a shooting with the police one year later. Several members of the JLP were shot at, at the time; some were killed. Kingston was plunged into darkness, and the PNP was no lamb to the slaughter. In 1978, the Jamaican realpolitik reached its peak when the police infiltrated a small JLP gang in Southside, in downtown Kingston. They promised ten kids a gun and a little job, and took them to the beach of Green Bay where some soldiers lied in ambush. Five of them were murdered on the spot, including the football player Glenroy Richards who died crying over his girlfriend. He left a prophetic song behind him, recorded a few weeks earlier, *Wicked Can't Run Away*. But in Jamaica, the wicked had all the luck. The incident became known as the Green Bay Massacre, and it shocked the entire nation—except Dudley Thompson. "*No angels died at Green Bay*," he coldly commented. But on which end of the guns were the devils? We still don't know exactly what the PNP feared from this little gang. It was affiliated to the JLP, but its members had nothing—not even guns as they hoped to get some when they followed the infiltrated policemen. What danger did they represent that it was necessary to eliminate them so brutally? "*They were about to bring the thing too far*," anonymously confessed a PNP activist, one day. "*We couldn't tolerate that.*" Mystery—and ballot papers.

The artists jumped on the latest fashionable rhythms to manifest their discontent over the Green Bay Massacre. The victims became the symbols of a whole nation misled by brotherly hate. Some communities partly bulldozed, others sacked, countless youths murdéred... Even the Dons started to wonder. What were they killing each other for? Who did all these murders and wars *truly* benefit? Certainly not the people in the communities—not even the *gunmen*. So they decided to quit, all of a sudden. It all started when a notorious PNP enforcer named Bucky Marshall and the Don of TG, Claudie Massop, met in jail. They had no guns, so they talked; and both agreed over a necessary peace truce. Within the twinkle of an eye, guns stopped barking; everyone gathered on the frontline of Pink Lane to smoke the chalice of peace, to play football and to embrace each other. Peace caught the politicians off-guard—Seaga was abroad, trying to convince the Western nations that Jamaica was about to catch fire. This popular and spontaneous movement was the only spark of reason in the middle of a decade of madness; and it came from the worst sprouts of the country, *gunmen*. "*I'm glad to see my brethren once more, I'm glad to see they ain't warring no more / Jungle and Rema are together, once more / Jungle and Rema, Tivoli Gardens, it's nice, it's cool to be like one brother and sister,*" sang Leroy Smart. But behind closed doors, the evil ones were planning their next move. For these hard-core warriors, peace was just a means to get unnoticed at their enemies. "*And if a man decide fi break this peace treaty (...), come make we kick out him two front teeth!*" warned another artist—big deal! As Claudie Massop and the Peace Council contacted Bob Marley in England so he would attend the reconciliation concert, Edward Seaga came back to Jamaica to celebrate peace while meditating war.

Bob Marley had almost been killed over politics in 1976 (see portrait), and had run away to England. But he came back for the One Love Peace Concert in 1978; he was welcomed as a national hero. Many *gunmen* came to his place to smoke a *spliff* (joint), and a few photographs show him rubbing shoulders with Claudie Massop and Bucky Marshall. Bob got along well with Massop—

the singer had grown up in Rema, the JLP part of Trench Town. Some say he even bought a BMW to the Don, who went on tour with him in the US. Bob had always been fascinated by *badmen*. He had a lot of them around him, including the footballer Alan "Skill" Cole, a part-time thug—one of his Trench Town obsessions, probably. Furthermore, Massop was no ordinary Don. Apart from an impressive criminal records, he also had charisma, a charming smile—you can feel his self-confidence by looking at his pictures. The Peace Treaty turned him into a providential angel of peace—a sort of redemption. He was celebrated everywhere, even in songs, and little kids called his name in the streets. He started to enjoy it. During the One Love Peace Concert, he witnessed the most curious event of the decade. Under an unusually low moon, almost in a trance, dancing on a hypnotic reggae rhythm, Bob Marley asked Manley and Seaga to join him on stage, right here, right now, to shake hands, to show the people that everything would be all right, that peace was at hand. The crowd shivered with emotion. Only Bob could unite the Montagues and the Capulets—he raised their hands over his head, singing: *one love, one heart, let's live together and feel all right*. But it was just a song. "*At that historic moment,*" commented Seaga, "*Jamaica was one people, one nation.*" That's almost all he had to say about this handshake. The photographs and the films still show how uneasy and uncomfortable he was. It was obviously a painful moment for him; especially as Manley took time to join him on stage. Seaga stood alone for a while, as if waiting on Manley's good will—what an outrage! To believe in peace at this fleeting instant was so comforting that many people forgot that the fragile reconciliation in the Shakespearian Verona had taken place over warm bodies. Did Seaga want peace, he who had built his political tactics on war? During the One Love Peace Concert, a cynical Peter Tosh almost spoilt the joy, giggling while talking about the peace concert where, he said, he had first refused to appear. To him, peace was the diploma you got when you entered a cemetery, *rest in peace*.

What did he advocate then? Justice. But this was even harder to find in Jamaica.

Claudie Massop started to enjoy his position at the head of the Peace Council, and declared that he would run for the seat of the constituency of Tivoli Gardens for the next election. But, wondered the journalists, what about Seaga? A warlord who didn't care for his community, retorted the Don. This was as good as an official declaration of war. And it is delicate to defy a blind man who has so many pistols at hand.

We can hardly understand what went on behind closed doors—we must stick to facts, and try to link them with one another, as logically as possible, without jumping to conclusion. As Massop fell out with Seaga, a young *gunman* was making sure he would benefit from the truce. His name was Lester Coke aka Jim Brown—a reference to the black protagonist of the movie *The Dirty Dozen* (1967). According to Don Taylor, the late manager of Bob Marley, he had personally led the assassination attempt perpetrated on the singer in 1976. During the truce, Jim Brown got close to some PNP enforcers. The most trusties ended up in a pool of blood. Was Jim Brown the providential man Seaga was looking for? Their ambitions appeared to be quite complementary, to say the least; especially as far as Claudie Massop was concerned.

On February 4, 1978, coming back from a football match with a friend, Massop spotted two policemen riding motorbikes in the wake of his taxi. The vehicle was stopped at the corner of Industrial Terrace and Marcus Garvey Drive, the passengers searched for—one gun was found inside the car. As they stood outside with their hands up, the two passengers and the driver saw one of the policemen walking towards a car parked nearby. He spoke to someone inside, then turned round and shout: "*Kill them!*" Massop started: "*Wai...*"—but was cut off by a shower of bullets. Some fifty were retrieved from his body, Seaga writes 129. This is the version of the driver who escaped from the shooting by crawling to the nearby sea and jumping into the water. The police claimed Massop had shot first. How come he had several wounds under his armpits, then? For one reason, the Don's hands were raised when he got shot. Seaga was apparently outraged by his man's brutal ending, and he denounced a *state murder* in his memoirs; but in the street some thought Jim Brown might have planned the murder on Seaga's orders—rumours, of course. Anyway, Massop's *dismissal* enabled Jim Brown to become the Don of TG at the break of the bloodiest election ever. At the same time, Seaga was getting rid of a dissenting voice—and a serious contender. Not to mention that this murder rang the end of the truce. Terror could start again. Thirty years later, the Tivolites still mourn Claudie Massop. His death is celebrated every year with a dance attended by the youths of the garrison. Massop's mother loves to turn up at the show—out of respect, she is handed the microphone; she sometimes talks for one hour straight. *"Respect to Jim Brown! Respect to Dudus, and respect to all the Dons!"* she shouts. *"But the greatest Don of all was my son, Claudie Massop; and he came from this womb!"* The kids patiently listen to her, until the party resumes.

After Massop's murder, Jamaica plunged back into chaos. But this time, the PNP was cornered. *The Gleaner*, seen as the servile tool of the opposition by the PNP, kept on pouring *daily lies* about the Manley's administration. At the Marxist International Congress of 1979, the Cuban delegate called Seaga a *fascist*. Eddie's plans were working out; the powerful turned their attention to this small island of the Caribbean, fearing a communist contagion. *"Jamaica was now the centre of an espionage and psychological war,"* triumphed the politician. A former agent named Philip Agee denounced some CIA agents operating in the island—they were all working at the US embassy. The leftist publication *Covert Action* published a list of names, and one of the incriminated had his house set afire. The incident made the front cover of the *New York Times*, the red threat was closing in. Did the CIA support Seaga—and did it provide him with guns? We can't help thinking about the shipment of guns that allegedly came to Jamaica in the same boat that carried the equipment for the One Love Peace Concert—cynicism to its peak. As people celebrated peace on stage, war was planned backstage. *Smile, you're in Jamaica.* It seemed logical for the CIA to support the JLP—they had common interests. But did they go that far? Was Seaga directly implied in firearms deliveries, or did he simply turn a blind eye? Who knew? Who acted? What about the trailer of shotgun cartridges seized in the Kingston Free Zone in 1978, and consigned to Moonex, *a parastatal organization of the government of Cuba*, to quote Seaga? The Minister of Security, Dudley Thompson, refused the trailer to be publicly opened. So who was doing evil? And to which extent? Hard to say, and harder to demonstrate. Anyway, Michael Manley himself was positive: the CIA had never been at work in Jamaica. All right.

In the streets, some people were killed, others starved—flour, coconut oil, rice or soap, everything was wanted. The shelves of the shops were like the pockets of the buyers, empty. *Joshua, your rod is digging out our eyes!* lamented the singer Bill Gentles, cunningly forging Max Romeo's *Let The Power Fall On I*. And the song hit the right chord—wrongfully blamed as the author, Max Romeo was rushed by a mob of enraged PNP supporters, and left the island shortly afterwards. Meanwhile, the shelves of the supermarkets remained empty—because of the irresponsible policies of the socialists, claimed the JLP; because of the international JLP plot aimed at destabilizing Manley's administration, retorted the PNP. Sent to the Middle East to collect some funds, Dudley Thompson publicly blamed the US support as a poison slowly killing those it pretended to help. The Libyans relayed his words, and the scandal took an international dimension; Manley tried to cope with this new tribulation. With his back against the wall, Manley had no choice but to call for anticipated election in 1980. The JLP exulted. Seaga was in a strong position, and he knew it—he could already hear the bell of victory ringing. The campaign was a bloody one—some police stations came under attack, and many innocent or guilty citizens fell under stray or straight bullets. In certain PNP communities, some people heard the blades of knives scraping the zinc fences. Like *duppies,* some devilish spirits giggled: *deliverance is near, deliverance is near*—the JLP slogan. It is said that Manley realized he couldn't win; that he spread the word to the PNP supporters not to resort to violence, and not to answer provocations. The 1980 election cost the lives of more than 800 people. Once the dust had settled, Jamaica woke up on the undisputed victory of Eddie.

On that evening of October 30, he was home when the news reached him. The JLP wan 51 parliamentary seats out of 60. But Eddie didn't rush out to rejoice, no. He called for an Anglican priest instead; and kneeled down with all his family, feeling *the need to humble* (him)*self before God and seek his blessing.* Amen. Shortly afterwards, our humble lamb triumphantly entered the bubbling JLP headquarters. After eight years of socialist dream—which had turned to a nightmare—, a victorious Seaga stepped on the ruins of the nation. Backstage, Jim Brown rejoiced—his advancement would follow his master's. At the break of the 1980s, Jamaica could breathe for the first time in almost ten years' time—not yet conscious that the scars are sometimes as painful as the wounds.

Seaganomics

At the turn of the 1980s, injured and recovering, Jamaica withdrew within herself. Music underwent a crucial and revealing change: it became less tensed, and the artists shifted from apocalyptic warnings to lighter topics like *slackness*, a sexually explicit genre that became the order of the day. Yellowman, an albino deejay with incredible talent took it all thanks to his humorous lyrics—and a few stolen rhymes. Nothing mattered apart from the ghetto and the Jamaican way of life. In dances, reports were improvised on the spot; the latest dance moves were commented while people *skanked* and *wined* on consensual rhythms. Microphones changed hand every minute in a celebration of the present moment. This new style was called *dance hall,* and it was a brutal change for Western amateurs. They were first surprised; then bored, and eventually disgusted by this new style. *Island Music* and *Virgin Records*, the two records companies that had established *Reggae music* on the international scene, lost interest in the genre after Bob Marley's passing in 1981. The Jamaican music went on in closed circuit, indifferent to the outside—but a self-centred mythology has never scared islanders.

Meanwhile, liberalism set foot in Jamaica. Seaga invited his old friend Ronald Reagan to Jamaica (Eddie had become the first foreign statesman officially invited to the White House after Reagan's victory). The US president's visit didn't last more than eighteen hours, but he still found time to blunder, evoking the *former communist regime* of Jamaica. Even *The Gleaner* confessed that his visit aroused little enthusiasm. But Eddie had a good reputation among the western liberals, and made good use of it by getting a fantastic loan from the IMF—681 million dollars over three years—while avoiding too drastic a devaluation of the Jamaican currency. His allegiance to liberalism had first comforted his partners, who nonetheless frowned at his nationalising the ESSO refinery, or his maintaining the Jamaican National Export Corporation set up by Manley. The IMF eventually grew disillusioned with him, and his relationship with the USA remained mixed—a result of the subtlety of what economists called the *Seaganomics*. Yet he had to comply with a few claims of the IMF, including the opening of a Free Zone in Kingston. Aimed at creating jobs, it was in fact a dream come true for foreign investors. Devaluation was unavoidable, as well as drastic cuts in social programs. The first years were promising as Jamaica was coming back from far with an unemployment rate of 27%, a plunging GDP, brain drain and capital flight. Within his first year in power, Edward Seaga put things back on an even keel—but imports remained very high and the local production almost inexistent. And when international funding stopped, the miracle stopped as well. The agriculture went down first; then followed the mining industry, and eventually trade on a whole. After three years in power, the JLP had mixed results—some already foretold the return of the PNP to power for 1985. Furthermore, Michael Manley, who had been down for a while, was recovering pretty fast. Re-elected at the head of his party, he appeared quite convincing as a man of principle willing to learn from his past mistakes. Invigorated and quite comfortable in his new role, he attacked Seaga, calling him an *inconsistent* politician.

On his part, Eddie grew fond of travels—did he have an ulterior motive? Indeed, in 1983 he became an international figure. Four years earlier, his prophecy of a red wave overwhelming the Caribbean came to pass—so to speak. It didn't take place in Jamaica but in Barbados, where a Marxist-Leninist *coup* supported by Cuba overthrew the regime. Nevertheless, the real problem didn't arise from the communists, but from the bloody counter-revolution of 1983, that ended up with the execution of the revolutionary leader Maurice Bishop. The neighbouring countries were shocked at the violence of this movement and called for an intervention of the United States. Edward Seaga proved himself a faithful partner of the Eagle by sending a contingent of troops in Barbados. The Jamaican population reacted so positively to his decision that the Prime Minister hastily dismissed the Parliament and called for an anticipated general election. This was a hard blow to the PNP that decided to boycott it—it stood no chance anyway. Eddie's triumph was complete. Thanks to his *stomach of iron*, he had subdued the island, stepped on the throat of the PNP and was now stretching forth his hand to the powerful liberal nations of the world. Five long years of happiness opened before him.

In the ghettoes, the Seaganomics also bore juicy fruits. The *gunmen* had become experts in trafficking, and intended to enjoy the remorseless splendour of the 1980s. Politics was cast in the background, and while Eddie publicly rejoiced at the decline in crime rate, the Tivolites set up an international branch in New York—one Vivian Blake became the executive director of this lucrative start-up. That's when the worms started to eat up the Big Apple—the 1980s. Crack, a new drug derived from coke, was cheaper and much more addictive—it became the secret weapon of the Jamaican *posses*, or gangs, in New York. Commercial prospects were boundless; cash started to flow in, and Jamaican *gunmen* rushed New York like mad dogs. The US gangsters learnt to fear these crazy guys who resorted to violence at the slightest provocation, piling corpses like old *spliff* tails, and perpetuating their folkloric traditions such as killing up to the dogs of their enemies. The Jamaicans had the reputation of being inflexible—and indeed, they didn't care to *flex* (get along) with anyone. They had come—end of the discussion. When the first public gun battles alerted the FBI, the Jamaican *posses* were already well established from Florida to California to New York.

The Jamaican-American Dons never forgot where they came from, and usually recruited their soldiers *ah yard* (in the island)—they were more loyal and efficient. They usually sent a good part of their money back to their community where the people celebrated their generosity. Some dances bore their names, their portraits were painted on the walls, and the kids saw them as role models who had gone to New York to *make it big inna life.*

Self-reliance and money soon generated a desire for independence; the Dons had grown sick and tired of politics. They kept one fighting over territories in Jamaica but these wars were now related to drugs and extortion rather than to ballots. The politicians couldn't tolerate such a shift of allegiance—a terrible arm-wrestling contest started. In 1982, a special unit was created; it bore the dreadful name of Eradication Squad. Its members were sent into the volatile communities to discipline the reluctant *gunmen*. "*Sometimes they make mistake,*" sang the artist Eek-A-Mouse, "*and kill pure innocent ones.*" But sometimes they didn't. Anyway, many youths—innocent or not—fell under their bullets. At the same time, the Americans imposed a drastic ban on marijuana. A helicopter from the DEA started to fly over the Blue Mountains, looking for the marijuana fields lost in the luxurious vegetation. Many farmers drawn to illegal activities by poverty saw their last hope of survival consumed by flames. "*But if you continue to burn up the herbs, we gonna burn down the cane-*

fields," warned a song at the time. This obsession to fight marijuana boosted the coke business in the island. The *posses* arriving in America was the last development of the policy of terror set up by the Jamaican politicians.

Eddie was neither a bad Prime Minister nor a good one. Just like his friend Reagan, he acted as a cowboy, jumping on any horse and whipping away the collateral damage with despising gestures—*what are a few broken skulls in the history of a nation?* once asked his mentor Busta.

For his part, Michael Manley stayed far from his former communist diatribes, and proved himself a humble repentant, denouncing the policy of terror orchestrated by the JLP while hobnobbing with the same old warlords of his own party. In 1986, the PNP wan the local election—people were dissatisfied with the Seaganomics. Eddie rejects this analysis, but at the same period he also rejected the joined demands of the IMF and the World Bank for more austerity. The country was at the end of the rope; teachers, doctors or transporters—everyone went on strike. People were suffering, and crime was spreading. To live under the yoke of organized crime is no bed of roses, and the era of Dons was far from fading away. In 1987, Lester "Jim Brown" Coke was freed of all charges in a case of murder—the notorious Rema Massacre of 1984. As he walked out of the tribunal, his men aligned in King Street and Tower Street fired a general gun salute in the open, creating panic. *Anarchy!* read the front page of *The Gleaner.* Several Jamaican cases involving drugs trafficking and organized crime were reported in foreign newspapers. Michael Manley officially asked for an inquiry over the links between Tivoli Gardens and the coke trade in the island. Meanwhile, CBS broadcast the compromising images of a Don giving an important sum of money to a politician during the PNP National Conference of 1987. The politicians' secrets were now open ones—but brought no dismissal, no demission, and no sanction. Crime and politics were so interwoven that it had become impossible to fight one without killing both. So they stuck together, holding tight while blaming crime and corruption. But Dons had become so powerful that the PNP and the JLP decided to unite against their new and common enemy—a gentlemen's agreement, so to speak. At the end of 1987, *The Gleaner* published the unexpected photograph of the two worst enemies of the Caribbean, Michael and Eddie, shaking hands once again. It was taken during a National Prayer Breakfast—a meaningful symbol. Bob Marley wasn't here anymore to cheer everyone up with a song. Anyway, no one in Jamaica listened to the music of this false prophet any more.

The Jim Brown Story

There is a powerful photograph from *The Gleaner* that tells a decade of complicity between one of the worst notorious gangster of Jamaica, Lester "Jim Brown" Coke, and his silent Lord, the blind man with a pistol—Edward Seaga. This photograph, just like the story, needs to be deciphered. Your eyes are first attracted to a widow clad in black and bent in front of a coffin, in the middle of the picture; there your eyes stop for a while over her expensive and ostentatious clothes. You still don't exactly know what you're looking at; then you naturally follow the widow's look, down to the dead face of Jim Brown. The Don is lying in a coffin, wearing a pair of sunglasses; the dreadful master of TG lies in satin and mahogany, but his face isn't covered with burns—the embalmer did a wonderful job. This is 1989, during Jim Brown's funeral in Kingston. Just as you are about to look away, you make out a blemish face in the top left-hand corner of the picture, dully overlooking the whole scene like an exterminator angel—Eddie! This is a breath-taking apparition that tells the whole Jamaican tragedy through a unique transversal axis of evil. It is a disturbing and cynical moment, as the most important statesman of the country is paying tribute to its most notorious criminal.*

---

* Just like Michael Manley and several Cabinet members led a 20,000 mourners at Winston "Burry Boy" Blake's funeral in 1975.

Furthermore, chances are that the former was involved in the murder of the latter. Indeed, when Jim Brown was burnt to death in his cell after he had threatened to reveal certain things, some evil-minded observers pointed their finger at the honourable Eddie. Indeed, his creature had become—how could we put it? *Embarrassing*. Jim Brown's links with the Shower Posse based in the US had attracted the attention of the FBI—they spied, observed, and accumulated evidences before asking for his extradition. America was a friend that Jamaica could hardly turn down. Jim Brown was arrested and jailed, and about to be delivered to the FBI. The Don panicked, and played what he thought was his trump card. Fearing his lord might be reluctant to openly support him, he warned: should he go down, many would follow—he had things to say! Shortly afterwards, a fire started in his cell. Half-burnt and half-suffocated, the Don who had taken twelve lives in a raw five years before, agonized for hours among several unmoved policemen. No one helped him out; no one intervened—somebody made sure he wouldn't survive.

Anyway, after the 1980 election the relationship between the politicians and their Dons wasn't as good as it used to. "*The intensive use of the gun in politically partisan rivalries of the 1970s left opposing forces in the 1980s with little to oppose after the rivalries ended,*" wrote Seaga. The *ganja* (marijuana) trade was now the most lucrative among *badmen*; the sums involved were colossal but, *traditionally, governments had turned a blind eye to the activity because prosecution was not taken as a serious mission*, explained Eddie. Everything changed when the US decided to eradicate the trade. Seaga had to launch the Drug Abuse Committee in 1983 to satisfy his powerful neighbours, and partners. But the Dons refused to obey. One of them, directly stigmatized by the Prime Minister in 1985, planned to kidnap Seaga's son, Andrew. The Special Branch intervened on time, said Eddie in 2010, and the Don ran away to another island, *from which he still continues to operate* (Seaga). In 1988, one Michael

Vogel quoted the name of Edward Seaga in front of an American Senate committee; but the witness wasn't credible, as he accused the Prime Minister of sheltering his own brother in his hidden property of the Cayman Islands—but Eddie never had any brother. Vogel wasn't the ordinary mule, or petty trafficker, though; he was charged for smuggling dozens of tons of herb and cocaine in the US between 1982 and 1984. He probably tried to belittle his sentence by giving away a *bigger head*—he was unsuccessful.

The body of evidence against Seaga is disturbing. But did he really organize the business, like a Mafioso, ordering some executions, diverting cargos, and arming his TG garrison? Was he an active warlord? The street will tell you he was—and has always been. But the street says many things. In 1995, the American journalist Laurie Gunst published her book *Born Fi' Dead*, openly accusing him of being an active warlord. When she went on a Jamaican TV show to confirm her writings, the politician sued her, demanding $500,000 damage. Laurie Gunst raged: "*Over my dead body!*" But she hasn't produced any concrete proof of Seaga's responsibility yet. Anyway, the suspicious death of Jim Brown unsettled politicians. The little local arrangements started to be exposed internationally, scandals weren't that easily covered up now, and who, in this still recovering Jamaica, could brag of being innocent? Eddie, maybe—who didn't write a sole line in his memoirs about Jim Brown, a man he yet accompanied to his final resting place—probably a regrettable oversight.

Gilbert 89

After the euphoria of 1983, Jamaica entered a dark era. The lightness turned into inconsistence, dirty money infiltrated every stratum of society, including music. Some suspicious producers supported their *badmen* friends with a musical inclination—it led to ostracism, and to the shameless glorification of sexual and criminal exploits. "*This was dance hall,*" explained Seaga, "*a renegade subculture that provided the ultimate in antisocial* outrage, 'badmanism', in retaliation for historical repression. This subculture venerated money, sex and drugs. It created its own revealing dress style to attract attention, adorned with 'bling bling'." Whereas Rasta music had always aimed at uplifting people, *dance hall* glorified Man in his mediocrity, flattered the ego and disrespected the values of a whole generation that had disappeared in the vapours of crack pipes. Meanwhile, people in the street saw their Dons as tragic heroes—Jamaicans have always been on the lookout for leaders. "*In Jamaica,*" wrote Seaga, "*support for a political party rests to a great extent on the popularity of the leader. It is the leader who rises and the leader who falls. This has been so throughout our modern political history. The popularity of the leader is of prime concern.*" It is true. And his entire career was built upon this phenomenon—Eddie was a cowboy who excited the crowd, terrorized his enemies, and cheered up his troops with authority. The scenario may have been weak, but the lead role was brilliant. Let's remember that before being the name of his garrison, Tivoli was the name of a movie theatre. Yet, Eddie lost ground in the 1980s, even considering retiring from politics to save his marriage. Furthermore, he had the feeling that Jamaicans weren't intelligent enough to understand the international economic situation. The devaluation of the Jamaican currency—which increased the price of basic commodities, the rate of unemployment and social insecurity—was due to the world price of bauxite. But trying to explain something that simple to the Jamaicans seemed useless. The JLP lost ground with the people, and its members were perceived as a corrupt bunch of cocktails-goers who visited their remote parishes only when ordered by Seaga. More than ever, the JLP was the party of the Haves. Except for the intervention in Barbados, Seaga's popularity rate remained very low all through his two mandates. And if external events had worked in favour of the JLP in 1983, Hurricane Gilbert reversed the trend six years later.

On September 12, 1989, Jamaica woke up under siege. Everyone was expecting Hurricane Gilbert, an undesirable guest.

It hit Jamaica and left it agonizing. Sitting in a sporting aeroplane and flying over the devastated parish of Saint Thomas, Edward Seaga beheld an apocalyptic landscape. The Prime Minister handled the situation quite good, federating people of good will—including Michael Manley—and rapidly raising funds from the World Bank. But a disruptive event wasted it all. In the middle of chaos, the 500,000 people left homeless by the hurricane were in need of everything, but mainly of corrugated zinc fences to rapidly build shelters—yet they couldn't find any. The PNP saw an opportunity, and launched a rumour: the JLP refused to give away zinc fences to the people in need. It created an immediate scandal. So that no matter how hard Seaga was working, building million dollars emergency plans, he remained far from the aspirations of the people who expected nothing but zinc fences. More than ever, the JLP officials appeared locked in their ivory tower whereas the PNP kept on claiming that it *put people first*—its official slogan for the 1989 campaign.

The JLP was defeated in 1989. Eddie was infuriated. Manley the populist, Manley the demagogue, had done it again—just like in the 1970s! Jamaicans would never learn, and would always give in the wishful thinking and dangerous promises of the PNP! The Jamaicans didn't vote with their brains but with their hearts—this was hopeless. No matter the consequences of his policies, Michael Manley remained the so-called friend of the Have-nots. Talk about the pot calling the kettle black! Posing as a dignified and rightful citizen painfully conscious of his duty, Seaga let the power go with contempt, stating in his memoirs that it was impossible to fight such an irrational thought. He also reflected on the zinc distribution scandal with anger, reminding that $400,000 of zinc handled by the JLP to the PNP after the elections were eventually distributed to gang members on both sides. He went further: "*Political activists became dealers in zinc and drove zinc factory (GI Industry) out of business. Zinc was used instead of money to bribe voters in the 1990 local government election.*"

The 1990s

Defeat always stunned Eddie. This time, several dissidents from the JLP tried to take advantage of his downfall, and silently gathered at night for secret meetings. There were five of them, and the journalist Carl Stone called them *the Gang of Five*—a reference to the pro-Mao Gang of Four. Backstage, they worked at destabilizing Eddie, whom they depicted as an authoritarian leader, a one-man band obsessed with controlling everything. According to the Gang of Five, Eddie had subdued the JLP. Poor Eddie, facing a conspiracy! He lost his temper, and sent these unruly children to *light a candle, sing a 'Sankey' and find their way back home*. The invective was rude and despising, as usual—but the Gang of Five wasn't that glorious either. Led by Charles Peanel, it durst not facing a dreaded Seaga, and contented itself with a guerrilla of misinformation. In politics, the most abject tactics are often the most efficient; this one almost worked out. For a while, Eddie's best friends apparently considered letting him down; they started to criticise him behind his back—even the street started to complain about him. But Seaga has always loved hardship—it brings the best out of him. Furthermore, the Gang of Five made a mistake; they didn't appoint any leader to compete with Seaga in people's minds. Their *coup* died by itself, and three of these five *rude boys* came back home in July 1991, accepting the harsh conditions imposed by their master—their Sankey.

In March 1992, the political face of Jamaica changed forever as Michael Manley retired from politics. He had been fighting against cancer for years, a battle he eventually lost in 1997. In the JLP garrisons, people rejoiced, convinced that Kapo, the occult counsellor of Seaga, had finally decided to send a curse to Joshua. Seaga publicly paid a moving tribute to his enemy, which sounded like a victory speech. Pretending to praise Manley's passion, he reproached him his extremism, and blamed him for all the misery of Jamaica. He nevertheless praised his intellectual honesty that enabled him to come back to reason in the 1980s by giving up his socialist aspirations. Edward Seaga congratulated him for that.

He couldn't go as far as denying Manley's intelligence, or his international vision of politics. Manley had always been a sophisticated man, and even cancer couldn't belittle his charisma. Seaga would never enjoy this kind of aura, and seemed painfully conscious of it. But show had to go on, with or without Manley. His successor PJ Patterson was a serious opponent although he had been dismissed from Cabinet the previous year, following the Shell Waiver scandal. Claiming to be the victim of superior interests, Patterson had stepped down, prophesising: *I will be back!* And he did come back a few months later, directly propelled to the highest position of the country—he entered the 1993 campaign with enthusiasm, travelling the island to meet people, shaking hands, and sharing his vision for Jamaica. His victory was the most contested ever by the JLP—it has always accused the PNP of rigging the election by filling the boxes with dead people's ballots—or people who were never born. But Eddie knew about low blows too. Always on the lookout for his enemies' weaknesses, he realized that PJ Patterson was single. Divorced, the Prime Minister was the father of two, but nobody ever saw him with a woman. How come? Backstage, the worried PNP activists winked to the journalists: "*PJ fucks like a rabbit, man! But him loves married women, so him do him thing secretly.*" Seaga had another story to tell, which he did in front of a JLP crowd in 1997: "*Nobody can sing* Boom Bye Bye *for me!*" The crowd went wild at the reference to Buju Banton's hit song. Buju Banton was only fifteen when, in 1988, he tried to make a name for himself in the music business with his homophobic song *Boom Bye Bye*. The lyrics advocated to burn homosexuals like *old tyres*. Re-released in 1992, it became an instant hit—and the curse of his career. He is still caught today* between the pressure of the street and the financial pressure imposed on him by international gay lobbies that prevent him from touring.

---

* Since this book was first published, Buju Banton was arrested for drug trafficking in America, where he is currently incarcerated.

Eddie giggled—a good one. Did he only believe in what he insinuated? Probably not. But in politics, you just need a small cloud of smoke to create a fire. And this one caught at once. Homophobia is very strong in Jamaica—justified without any ambiguity by the Holy Bible and encouraged by society at large, it is openly expressed. As a matter of fact it must be the most federating opinion in the island—a blessing for any artist longing for recognition. The first homophobic songs appeared in the early 1980s, as anyone could grab the microphone in a dance to say whatever he had on the top of his mind. The audience was hard to please, and the exercise quite risky—when the crowd wasn't responding, the artist started to insult *battymen,* or *chi chi men*—two patois words for homosexuals. Edward Seaga probably knew what he was talking about when he invoked populism about Manley—after all, he proved he was very good at it himself. As Patterson went on TV to justify his sexual orientation, a wave of homophobic songs hit Jamaica. Eddie didn't care; he had always fought as a blind man, shooting at random and waiting for one of his stray bullets to hit something—upon hearing *Ouch!,* he knew he had hit a target, and he started to fire restlessly. Thus, during the local election in the parish of St Ann, the JLP had the brilliant idea to use the song *Chi Chi Man* by T.O.K as an official campaign hymn. "*From them a par inna chi chi man car / Blaze the fire make me bu(r)n dem / From them a drink inna chi chi man bar / Blaze the fire make we bu(r)n them.*" When Eddie sawed, it was no mustard grain, but the seed of discord. In the middle of the ensuing tempest, he reaped the power and the glory.

And no one would sing *Chi Chi Man* for him, indeed. Divorced from the beautiful and black Misty, he remarried a former female collaborator from the 1980s, thirty years younger than him, the less beautiful, but whiter Carla Vendryes—she gave him a daughter in September 2002. Meanwhile, he failed as a businessman. His property of Enchanted Garden near Turtle Beach, with its three waterfalls—one of them named by Mick Jagger himself—, was a small lot of paradise when he bought it.

But he hardly knew how to make it lucrative. First conceived as a natural reservation for some wealthy American tourists, it became a touristic complex before declining; it eventually resurfaced as a housing scheme before being placed into liquidation in 1999. This was the end of the enchanted garden, back to Tivoli Gardens.

TG Raid

June 2010. Invited to a local TV show, Edward Seaga cried over his poor little garrison of Tivoli Gardens. A few days earlier, the army and the police had raided his turf in armoured cars, looking for Tivoli's Don, Christopher "Dudus" Coke—Jim Brown's adoptive son and heir. For the past twenty years, the Don had ruled the most notorious community of Jamaica. A secretive man, he was described by his supporters as an honourable businessman—and a providential bread-giver. The whole world suddenly discovered his face through the only two pictures of him then available—one of them was a nice black and white shot, upon which he appeared quite charismatic, wearing sunglasses and a gentle smile. Dudus' case had been the order of the day for the past six months. It all started when the FBI demanded the extradition of the Don, whose name had popped up in a case instructed by the DEA—some phone discussions involved the Don into an international drug trade. The JLP Prime Minister then in power, Bruce Golding, was deeply embarrassed. History repeated itself, but Christopher was no Lester, and Golding no Seaga.

Eddie did his best to dry his tears in front of the camera—in fact, he cried over himself rather than over Tivoli, but it's almost the same. He had a thought for his relatives, too; whom he had neglected all these years. How sad and beautiful! In fact, Seaga probably rejoiced at Bruce Golding's downfall. This ungrateful creature, the only one who ever forced him to bow, the unworthy heir of the mighty kingdom of Tivoli Gardens, publicly failing! Seaga had retired in 2005 and could at last peacefully enjoy some rest—no one could beat him. His glory would remain unstained. But the baby he gave to Golding had been sick for a long time. Eddie's dream, the beautiful Tivoli, had become an independent *republic*—to be honest, it was more of a dictatorship ruled by Jim Brown's son, Christopher. The latter had a nickname, Dudus. Whispered in fear or proudly shouted out, it had been all over Kingston ever since the DEA had asked for him. Little was known about him, except that he had been a peaceful Don, who had lived in peace with the rival PNP Don of downtown Kingston, Donald "Zeeks" Phipps. Dudus was a modern Don who wore suits and ties, just like an ordinary businessman—a sort of white-collar criminal. He even owned a construction enterprise; convenient to get public contracts. But he also had various activities that were of interest to the FBI and the DEA. When he learnt about the extradition warrant, Dudus didn't make the same mistake than his father. Advised by his lawyer, Jim Brown had agreed to negotiate with the government; when he had reached the meeting, he had been arrested—and then chewed up by the big bad wolf.

Dudus decided to barricade himself in TG. His new Lord, Prime Minister Golding, was behind him; he even hired an American lobby firm to try to cover up the case in Washington—another failure, another scandal. Of course, people wondered where was so much zeal coming from. Did he fear what the Don might say to the US authorities? Obviously, this is what had cost his father's life in 1989. But something else was a stake with Golding, something deeper. He had to be up to it, to prove he was as tough as Seaga. The street was clear about the whole situation: a good leader with *a heart of gold and a stomach of iron* would never let his man down—not to mention his party that could be compromised. The street credibility of Golding was at stake—a real leader *nah bow,* never bows. A leader's garrison is his castle. Jamaica is a tough men country; you need to have guts to earn the respect of your pairs. Especially when you're in the construction business. Unfortunately, Golding never lived up to the challenge—not everyone could match Eddie's standards.

Within a few months, the situation reached a dead-end. *Was Golding qualified to deal with this?* asked the TV journalist. Seaga shook his head in despair. He stared at the journalist and confessed he had never really trusted Golding—not authoritarian enough to rule Tivoli. Unfortunately, aged 75, Eddie *had* to retire—because of his family, etc. So he had appointed his less evil creature as a successor, Golding. The latter had yet been a rebellious disciple. He had stood by Seaga for more than twenty years but was too proud a man, and consequently not fully reliable. Eddie probably lost faith in Bruce after his betrayal of 1995 when, tired of his tyrannical master, Golding decided to rebel with a handful of accomplices—the Gang of Five. Seaga was then facing serious hardship. Indeed, the JLP community of Rema, in Trench Town, had just shifted alliance to the PNP—a mark of distrust from West Kingston was the worse backlash the politician could ever get. The *gunmen* from Rema and their new PNP friends of Concrete Jungle had started to retaliate for many years of ill treatment. This political shift pushed them to attack the neighbouring JLP community of Denham Town—*as they weren't powerful enough to deal with Tivoli Gardens*, stated Seaga. Denham Town was indeed a far easier target, and the terrorised inhabitants started to leave it by the hundreds—a worrying haemorrhage of ballots. For the first time, Seaga was losing ground in his own turf.

The JLP dissidents pretended to be concerned, and sympathized with the old blind man: *let's not criticize him*, they said, *he's got enough problems for the time being*. Eddie felt that things might get out of hands, so he jumped on his horse and asked for a vote of confidence within his party—he wan by a landside. Generous and brutal, he dropped: *"Argument done!"*, in a pure John Wayne style. But the argument wasn't exactly done. In November 1995, Golding resigned from the JLP, and launched his own party, the National Democratic Movement (NDM). He was weaker than his master, and had no choice but to openly oppose him. He denounced tribalism—political warfare—, and corruption as two poisons slowly killing Jamaica. This was a clever position, as Seaga was unanimously associated to political violence in Jamaica. The NDM centred its clean-hands campaign on this argument. Eddie was surprised. A violent man, him? Maybe a little bit impassioned at times, but could we expect less from a man with a heart of gold? After all, Golding wasn't wrong. But who is free of sin? For a while, Golding had embodied a new generation of politicians who claimed to condemn tribalism—a possible redemption for Jamaica. Fifteen years later, after he had run out of ideas to save the head of the most notorious criminal of his country, he jumped on his fierce stallion to publicly declare he would never let Dudus down—didn't that sound like the good ol' Eddie?

After a promising start—Jamaicans love novelty—the NMD was washed out during the 1997 election. An obvious failure, indeed; but over all a good move for Golding who came back home, indeed—but not without imposing a change of direction in the party. Golding sang his *Sankey* off-key, and Eddie was upset—but Bruce remained his creature, though a second best option.

When the police and the army entered the stronghold of Tivoli Gardens in May 2010, two former governments had already failed to take it. But there was something different, this time, as the raid was led by a JLP administration. It was logical for the PNP to overthrow its enemy's stronghold. But TG had always resisted—and Eddie had always risen to the occasion. In 1997, he stepped in the middle of the gun battle to denounce a conspiracy. The army, he said, was shooting up the place to leave false evidences of a tough gun battle. A kid from Denham Town was shot dead by a bullet while looking through his window—was it a stray bullet? Seaga claimed the police had deliberately shot the kid. The fight lasted for several days before the police withdrew from Tivoli Gardens—empty-handed. No *gunmen* corpses, no gun storage, no coke, no cash—nothing. All they had to show were an injured little girl, a dead boy, and three buried women. Commissioner Francis Forbes said the *gunmen* had run away through escape tunnels—but gave no evidence of such tunnels. A few months later, it was election time and the JLP paid the consequences of what Eddie viewed as a political propaganda: *"The damage had been done,"* he wrote. *"The strategy had worked. Electoral corruption still ruled, triggered by state terrorism."*

Good Ol' Eddie

Edward Seaga retired from business, exhausted after so many years of disinterested devotion. Honours poured like rain—some intellectuals from the University of the West Indies where he was appointed speaker, wrote so moving eulogies that he reproduced them at the end of his memoirs. Celebrated Eddie—a man about whom circulates so many dark tales. The *eminence grise* of Jamaica, a blind man with his pockets full of loaded pistols, who has shot at random all his life, feeding his herd of mad dogs in Tivoli, and rooting his power in the stinking ground of *obeah*. Even his worst detractors can't evoke his name without a tang of fear. What's the most powerful turf of one of the crime capitals of the world? Tivoli Gardens—Eddie's Eden.

Nevertheless, what's the part of fantasy in the portrait of a devilish Eddie leading some legions of devils to sack the green pastures of Jamaica? After all, the last—and successful—raid on TG revealed quite a contrasted reality. Yes, the *gunmen* fought back—Dudus even recruited some PNP gun fighters in his army. Times have changed, politics remain in the background but crime is now perceived as a free-lance career. Once the powder had settled, there were 70 dead—*gunmen*, policemen and civilians included. But the stronghold was taken. Where were the dreaded bazookas, the heavy machine gun mounted on a tripod and the other war rifles the Tivolites supposedly owned? Before the raid, some Tivolites marched to support Dudus, publicly advocating his generosity and his love for his people. Some had tied a piece of board on a *maga* (meagre) dog: *Jesus died for us. We'll die for Dudus.* A majority of the community seemed to be behind him—

the Stockholm Syndrom, suggested a psychologist. But the hero finally fell. He was caught a few days later, sitting on the passenger seat of a car; dressed as a woman—including a ridiculous wig—, he wet his pants when stopped—so the police reported. He thought his last hour had come, and we can't blame him. It was quite likely—this is Jamaica. But he was arrested, locked—and his cell didn't catch fire—, and then extradited to America where he was tried and condemned. But we're still waiting for his supposedly devastating revelations about the JLP, Eddie or Golding. Meanwhile, the post-raid investigations in TG excited the whole nation. What would the police find in this terrible place forgotten by God? Escape tunnels loaded with machine guns? None. Dozen of corpses piled in common pits? Only two were found, who had apparently been executed—no big deal in Jamaica. Morbid and scary torture rooms, maybe? One alleged interrogation room was put to light—it was empty. They found some crocodiles, though! And everybody started to speculate about their diet. The animals were killed, but no human flesh was found in their stomachs. What about the booty, then? A few dozens of firearms, and a few thousand rounds of ammunition—and a Don, who wet his pants. So, what? That was Tivoli? The community that terrorized the entire nation for decades? The headquarters of crime in Jamaica? Maybe the place had been cleared off before the raid? Or maybe crime isn't that glamorous, after all—maybe it is just a dull business. But a lucrative one: the fortune of Dudus was estimated at several dozens of million dollars.

 Seaga clearly built his career, and his life, around Tivoli Gardens—he never lost his seat as a Member of Parliament thanks to it. He has preached violence, at least verbally, benefited from its perverted effects, and almost overturned the ship just to grab the helm. The unfortunates who went overboard? Gone with the foam. Maybe Eddie has never been that mean, after all? No *obeah*—just a few guns and a big mouth. His memoirs have just been published in two volumes—they are disappointing. Many dead-ends, even more justifications, and an obvious self-satisfaction. They are sometimes interesting—but never brilliant. No real passion, no in-depth political analysis, not even a good literary style—but gall for his enemies, mostly when he pretends to depict their qualities; contempt for all, and an ever-burning arrogance. Eddie hasn't cooled down, he's the same petty king who stood on the tarmac of the airport in 1966. The good ol' Eddie, man. Has he been the curse of a whole nation? It seems like Eddie has always been a slave to his temper—the prisoner of a system he has applied without remorse or mercy: to sack and rule. A blind man—with lots of pistols.

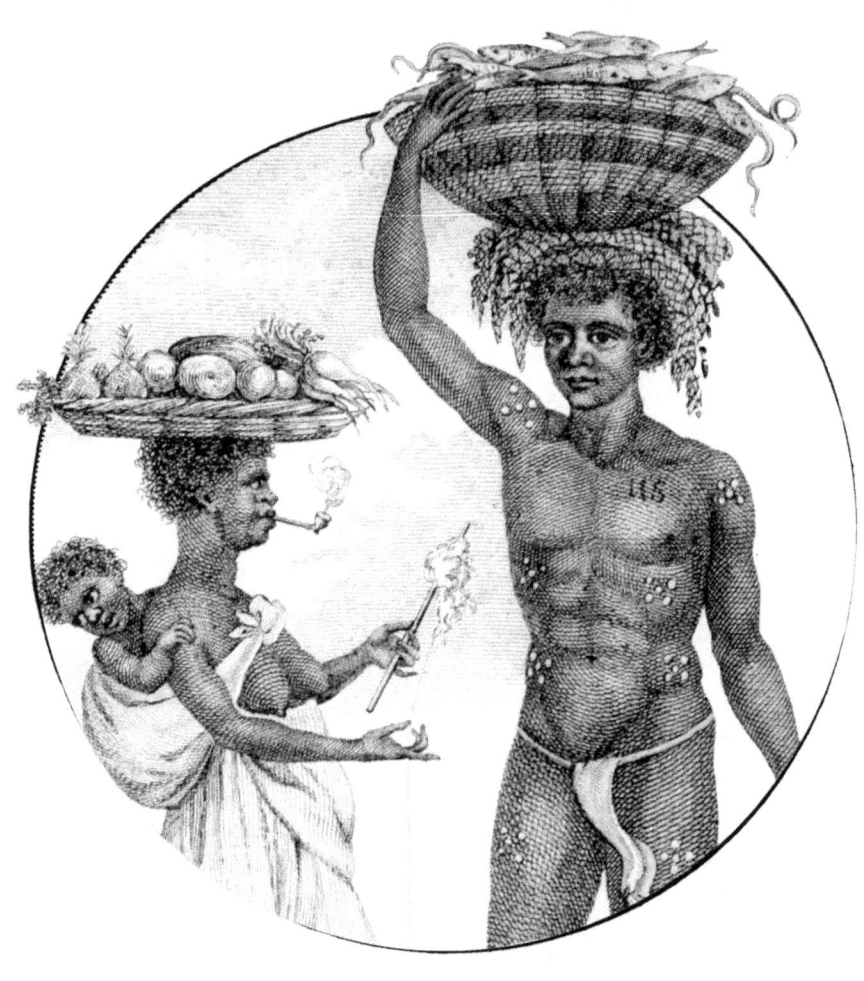

There's no portrait of Tacky. This is a family of slaves
drawn by G. Stedman in the 18th century.
(Dread archives)

Tacky
(unknown -1760)
Not Enough with You, Mr Long!

When Christopher Columbus related his discovery of the New World to the Court of Spain in 1492, he stirred the imagination of the Nobles, who rammed the vessels of his second expedition. They envisioned the wonderful lands described by Marco Polo—Columbus thought he had reached the Indies by circumnavigating the globe—as covered with gold and diamonds. But it wasn't so. The riches of the West Indian islands mostly lied in their fertile soil and their inhabitants that could be exploited at will. In the name of God—and entitled by a bull of Alexander VI, the most corrupt Pope ever—, the Spaniards took possession of these pagan lands, shared them among themselves and put the Indians to hard work. These innocent creatures accustomed to an idle life perished by the thousands from diseases and exhaustion. Not to mention the cruelties they suffered from the Spaniards, who ran amok in the New World. Their daily occupations consisted in cutting Indian babies asunder, breaking children against the rock, cutting off noses, ears and hands, raping and torturing—a Christian's work is never done.

When Father Las Casas went to the New World in 1502, it was to get rich—like everyone else. But the horrors he witnessed were too much to bear. His barbarous countrymen didn't even care about baptizing their victims. Standing up as the *Protector of the Indians*, Las Casas made himself some powerful enemies in Spain; so powerful he had to compromise with them at some point. The Spaniards needed free workers in the West Indies, and they needed them badly. Las Casas then had the worst idea of his life: he suggested replacing the Indians by some Africans. The latter were more resistant and accustomed to tropical climates. Furthermore, they were said to be immortal—unless hanged. Cardinal Ximenes, then regent of the kingdom of Spain, opposed the idea. The Negroes from Africa, he thought, were too aggressive; they might overthrow their masters and establish a black kingdom in America. But Las Casas insisted; he used his connections, and had the ban lifted. The Indians were saved, and the Negroes were doomed. Thus the road to hell of more than eleven million people was paved with the good intentions of one of the most brilliant men of his time—and a true humanist. Let's put this into context, Las Casas' idea didn't shock at the time, and slavery didn't stop when he died. Nevertheless, blinded by the comfort of *his dear Indians*—as the historian Thomas-Guillaume Raynal ironically put it—, he was prejudice to all mankind. The regrets he expressed in his memoirs were sincere, but they came too late. When he passed away aged 92, dozens of slave ships were already crossing the Ocean loaded with their shameful cargo—and there was no Las Casas to stand up in their favour.

The Coromantins

The Europeans were far outnumbered by their slaves in the New World—up to one to twenty; in order to control them, they did everything such *tour de force* required. The Africans weren't prepared to the white invasion—their enemies were far too advanced, and worked hand in hand with some African Kings from the West Coast, who captured the slaves inland, and then sold them to the Whites. They traded them for firearms and various more or less valuable goods. Captured, beaten, separated from their kinsmen, brought across the Ocean to a foreign land, slaves reacted in different ways. Some adapted themselves, others fought back. The history of the Americas is filled with slave revolts, whether coordinated or spontaneous. And Jamaica, where the allegedly most turbulent slaves were disembarked in haste, went through many of these bloody upheavals. The most formidable one happened in 1760; it was planned and led by a slave named Tacky, a Coromantin—the most feared race of slaves. Unruly, resistant and bold, the Coromantins also represented the most lucrative investment for planters—the most dangerous one too. "*Their language is copious, and more regular than any other of the Negroe dialects,*" noted the historian Edward Long in 1774. "*Their music too is livelier, and their dances entirely martial (...) Their dances serve to keep alive that military spirit, for which they are so distinguished; and the figure consists in throwing themselves into all the positions and attitude, customary to them in the heat of an engagement.*" Coromantin is a generic name given to them by the Europeans, and inspired by one of the first English trading posts in Guinea—the Dutch later took it from them. "*This insignificant village, or factory,*" wrote the resentful historian Bryan Edwards in 1793, "*is situated in the kingdom of Fantyn, two miles from the fort of Anamaboe.*" Originating from the entire West Coast of Africa, the Coromantins—or *Koromantyns* according to Edwards' spelling—were from the Ashanti, Fantin and Quamboo tribes. "*Firmness of mind and body, and a ferociousness of disposition, distinguish the Koromantyn or Gold Coast Negroes from all others,*" continued Edwards. "*But with these, they possess activity, courage, and a degree of magnanimity, which incites them to difficult and dangerous enterprises, and enables them to meet death in its most terrible shape, with either fortitude or contempt.*" As far as their fortitude was concerned, Edwards knew what he was talking about, having witnessed it himself—as we shall see.

The Coromantins also maintained a very tight tribal social cohesion. On some plantations, they refused to mingle with other slaves. This secrecy enabled them to celebrate their pagan cults for dozens of years without their masters noticing. These rites, orchestrated by some spiritual guides called *Obeahmen*, came to light during the revolt of 1760.

* * *

On the night preceding Easter Monday of 1760, some fifty slaves rebelled in Port Maria, in the parish of St Mary; and they soon dragged the whole island in their bloody wake. The white Jamaica was caught off guard. «*The conspiracy had been conducted with such profound secrecy that almost all the Coromantin slaves throughout the island were privy to it, without any suspicion from the Whites,*» wrote Edward Long. The aim of this insurrection—if freedom wasn't enough—remains obscure. Some claimed the Coromantins demanded the same privileges obtained by the Maroons, these former slaves who had conquered their semi-liberty with their rifles. They were said to discuss with the same Maroons, as a matter of fact—and fear seized those who foresaw the dreadful consequences of so powerful an alliance: nothing less than the birth of a black kingdom in Jamaica! In England, the *Gentleman's Magazine, Vol. XXX* (1760), claimed that the insurrection was *occasioned by the Negroes being refused a holiday, by one of their masters, on Easter-Monday*—which, of course, was never the case. The same article contradicts itself, as a matter of fact, stating: *the two Coromantin Negroes (...) having long been concerting a rebellion...* This rebellion—the most important one in the history of the West Indies at the time—was indeed a concerted one, and was first and foremost dictated by the refusal of slavery. It wasn't the fruit of the Creole slaves born in Jamaica and more inclined to accept their fate. No, this one was led by some recently disembarked Coromantins, who could still smell the natural scent of freedom. Their hatred for their oppressors was fresh, and their will was strong.

The way slaves were forced across the Ocean, also known as the Middle Passage, was painful and stressful—they were crammed together in a boat's bilge, ill treated and ill fed. Extracted from their lives in Africa, they were thrown into a world of violence in the devilish hands of some horrid creatures. Their children were kidnapped, their women raped—many fell into despair; others rebelled, slaughtered the crew, then drifted to death on board of a ship they couldn't control. The dark triangular trade that started in the 16th century between Europe, Africa and America evolved along the centuries. Less brutal and more regulated, it supposedly abode by some so-called rules in the 18th century. The number of slaves had to be proportionate to the tonnage of the ships, for instance; slaves were also to be properly fed, and some fans insured a better sanity in the bilge. But concretely, some merchants regularly emptied their ships a few hundred meters from the shore, drowning their cargo to get the insurance premium. But the majority reached Kingston, where a poster promoted the sale. The planters visited the new comers directly on the deck of the ship—it was crowded with curious who had come to make fun at the Negroes by letting them think that they were about to eat them up. Let's imagine the resentment of the proud Coromantins, their burning looks and theirs faces of steel—they were forced to go with it, but retaliation was already at work in their minds. And when given the opportunity to lay their hands on a white man, they sawed his skull asunder, threw away the brain, and joyfully drank the wine of revenge from these cups of victory. The planters in Jamaica have always feared their slaves—the 1760 insurrection proved them right.

The Slaughter of Hallard's Valley

Bryan Edwards wrote that the rebellion broke out *on the frontier plantation in St. Mary's parish, belonging to the late Ballard Beckford, and the neighbouring estate of Trinity, the property of Zacahary Bayly*—the latter was Edwards' benefactor, who had raised him after his parents' death, and left him his fortune. This very day, some fifty slaves led by Tacky marched on Port Maria where they murdered the sentinel of the fort, and furnished themselves with rifles and ammunitions; the only ones they could find were bullets drilled used by the fishermen as leaden sinkers for their nets—fired at the enemy, they proved inefficient. The aforementioned issue of the *Gentleman's Magazine* said they took four barrels of powder and about 40 serviceable rifles; they then went to *James Keily's store from which they took a pair of silver mounted pistols.*

Bayly—or Bayley—was an enlightened planter who cared about the well being of his slaves. He never tortured them and punished them only when necessary, and only with moderation—Bayley was a God-fearing man, and a true Christian. Didn't Edward Long write that the Whites should treat their slaves with *the conciliating affection of an ancient patriarch*? In 1780, French philosopher Diderot, hiding behind the feather of his friend Guillaume-Thomas Raynal, giggled: *"Your Negroes are mean? Not enough with you!"* But the abolitionist movement was just starting, and Bayley was probably genuinely thinking that his loving attitude would protect him from the anger of his slaves; convinced he could negotiate with them, he galloped toward them when they came back to Ballard's Valley at the breaking of dawn. What a shock it must have been when his tender and beloved slaves opened fire at him! He went backward and rode directly to the neighbouring estate, *alarming them as he went* (Long)—looks like he remembered which side he was on, after all. Tacky who had just been joined by more rebels from the nearby plantations attacked Ballard's Valley, where ten white people were lying in bed. *"All these they put to death in the most savage manner,"* wrote Bryan Edwards, *"and they drank their blood mixed with rum."* Tacky and his men then made it to Esther, the plantation of the famous William Beckford. En route, they came across *a poor white man who was travelling on foot* (Long), and killed him on the spot. At Esther, they set fire to a cane piece and a windmill, and then they surrounded a house where a dozen of Whites had sought refuge—being without ammunitions, they couldn't resist very long, and the infuriated slaves soon took the house. One doctor was mutilated, dragged by one foot and thrown onto a pile of bodies where he was left for dead. Leaving the house, one of the rebels noticed that the doctor was still breathing, so he shot him five times in the back—the doctor miraculously survived his wounds. "*They murdered in one morning between thirty and forty whites,*" underlined Edwards, "*without even sparing infants at the breast.*" Tacky and his men then proceeded to Ballard's Valley and Heywood Hall, where *having therefore a good magazine of hogs, poultry, rum, and other plunder of the like kind, they chose out a convenient spot, where they spread their provision, and started to carouze* (Long). Many other rebels had joined them, and their total number amounted four hundred at this point. Very soon, Bayley attacked them with 130 men, and forced them into the woods where they started to fire their useless bullets. Bayley and his troop apparently killed eight rebels and captured several others.

Several skirmishes took place during the following days; none was decisive but the Whites started to organize themselves, and to gather some reinforcements. Two faithful slaves ran to Spanish Town to inform Governor Sir Henry Moore about the situation. A man of action, Moore immediately dispatched a regiment to St Mary and called upon the Maroons of Scott's Hall. The 1739 Treaty stipulated that the Maroons had to assist the British during slave rebellions. The Maroons were the secret weapons of white Jamaica—yet, their leader Cudjoe was a former runaway slave himself. In 1690, he had drunk a mixture of blood and rum from his master's skull. Then he had run away, and fought against the English like a mad dog for fifty years without rest or mercy. There were Maroons—the name derives from the Spanish word *cimarron*, savage—all over the Spanish Americas. They lived a free life of misery, surviving in makeshift hideouts in the hills. In Jamaica, they attacked isolated travellers or remote settlements; the slaves on the plantations supported them, informed them of the masters' whereabouts, and offered them shelter whenever they could—and sometimes joined them in the fight. In a few decades' time, the Maroons had colonized the whole inside part of the island, leaving the shores only to the Whites—it was impossible for them to cross the island, or to travel in small groups. The British troops were ill adapted to the topography of the Blue Mountains, and the Maroons regularly humiliated them, fighting according to the practical rules of guerrilla—the stiff necked English officers saw it as a despicable form of war, and refused to adopt it. Jamaica was paralyzed—to such an extent the Whites were eventually forced to ask for peace. A peace treaty was signed in 1739—and the whole colony suddenly came back to life. In fact, the beginning of the prosperity of Jamaica can be traced back to the treaty—that's how powerful the Maroons had been! The treaty was like a miracle for the English. Not only did the Maroons stop being their worst enemies but they also became their protectors as a clause specified they should defend the colony from slave rebellions; and the Maroons happened to be far too willing to chase their runaway brothers to be considered with any complacency today. But war was at the heart of their precarious society; it was its corner stone. They knew how to fight and how to kill— but not much else. So that when Tacky and his likes rebelled, the Maroons came after them without any hesitation. They even proved barbarous, according to Bryan Edwards who didn't like them, and who conscientiously underlined their misdeeds. When the Maroons reached St Mary, they behaved *extremely ill*, wrote Edward Long, refusing to fight before being paid some arrears due to them. Once the English had complied, they marched unto the slaves, but were repelled. And as Tacky's troops bravely resisted, the insurrection spread throughout the island.

Black Magic
During the insurrection, the Whites discovered an unknown

part of their slaves' culture, *obeah*—or voodoo. Several authors had studied their spiritual beliefs before, noticing that they knew of two gods, the good Naskew and the evil Tunnew. But none had gone deep enough to uncover the secret of their black sorcerers—these *obeahmen* practiced a pagan cult that celebrated the occult forces of nature. "*Their incantations, to which the midnight hours are allotted, are studiously veiled in mystery,*" wrote Edwards. *Obeah* became a main issue during the revolt of 1760, as the rebels believed that a magical body powder protected their leader. Thus reputed to be invulnerable, Tacky was also said to catch the English bullets with his hands, before throwing them back at his enemies. Faith can move mountains, and the colonists feared these irrational beliefs—they rejoiced when a sorcerer, said by the English to be Tacky's personal *obeahman*, was captured in the parish of St Mary. "*This old impostor was caught whilst he was tricked up with all his feathers, teeth, and other implements of magic, and in this attire suffered military execution by hanging: many of his disciples, when they found that he was so easily put to death, notwithstanding all the boasted feats of his powder and incantation, soon altered their opinion of him, and determined not to joint their countrymen, in a cause which hitherto had been unattended with success,*" triumphed Edward Long. The invulnerability of Tacky wasn't questioned among the Coromantins yet; he had never been injured when fighting the English—one of the rare details about him. To belittle the power of *obeah*, the Assembly passed a law that became article 21 of the Slave Code; it read: "*Obeiah-men, pretended conjurors, or priests, upon conviction before two justices and three freeholders of their practising as such, to suffer death or transportation, at the discretion of the Court.*" Meanwhile, the insurrection spread out.

At Forrest's Estate, in Westmoreland, the Coromantins raided the owner's house as he was dining with his lawyer and some friends of his. Informed about the situation by three faithful slaves, the neighbour planter endeavoured at once to equip a militia of twenty slaves—and gave them weapons. Described by

Edward Long as *remarkable for his humanity and kind treatments of his slaves*, the white planter suddenly faced twenty armed Coromantins who paid back his kindness by leaving him unharmed. "*Saluting him with their hats, they every one marched off,*" concluded Long. Among them were a few slaves recently captured in the French colony of Guadeloupe, where they had been initiated into the art of war. They looted several houses, and then went to the woods to build a long breastwork. That's where the militia found them—but the Whites were repelled and dramatically disbanded. "*The whole part was thrust into the utmost confusion, and routed,*" wrote Long. "*Each strove to shift for himself, and whilst they ran different ways, scarcely knowing what they were about, several were butchered, others broke their limbs over precipices, and the rest with difficulty found their way back again.*" Excited over this victory, thousand new comers joined the Guadeloupian's band. But the breastwork was eventually taken by the cumulated efforts of the 49th Regiment of Captain Forsyth and the Leeward Maroons. The fight was fierce, the slaves ran for cover into the woods; then came back to their settlement, trying to recover it. The Maroons were this time decisive. They murdered a majority of the slaves, and forced the rest to flee disorderly. According to Long, after this overthrow, *the Westmoreland rebels were never able to act any otherwise than on the defensive; several skirmishes happened, in which they were constantly put to flight; their numbers were gradually reduced, and many destroyed themselves.*

The rest of the island was still at war. In Val of Luidas, a conspiracy failed, and the leaders were hanged. In St Thomas, a huge revolt was prevented thanks to a traitor, who had pretended to join the rebels to betray them. From the Carpenter's Mountain in St James to the short-lived revolt of Damon in Clarendon, Jamaica was on fire. In Kingston, the Coromantins had even crowned a Queen called Cubah. Long grew ironical: "*Her majesty was seized, and ordered for transportation.*" She nevertheless succeeded in disembarking close to Leeward where she continued undiscovered for a while before being caught and executed—her story has never been thoroughly researched.

* * *

The colonists were gaining ground while the rebels proved unable to federate their action. In St Mary, Tacky's troops ended up in a critical situation. Dislodged from their advantageous position, they started to lose ground as the English coordinated their efforts, sending a frigate in Port Maria to be used as a floating jail—freed from its prisoners, the militia then concentrated on the last breastwork of the rebels. The grenades and the efforts of the Maroons finally paid, and the rebels disbanded. *"Tacky, their leader, having separated from the rest, was closely pursued by lieut. Davy of the Maroons, who fired at him while they were both running at full speed, and shot him dead,"* reported Long—which tells a lot about the ability of the Maroons to handle a firearm. Edwards didn't like the Maroons, and his relation of the last instants of Tacky was quite different from Long's. He wrote about an isolated, unarmed and disorientated man lost in the woods with no clothes on. The Maroons eventually spotted him, and started to chase him while yelling out loud—they eventually cornered him, and shot him in the head. His severed head was then brought to Kingston and exposed in Spanish Town—but the slaves stole it away, thus depriving their masters of their trophy. What Long didn't say, and what Edwards reported from allegedly irrefutable witnesses—including some Maroons themselves—, is what happened to the rest of Tacky's body. He said the Maroons *roasted and actually devoured the heart, and the entrails of the wretched victim*. He added that far from concealing this horrible deed, they actually boasted of it. Edward Long gave a short portrait of Tacky: *"He was a young man of good nature, and well made; his countenance handsome, but rather of an effeminate than manly cast. (...) He did not appear to be a man of any extraordinary genius, and probably was chosen general, from his similitude in person to some favourite leader of their nation in Africa."* Such is told the story of the weak by the powerful. The tone is casual, almost derisory—paternalistic. We must put Long's speech into context—and underline that he was contemporary to Voltaire, Diderot and many humanists who described slavery for what it was, an inhuman and cruel ordeal. Edward Long was a mean man, that's for sure. And his slaves were probably not mean enough with him.

Blood and Tears

Desperate and cornered, Tacky's men sought refuge into a nearby cave, where the Maroons found them. For every slave they slaughtered, the Maroons received a reward; but the English were usually satisfied with a mere pair of ears. In this particular case, it was established that the rebels had killed themselves before their enemies found them. The Maroons simply chopped the ears off the corpses—*seventeen pairs are brought in*, said *Gentleman's Magazine*. According to Edwards the Maroons had recovered these ears from the bodies of the slaves killed earlier in Heywood Hall. The English never had the time to bury them, and the Maroons hastily mutilated the corpses to make money. This version seems quite acceptable.

The survivors spent several days wandering in the woods. Their situation was terrible and, according to the same magazine, *there were so much dissensions among them that several were killed in their own quarrels*; the magazine even added that when one of them was wounded, the others put him to death to prevent his giving intelligence. The fugitives having ran out of food eventually came to an agreement with Mr Gordon, a planter who promised they would be spared should they surrender. Handfuls of rebels were still fighting in Westmoreland or St James, but the end was near. The triumphing Governor decided to make an example out of three Negroes, who had partaken in the massacre of Ballard's Valley. The first one was burnt alive—very slowly. He was first chained on a scaffold on Parade, the main square of Kingston.

Bryan Edwards witnessed the scene and described it as follow: "*The fire was applied to his feet. But his torments could not force him a groan; and he saw his legs reduced to ashes, with the utmost fortitude and composure. After his legs were consumed, one of his arms happening to get loose, he snatched a brand from the fire, and hurled it at the face of the executioner.*" Thus die the brave, with an almost incredible *fortitude*—had it not come from a white witness, we could have honestly doubted its accuracy.

The last two slaves, named Kingston and Fortune, were locked in iron cages suspended at Parade, where they were left to die in the open. "*The Negroes who have rebelled and killed their masters,*" explained the French traveller Father Labat, "*are condemned to be put to the mill, to be burnt alive or to be exposed in iron cages that are so tight they can't move an arm. They are then suspended to a branch and left to die from hunger and anger. We call it, to put a man on a dry diet.*" But then again, the fortitude of both Kingston and Fortune put their executioners to shame—and awoke their fearful and admiring respect. "*From that time till they expired they did not utter the least complaint, except of cold in the night; but diverting themselves, from morning until night, in conversation with their countrymen, who very improperly were permitted to surround the gibbet,*" wrote Edwards. They even mocked the said Edwards at one point, pretending to have something important to say. Appointed as a mediator by the officer in charge, the historian was asked to approach the Negroes in their iron cages. With the help of an interpreter, Edwards addressed them but couldn't understand their answer. "*However, both (...) laughed immoderately at some circumstance that occurred.*" The historian was probably the object of some joke, but it was their last one. "*The next morning, one of them expired with great silence; and this was the case with the other, on the morning of the ninth day.*" About Kingston's death, Edward Long gave more details: "*The morning before* (he) *expired, he appeared to be convulsed from head to foot; and upon being opened, after his decease, his lungs were found adhering to the back so tightly, that it required some force to* disengage them. *The murders and outrages they had committed, were thought to justify this cruel punishment inflicted upon them in terrorem to others; but they appeared to be very little affected by it themselves; behaving all the time with a degree of hardened insolence, and brutal insensibility."* Your Negroes were insolent and brutal, Mr Long?

The End of Slavery

The revolt led by Tacky was subdued in blood; but slaves had spilled so much already, it didn't discourage them. Five years later, Blackwall—one of Tacky's men who had escaped retaliation—led a new insurrection. With the help of several other Coromantins, he cut a white man into pieces in Whitehall, and then tried to take the neighbouring plantation. But the unexpected resistance of the Whites and the killing of one of their leaders disconcerted the rebels who disbanded. This aborted movement was yet quite important—not less than seventeen plantations were involved. Following the governmental inquiry, seventeen slaves were executed and twenty-three others transported. These were the last fiery ashes of Tacky's furnace—but the flames always sprung somewhere. The following year, some thirty Coromantins murdered nineteen Whites in one hour's time. As usual, bloodshed put an end to the rebellion.

All these revolts proved the planters wrong, who kept on retorting the European abolitionists that, except a few isolated and deplorable cases, their slaves led a better life than the poorest people of London. Yes, their slaves were happy—they quartered those who weren't, anyway. But resignation slowly shifted sides. Slavery became ugly to the Europeans—who also grew jealous of the planters' wealth and power. Free labour was regarded as unfair competition, and the way the planters treated their slaves was condemned all through philosophical pamphlets. As the neighbouring island of Saint-Domingue sank into blood to reborn under the triumphant black name of Haiti in 1804, slavery in

Jamaica was living its last hours. After a period of so-called
apprenticeship, slavery was abolished on August 1,
1838; some 78 years after the insurrection
led by Tacky and his men, who
lived as slaves—but
died as free
men.

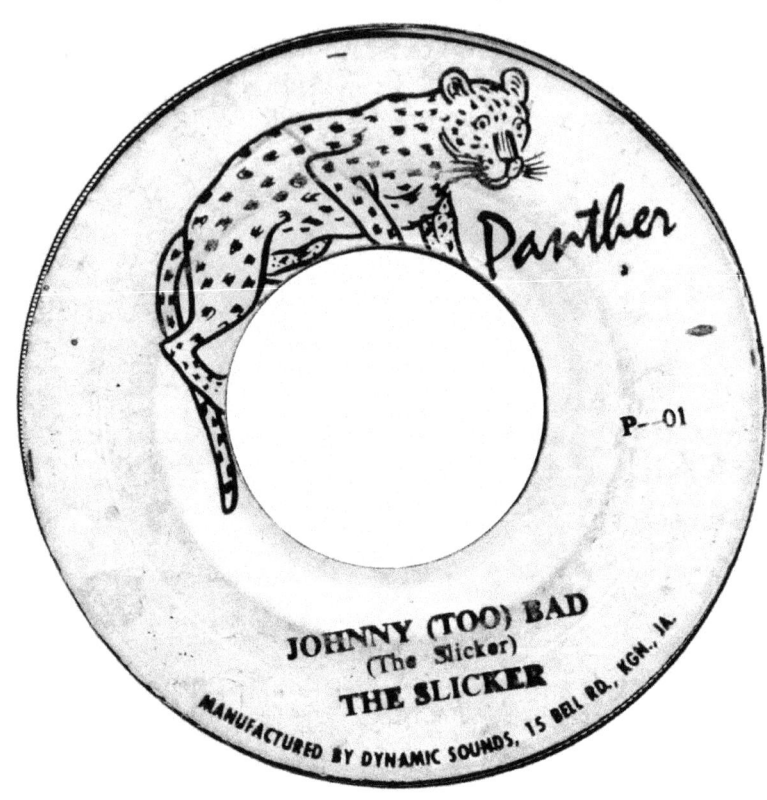

The original 45 of *Johnny (Too) Bad*, by the Slickers.
(DREAD Archives)

Wilson, Trevor
(1949-1972)
Johnny-Too-Bad

The ghetto of Trench Town in West Kingston has bred many disturbing creatures floating between light and darkness; such was Trevor Wilson, a youth with a voice; he could write songs, too—just like his brother Delroy; but he never had the same musical determination. He was far too inclined to do evil. In fact, he was a juvenile delinquent—a mutating one, the missing link between the *rudies* of the 1960s and the *badmen* of the 1970s. The former had been at the centre of a cultural revolution initiated in the 1960s by a handful of local musicians who drifted from the American musical codes to create an original music. This enabled the singers to tell their own stories. The *rudies*, leading dramatic and violent existences, became a natural topic to sing about; and a very popular one. This generation built an urban mythology with music as sole cement. But as violence intensified under political pressure at the turn of the 1970s, the *rudies* picked up guns and turned *badmen*. The transition took a few years, and Trevor was right in the middle of it. Indeed, he was one of these modern heroes reminiscent of the ancient ones—doomed from the start. He could handle a *ratchet*—a small German knife with a flashing blade—or a gun, as well as singing or writing songs. Unfortunately, he loved *badman* life too much. Girls, guns, and dancing all night long to his brother's hit songs—such was the furious life of Trevor Wilson. In fact, there was no way he could have become someone else. His fate was written on the wall, he wasn't meant to be a singer—he was *Johnny-too-bad*.

Armed descending a staircase

One fine day of 1969, in Trench Town, Trevor Wilson crossed his yard on 2nd Street, climbed the ladder leaning against the back wall, and then jumped into the next yard, on 1st Street. "*Roy!*" he called, climbing the stairs leading to his friend's place. Roy was a little youth from Morant Bay, in the parish of St Thomas, who had recently come to live on 1st Street. His aunt rented him a room upstairs. The two kids knew each other well, and regularly sang together. But this very day, Trevor had come for a suit to attend a party the next Friday—Roy Beckford was a tailor by trade. "*Roy!*" Trevor repeated, knocking on the door. "*Who dat?*" came a voice from inside. "*Me, Batman!*" retorted Trevor. He was known as Batman in the community because as a kid, he could perform incredible acrobatics—he was a good boy then.

When Roy asked him to tuck his shirttail into his pants to take his measurement, the *rudie* took a gun from his waist, and heavily dropped it on the sewing machine. He then laid a *ratchet* knife beside it. Roy was impressed, but didn't say a word. He silently took Roy's measurement. Then Batman took back his gun and knife, slid them back into his pants, and covered them up. He asked the tailor a cigarette, lit it on the threshold, and then walked down the stairs. Standing back, Roy couldn't take his eyes off him. A song came to him as he heard the rhythm of Batman's feet battering the stairs. *Walking down the stairs with a pistol in your waist, Trevor you're too bad.* Yes, such was Trevor Wilson—too bad. The melody was catchy, and Roy sang it over and over all day long in front of his worried aunt. "*You know, Roy,*" she said at last, "*I'm not too sure Trevor would appreciate your quoting his name in a song.*" Roy paused—he hadn't thought about that. But his aunt was right. So he changed Trevor into Johnny. The staircase wasn't meaningful enough, Roy placed his bad boy in the street and sang: *Walking down the street with a pistol in your waist, Johnny you're too bad.* He had just written one of the most famous songs of the history of reggae music.

* * *

A few days later, Roy was in his yard, playing guitar. Sitting in front of him, Trevor was rolling a *spliff of ganja* (joint of marijuana) while listening to his friend's new song. *Walking down the road with a pistol in your waist, Johnny you're too bad...* Batman didn't even look up. The notes came naturally to him, and he let out some wonderful harmonies: *Ooooo-oooooh ooooy!* He had just signed his musical biography.

This song is an urban parable, the tragic tale of a soul lost in crime and violence—this is the sad story of all the *Johnnies-too-bad* in the world. *Rudies* knew of the implications of their lifestyle. They loved to be celebrated in songs, but they also usually accepted the moralist warnings sent by the singers—most of them were carefully picked up in the Bible and couldn't be argued over, anyway. The *badman* described by Roy in this particular song was no stranger to Trevor—he knew him well. This guy with a gun in his waist, who restlessly meditated evil, was his musical alter ego. He was on a slippery slope, and he knew it. One day, a voice would tell him that his time has come. He would then try *to hide behind a rock*, as the song goes—*but there'd be no rock.* Johnny was a prisoner of fate, the victim of a foretold destiny. His tragedy was every Johnny-too-bad's—a moving waste. Thus perished all these bad boys from Trench Town who picked up a gun. They died young—but would rather be *free men in their graves, than living as puppets or slaves.* The romantic image of the *rudie* isn't totally false. But beware, before you feel sorry for them! *Maga dogs*—skinny dogs that haunt Kingston's sidewalks—usually bite the hand that feed them. Peter Tosh who knew Trench Town well, wrote one of his best songs about them. So, get it right: *Johnnies-too-bad* are vipers; they've always been—and Trevor was one of the worst. He had a talent, though. Guitarist Earl "Chinna" Smith, who lived in the nearby community of Greenwich Farm, knew him well. Trevor usually hung out in the area where he was known as *Badman*, a significant nickname in Jamaica. One fine day, Chinna saw him sitting on the veranda of Earl Zero, a young singer from the community. The latter played guitar and Trevor was singing: *As I entered the gate of Zion, I could hear the choir singing.* This is the first couplet of another historical hit song, *None Shall Escape the Judgement*—written by Earl Zero it led singer Johnny Clarke to fame in 1975. Was it partly written by Trevor Wilson? Chinna was wondering. But Earl Zero firmly denied. Nevertheless, it was quite ironic for Trevor to sing such a song—not to mention *Badness No Pay* that he recorded as a duet with his brother.

Slick Boys From Saint Thomas

Roy hadn't become a tailor by chance. He had always been crazy over clothes. So that when he formed a musical group with his childhood friends, they called it The Slickers. By 1969, they had already recorded a handful of singles, including for legendary producers Duke Reid or Joe Gibbs. No hit song yet, just ordinary *little tunes*. But one day, they stepped into the yard of the sound engineer Syd Bucknor for an impromptu audition. Fortune favours the brave: the engineer liked what we heard and introduced the youths to Byron Lee, a juggernaut of the local production for whom they recorded *Johnny Too Bad* on October 1, 1969. The sound was clear, the vocal harmonies well put together and the melody catchy—not to mention the lyrics that betrayed the evolution of the rebellious *rudies* into ruthless criminals. This dramatic change came from the politicians who had been recruiting their henchmen among gangsters for the last few years—could they dream of better political enforcers? Everybody feared them, especially since the police left them alone. The gangsters who refused to work for the politicians like Busbie (see Bob Marley portrait) were eliminated. Others soon foresaw the opportunities offered by this reshuffling of cards: crime with impunity. Was Trevor into politics? Did he refuse to work for the politicians? The problem with criminals is that they tend to be secretive. Trevor had at least one strong political connection, Bunny "Striker" Lee. Originated from Greenwich Farm, Lee was a musical producer who worked with Trevor's brother, Delroy—and who soon took care of Trevor too. As he once stated: "*I have many friends, criminals, police, preachers, politicians, thieves. They are all my friends. You never know when you're going to need their help.*" As a matter of fact, he always had *badmen* around him—music was a dangerous environment— and he apparently took Trevor out of jail a couple of times.

The Wolf's Share

The recording session of *Johnny Too Bad* filled everyone with enthusiasm, especially Byron Lee who pressed an acetate copy for the group. The three singers headed straight to downtown Kingston, to Clancy Eccles' shop. A *rudie* himself, Clancy was a streetwise producer; he almost suffocated when he heard the song: "*Me can't play that, my youth! The gunman-them ah-gwaan mash up me shop (are going to mash up my shop)!*" This was almost a prophecy. But Byron Lee had heavy commercial arguments, and didn't care about what the street would say—the song reached number 29 in the national charts one week after its release. Ten days later, it was number one on the two national radio stations. When they first heard it, the *rudies* from Trench Town were outraged. "*With a pistol in your waist?! Who the bloodclaat (hell) is telling on us 'bout guns? Ah Roy dat! Which Roy? The little youth from 1st Street?*" Clancy Eccles knew the *rudies* well, he hadn't warned the Slickers in vain. Roy was peacefully at home when a group of them rushed into his yard. They were after him, and they were in a bad mood. Roy jumped through the window, and ran away.

After the incident, he remained for a while in Saint Thomas, and when he came back, *Johnny Too Bad* had become the most popular song in town. The *rudies* had changed their minds, and now considered the song as a tribute to their lifestyle—it talked about them, and as soon as it started in a dance, they drew their pistols and fired shots in the air to express their manly approbation—the *gun salute*. For his part, Trevor "Badman" Wilson was upset. He thought that Roy and his two stupid friends were making a lot of money. He didn't know he had inspired the song, but he knew he had played his part in the writing. Well, to say the truth, opinions diverge on the matter. Delroy Wilson later told a journalist that his brother had written the entire song; Bunny Wailer, from the original Wailers, confirmed. Winston Bailey and Derrick Crooks, the two other members of the Slickers, claimed he hadn't written the slightest word, and Roy Beckford acknowledged him for the harmonies part—*Ooooo-oooooh ooooy!* Anyway, Badman was determined to get his share. He preyed upon Roy one evening in the yard of 1st Street. Roy was coming back from Saint Thomas when he made out Trevor's silhouette from afar; he wondered what he was up to, but upon reaching his place, he was brutally assaulted and thrown on the ground. Johnny-too-bad, wearing a piece of cloth over his face, put the mouth of his gun in Roy's face, violently asking for money. Stunned, Roy asked: "*Trevor? Wha gwaan (what's going on)?*" Identified, Trevor calmed down, and let Roy get back to his feet. He took off his piece of cloth, but he wanted his share, and he wanted it now. Roy knew how serious Trevor could be, and he promised him a brand new pair of Clark's shoes. The idea pleased Badman. There was nothing above Clark's in Trench Town. The happy few who owned a pair cleaned them with a toothbrush and suspended them in a plastic bag to keep them away from dust and dirt—*badman shoes*, as Jamaicans respectfully call them. A few days later, Trevor walked down the streets of Rema in his brand new Clark's. But some suspicious things happened around the song at the time. Winston Bailey and Derrick Crooks refused to give anything to Trevor. Byron Lee also claimed he had written *Johnny Too Bad* now that it generated royalties. Winston Bailey talked to a journalist in the 1980s, reporting a meeting with Byron Lee, one Tommy—probably Tommy Cowan, an associate of Byron Lee—, the Slickers and Trevor Wilson. The idea was to find a common ground, but Winston claimed that Byron Lee only tried to rob the group. For his part, he refused to let anything go—not even to Trevor, who suddenly ran out of patience and drew his biggest argument, his gun; he allegedly pointed it at Winston's head. But at the end of the day, the Slickers held on strong in front of Byron Lee, and Trevor apparently got his share of the royalties on a song soon covered by international acts like Taj Mahal or UB 40—he never benefited from it, though. Some say he also obtained a S90, the most popular motorbike of the time— but this story wasn't confirmed. One thing is for sure, he was riding a bicycle when, on January 15, 1971, he was approached by a police car on Spanish Town Road around 10:30 p.m. His bicycle had no lights on, so the police officer asked Trevor to come off it. Badman suddenly threw his bike away and started to run. Rapidly joined by the officer, he struggled with him for a few seconds, trying to draw his pistol—the loaded firearm fell on the ground. Trevor had no license, of course—and this might be one of the occasions when Bunny Lee took him out of jail. He was free a few months later, anyway—and was *walking down the road with two pistols in his waist,* heading to a party in Trench Town. This would be his ultimate dance. A remote voice had started to whisper from afar—the time had come. And there was no rock.

Johnny Fi' Dead

Johnny Too Bad became a legendary song mostly because it was featured on the original soundtrack of Perry Henzell's movie *The Harder They Come,* in 1972 (see Vincent "Ryghin" Martin portrait). The liner notes of this brilliant compilation put out by *Island Records* contributed to the mythology of the Slickers: "*Johnny you're too bad warn the Slickers, and they should know:*

when the lawyer was getting copyright clearance on that tune, one of the writers was underground. The other was in death row." This led everyone to believe the group was no longer in existence—and it probably prevented them from fully benefiting the success of the album. But after all, underlined Roy, this was only half-wrong. Indeed, when the record came out, one of the writers was lying underground, Trevor Wilson.

On February 25, Trevor was spending the evening with his girlfriend; but she got tired, and asked him to take her home in a nearby community. Trevor had other plans, so he went to check Roy to see if he could do that for him. But it was late, Roy refused—during the meeting, he noticed that Trevor was carrying *two* guns this evening. Turned down by Roy, Johnny-too-bad went to Columbus Drive to ask Nancy, another friend of his, to take his girlfriend home. What happened afterwards? We only know that half an hour later, Trevor was alone on 9th Street, in the upper part of Trench Town—and that he decided to buy a beer in a yard. As he came out, a voice suddenly shouted to his ear—three shots! Hit in the head by a shower of buckshot, Johnny-too-bad fell on the ground. When Roy heard the gunshots on 1st Street, he identified the type of weapon that had just fired, and thought Trevor—who only carried handguns—wasn't involved. But a few minutes later, Nancy came knocking on his door. He hastily put on his shirt and ran to 9th Street, where he saw Trevor lying in a pool of blood. He had had time to draw one of his guns, but not to fire it. Taken to the hospital, he was pronounced dead on arrival.

Thus perished Johnny-too-bad, murdered by one Johnny-badder. Curiously, the *Sunday Gleaner* mentioned his death; a few laconic lines, but on the front page—this is quite peculiar and might indicate an ulterior motive for the killing. Could those few lines be a discreet political allusion? After all, Trevor lived in Rema, the part of Trench Town controlled by the Jamaican Labour Party (JLP), and was shot in Concrete Jungle, a stronghold of the rival People's National Party (PNP), only a few days before the general election. Had Trevor grown over-confident because the PNP used *Better Must Come*, one of his brother's songs—produced by Bunny Lee—, as a campaign slogan? Or did he meet some resentful JLP enforcer? Might be, might not. In Trench Town, some people remembered he had recently beaten a *badman* from Rema, leaving him alive—his deadly mistake?

The destiny of Trevor Wilson, unlike the ancient heroes', wasn't written—but sung; by his neighbour, a country boy from Saint Thomas. And it went:

> *Walking down the road with a pistol in your waist*
> *Johnny you're too bad—Ooooo-oooooh ooooy!*
>
> *Walking down the road with a ratchet in your waist*
> *Johnny you're too bad—Ooooo-oooooh ooooy!*
>
> *You're just robbing and stabbing and looting and shooting*
> *Johnny you're too bad*
>
> *One of these days when you hear a voice say come*
> *Where you gonna run to?*
>
> *You gonna run to the rock for rescue*
> *There will be no rock.*

End of *Jamaican Greats.*

About the author

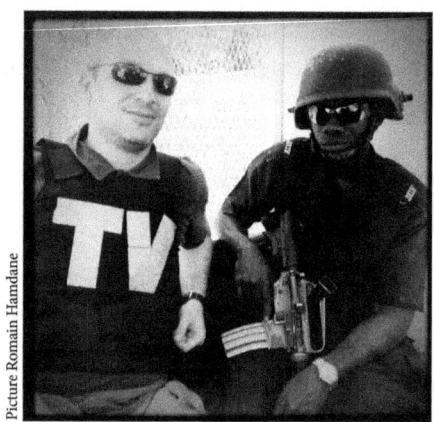

Picture Romain Hamdane

Thibault Ehrengardt is a French independent journalist. The former chief editor of the leading European reggae magazine Natty Dread from 2000 to 2010, and the current head of **DREAD Editions**, he's been to Jamaica many times, and has written several books in the **Jamaica Insula** series, including the first *History of Jamaica* to be published in French for 250 years as well as an *Historical Atlas of the First Maps of Jamaica*. He has recently published *Gangs of Jamaica* in English, an inquiry into the world of gangs. He is also the author of a book about the discovery of the New World in the **Le Moine marin series**, *La Fureur mensongère* (DREAD Editions).

* * *

www.jamaica-insula.com

www.ingramcontent.com/pod-product-compliance
Lightning Source LLC
Chambersburg PA
CBHW050203230526
45470CB00001B/213